How to Succeed in Business Using

How to Succeed in Business Using

Making Connections and Capturing Opportunities
on the Web's #1 Business Networking Site

Eric Butow
and Kathleen Taylor

⊿AMACOM

American Management Association
New York • Atlanta • Brussels • Chicago • Mexico City • San Francisco
Shanghai • Tokyo • Toronto • Washington, D.C.

Special discounts on bulk quantities of AMACOM books are
available to corporations, professional associations, and other
organizations. For details, contact Special Sales Department,
AMACOM, a division of American Management Association,
1601 Broadway, New York, NY 10019.
Tel.: 212-903-8316.   Fax: 212-903-8083.
Website: www.amacombooks.org/go/specialsales

This publication is designed to provide accurate and authoritative
information in regard to the subject matter covered. It is sold with the
understanding that the publisher is not engaged in rendering legal,
accounting, or other professional service. If legal advice or other expert
assistance is required, the services of a competent professional person
should be sought.

Library of Congress Cataloging-in-Publication Data

Butow, Eric.
    How to succeed in business using LinkedIn / Eric Butow and Kathleen Taylor.
        p.   cm.
    Includes bibliographical references and index.
    ISBN-13: 978-0-8144-1074-5
    ISBN-10: 0-8144-1074-X
    1. Business networks.   2. Online social networks.   I. Taylor, Kathleen.   II. Title.

    HD69.S8B88 2008
    025.06'65—dc22

                                                        2008007622

Printing number

10 9 8 7 6 5 4 3 2 1

Contents

How to Succeed in Business Using

Using LinkedIn to Your Advantage

You may have heard about social networking sites on the Web. If you view a list of social networking Web sites (http://en.wikipedia.org/wiki/List_of_social_networking_websites) on Wikipedia, a popular reference site, you will see links to more than 100 networking sites, available from around the world and catering to every taste. The sites range from general, including the very popular MySpace and Facebook, to the particular, focusing on different topics such as photo sharing, wine, and music. LinkedIn (http://www.linkedin.com) is a Web site designed to connect business professionals and enable them to share information, get answers, and promote themselves and their businesses.

Though LinkedIn was founded in 2003, it has experienced explosive growth only since 2006. For example, according to Nielsen Online rankings as of October 2007 (http://www.webpronews.com/blogtalk/2007/11/19/linkedin-growing-more-quickly-than-facebook), LinkedIn subscribers jumped from more than 1.7 million users to more than 4.9 million users, a jump of more than 189 percent, between October 2006 and October 2007. In terms of percentage growth, that put LinkedIn among the top 10 fastest growing social networking sites, beating the growth even of Facebook and MySpace. What makes LinkedIn so popular?

The answer: LinkedIn offers subscribers a number of high-value benefits.

Promote Yourself

LinkedIn is designed for business professionals and business owners instead of for the general public. You establish yourself on LinkedIn by creating a profile that summarizes your professional and/or business accomplishments. Without a profile you can't link to anyone else in LinkedIn, and no other LinkedIn users can learn more about you. So creating a profile is one of the first tasks you need to complete. For example, when I joined LinkedIn, I set up a profile for my business and linked the profile to several colleagues.

The text that you include in your profile is searchable. So, if you're looking for work in a particular area, such as telecommunications, be sure to add this information in your profile. As an example, Penelope Trunk, a syndicated career columnist for *The Boston Globe*, who uses LinkedIn extensively to network with others, pointed out in her April 24, 2007, blog entry about 10 ways that journalists can use LinkedIn (http://blog.penelopetrunk.com/2007/04/24/ten-ways-journalists-can-use-linkedin/). A thoughtfully completed and properly linked profile is an excellent way of promoting yourself and/or your business.

You'll learn more about creating your profile in Chapter 3.

Grow Your Network Fast

LinkedIn offers subscribers a remarkably fast way to grow their networks. When I joined LinkedIn, about 14 of my colleagues asked to link with me, and I asked to link with some of them. By degrees I expanded my link network to hundreds of LinkedIn members because my originally linked members have links to hundreds of other connections. And those hundreds of connections have thousands more. In a very short time you'll have more connections than you ever thought possible. Fortunately, LinkedIn makes it easy to search for other LinkedIn members who share your interests, including, for example, the company you work for (or the company you worked for sometime in the hazy past), as well as for people you went to school with (in the even more hazier past).

Guy Kawasaki, former Apple evangelist, managing director of the venture capital firm Garage Technology Ventures, author, and LinkedIn user, offers a valuable tip. He notes in his January 4, 2007 blog that if you make your profile available to everyone and use your actual name for your public profile URL (also known as a Web site address), you make your profile information easier for search engines to index. (You can read this tip and more of Kawasaki's recommendations for using LinkedIn effectively at http://blog.guykawasaki.com/2007/01/ten_ways_to_use.html.) This is especially true when people use Google to search for you because your site has a higher Google PageRank, that is, your profile comes up more quickly in search results when people search for your name, giving you more opportunities for people to network with you.

You'll learn more about customizing your profile name in Chapter 3, about searching for people in Chapter 4, and about adding new contacts in Chapter 5. As you connect with people, you'll also learn more about the appropriate methods for introducing yourself to other LinkedIn members in Chapter 10. If you're trying to reach someone on LinkedIn but can't get through, you'll learn about managing non-responders in Chapter 11.

Get a Job, Man!

When a friend of mine told me recently that he was looking for a job, one of the first things I told him was to sign onto LinkedIn and let me know when he did, so that I could not only link to his site but also write a recommendation for him. When you write recommendations for other users, they appear in the users' profiles so that others can read about how great your contacts are. Not only are other LinkedIn users searching for fellow users with similar interests, but recruiters and business owners also use LinkedIn to find great employees by posting job listings. And your LinkedIn home page shows you who's hiring in your network.

In addition, as Guy Kawasaki notes in the same blog entry, LinkedIn also enables you to perform reverse checks on your prospective manager as well as the company you're thinking of working for. You can use LinkedIn to contact people who have worked at the company, get feedback from them, and find out about the current rate of turnover.

You'll learn more about finding and recruiting for jobs in Chapter 6 and about placing references on your LinkedIn profile in Chapter 8.

Give and Get Inside Information

LinkedIn is also a great place for members to collaborate. You can question only the people in your network, or you can expand your search for information in LinkedIn Answers, which is a section for asking and answering questions at-large. You can ask a question in as many as 16 different forums, from issues about business administration to using LinkedIn. You also can participate in discussions and answer questions from other users.

What's more, as Penelope Trunk notes (in the same blog entry), you can get ideas for topics and trends in your industry. For example, she notes that, if you look for information about the iPhone, you get some of the buzz about the product from other LinkedIn users. If you're looking to work or start a business in a particular industry, Guy Kawasaki points out that you can use LinkedIn to find out who worked for your competitors and see who's starting up businesses in the same industry.

The more questions you answer, the more you become recognized as an expert in the LinkedIn community, and that leads to more opportunities for you. You'll learn more about searching for answers, answering questions, and raising your profile in Chapter 9.

Compare and Contrast

LinkedIn is not the only business networking site around, but it's become the most popular because it's easy to use and it's free. Like many sites that offer free services, LinkedIn relies on advertising revenue to pay the bills and employees' salaries. You'll see these advertisements in many places on the LinkedIn site, and they come from companies that are targeting professionals like you.

Also like many free service Web sites, there's a catch: the free service that LinkedIn provides gives you only so much. The free part of the service provides a network of unlimited size but a limited number of introductions to other members. LinkedIn offers (at the time of this writing) four "premium" plans that give you more powerful communication and search tools, as well as enhanced access, so that you can zero in on the people and resources you need. The prices range from $19.95 per month (or $199.50 a year if you want to pay in a lump sum and get two months free) for the Business plan to $200 a month for the full-blown Pro account (or pay $2,000 for the year and get two months of service free). As the well-worn disclaimer in the automobile commercials goes, "Your mileage may vary." So decide for yourself what you need. View the latest LinkedIn Premium Accounts at http://www.linkedin .com/static?key=customer_service_premium, and decide which one (if any) is right for you.

If you want to learn more about other business networking sites, turn to

Chapter 12 for a review of such sites, how they compare to LinkedIn, and their Web site addresses so that you can check them out for yourself.

Increase Your Chances of Success

David Teten and Scott Allen, in their book *The Virtual Handshake: Opening Doors and Closing Deals Online* (AMACOM, 2005), provides some quick ideas on how to increase your chance of business success using LinkedIn:

- "Answer questions well. Don't rattle off a quick opinion. Put some thought into it. Provide some additional resources. Refer people to an appropriate expert from within your network. Most of the questions on LinkedIn Answers are from people actually trying to solve a problem or accomplish something, not just looking for something to talk about. What better way to be of service than to actually help someone accomplish something?"

- "Add value to introduction requests. If you buy into the idea that LinkedIn is designed for 'trusted referrals,' then you need to participate in that. A trusted referral isn't just, 'Joe meet Sally, Sally meet Joe.' A trusted referral adds context to the introduction that helps the two people get off to a good start. How do you know this person? How can you recommend them in the context of their request?"

- "Make good recommendations. Don't just wait for people to recommend you and then reciprocate. Be proactive. Go through your network. Who among them do you feel strongly about that you could give a good recommendation to for their profile? When you add someone new, do you know them well enough to go ahead and recommend them? Also, recommendations on your own profile are a great way to show your own reputation, and the best way to ask for an endorsement is to give one. Don't write empty, generic recommendations."

- "Respond in a timely manner. Forward introduction requests right away. As to the rest, get to them as quickly as you can. Allen admits in his book that he is pretty slow in responding to invitations and to introduction requests if they are just general 'I'd like to meet you' requests because he places his existing clients, business associates, and family in front of new networking contacts. But he almost always handles forwarding requests within 24 hours and 2 days at the most."

- "Help your contacts learn how to use LinkedIn effectively. Most people don't have a clue how to get beyond the basics of a simple profile with their last couple of jobs and connecting with a few colleagues they keep up with. Help them! Go through your contacts list and see which people have less than 10 connections. Send them an e-mail message asking them if there's anything you can do to help them make better use of the system. Doing so not only helps them, it also helps you and all of your network if more people become actively engaged."

- "Be proactive. One of LinkedIn's shortcomings is that it doesn't have a mechanism for proactively introducing two people that you know. That doesn't mean you can't use it for that. For example, let's say you meet somebody new and they're looking to meet people with an interest in, say process management. Now, even though you know your contacts fairly well, you may not be able to remember (or even know) which of them have a background in process management, and I'm betting that's not in your contact management system either. But it is in LinkedIn. Search your network. Find the matches. Copy their profile URLs and send them to the new person you met and then say you'd be happy to make an introduction. Or say someone needs to a fill a certain position. Search your LinkedIn network and send them the list of people in your first and second degree and tell them you'd be glad to introduce the ones they're interested in talking to. Great networking is proactive, not just reactive."

- "Finally, use LinkedIn to enhance face to face meetings. Having a connection on LinkedIn is a great ice breaker in a conversation as you can share mutual connections and be able to establish some rapport rather quickly."

The Best Examples of LinkedIn Success

Many people have used LinkedIn to become successful, and their stories may help you think about ways you can use LinkedIn to increase your own success.

Promote and Grow Your Career

If you're looking to promote and grow your career, Jason Alba, the CEO of Jibber Jobber.com, offers the following tips about how to create an appropriate LinkedIn profile (http://www.jibberjobber.com/blog/archives/589):

- "Set up a meaty profile. This is something that recruiters and hiring managers will find when looking for candidates, which means have the right keywords in there."

- "Make your profile public, or at least a lot of it, so non-LinkedIn folks can still get value out of it without logging in or creating a new account."

- "Make connections. If you have 1 or 2 connections, start growing your account. Your goal should be to get it up to 60 people to make it start to pay off for you."

Leverage Profiles and Other Connectivity Tools

Liz Ryan is CEO of WorldWIT (http://www.asklizryan.com) and has more than 25 years of experience as a human resources professional. She offers a number of methods for leveraging your profiles and other connectivity tools from her blog (linkedin-notes.blogspot.com/2005/11/build-your-business-with-liz-ryans-ten.html):

- "Update your connections on new projects you are working on and it provides an opportunity to give them a call."

- "Advance your understanding of relationships between people you are linked to."

- "Connect with former colleagues from every past company, you never know where those former relationships can take you or your business."

- "Connect beyond the obvious. If you can't get into the company you are trying to, find a vendor or a partner that works with them and look for an introduction in."

- "Use LinkedIn to understand more about your prospects, look at where they used to work and where they went to school. Find your connections to those previous employers and alma maters to help you 'get over the wall.'"

- "What's in it for them? Don't reach out to brand new contacts that you don't know and ask them to do something for you or buy something from you. Look at their profile and see if there is something you can do for them in the way of an introduction or just market information."

- "Your contacts may be even more valuable to others than they are to you. You may have connections that would receive value from your network. Be generous and offer to make an introduction. It will come back to you."

- "When you spot a cluster of people who all know each other and are all accomplished in the same arena, that's a really special thing. It means that there is a mother lode of knowledge around these people that could be beneficial to your business. Reach out to one or two of them and express your interest in their topic and ask if you could send along a question or two. If they could possibly share the question in the group and tap into the rich repository of information it would be highly beneficial to you. Again remember to offer something in return for their knowledge."

- "Use LinkedIn with Google Alerts (http://www.google.com/alerts), which is a great business tool. For example, maybe you want to reach someone at Fidelity Investments (https://www.fidelity.com). Do a LinkedIn search on the company and you will probably come up with a couple of names that you will want to speak to. Set up a Google Alert on those people. This kind of intelligence will tell you what she cares about, etc. What's more flattering than a LinkedIn outreach message that says, 'I was sorry to miss your speech at the Financial Summit, but I was fortunate enough to read your thoughts on petro-dollars on Money.com and to catch your NPR interview last week.' Be diligent, but don't sound like a business stalker either."

- "Vendors like to reach out to former clients, and that's good, but it can be awkward when you haven't kept up and have no idea what the former client is now up to. Now you have LinkedIn to find him/her and catch up on what s/he is doing, so when you email it is not the 'let's catch up' message, but rather, 'Wow! You're at Fidelity! You know I see you've only been in the job a few months, so we should talk. It so happens that I've become something of an expert on Fidelity lately. . . .'"

Use Profiles to Find Common Connections

Make the Connection, Close the Deal

Al Chase is an East Coast recruiter who uses LinkedIn as his personal home page. Al checks his LinkedIn profile every day to see what his contacts are doing in the way of adding connections, moving to new jobs, and/or being promoted.
Al recently was contacted by a prospective client who found him on LinkedIn and who was motivated to call because:

- Al not only had a large number of connections, but also his connections were high quality.
- The client was attracted by the number and consistency of Al's endorsers and by their comments about his unusual approach to recruiting.
- The client and he were two connection degrees away from one another with LinkedIn; they were separated by an attorney in Boston with whom they both had worked in the past.

Al recognized that the potential client was in an area outside his range of experience and that he was competing with large retained executive search firms in Boston for the right to do the search. So Al quickly went to the client's LinkedIn profile to look for any similarities and/or connections that he might have had with this prospective client to help him turn this possible client into a paying one.

Al learned that both he and the client had a background in choreography and dance, which helped Al strike up a conversation. Despite Al's lack of experience in the potential client's field of expertise, he made the client feel comfortable to get himself hired. Al then used LinkedIn to identify the top talent in the industry, matched his new client with the talent, and closed a successful search.

Fill in Your Business Trip

David Teten and Scott Allen (in their book) note that LinkedIn is a very good way to schedule new appointments on your next business trip:

> Very often when you are on a business trip, you have holes in your day due to not enough appointments. Use LinkedIn by doing an Advanced Search to find people in the industry and geographic location you are traveling to. It's best to focus on the people that are one or two connection degrees away from you so the response time should be fairly timely. You can also reach out to one of your connections who you think may know people in a certain industry and location and ask that they scan their first degree connections for you and see if they can provide an introduction or two. In no time you will have filled up your travel schedule with new appointments.

You'll learn more about using degrees of connections in Chapter 10.

Boost Sales and Sales Delivery

Teten and Allen also offers advice in his book not only for closing the deal but also for bringing together people with the right skill sets to get the deal done.

> Quite often, especially for small businesses, you can't do it all yourself. LinkedIn is invaluable for finding partners with particular skill sets who can help you deliver the total solution. In addition to searching, you can post questions asking about the solution area you need expertise in and use that as a way to attract potential partners.
>
> Search for people at your potential customers who are not closely involved in your deal—preferably second degree contacts, not third degree.

> Ask for an informational interview. This is where strong, trusted relation-
> ships count for a lot—"light linking" (not a strong bond) breaks down
> here. Ask your interview subject about the priorities that are going on at
> the company—what are the high level factors that might be influencing
> the buying process. Be completely open and transparent. If you have a
> good solution and a really good referral to a true "friend of a friend," you
> will very likely find an internal champion in that person. This is the num-
> ber one technique that LinkedIn supports better than any other tool.

Streamline Your Sales Pipeline

Erik Hoogerhuis, vice president of business development at Pentaho (http://www
.pentaho.com), has a unique way to use LinkedIn. Erik used Salesforce.com as a way
to track the company's sales pipeline and to find new customers. Pentaho has a direct
link with Salesforce and LinkedIn. So when Pentaho finds a prospective client
through Salesforce, it immediately sends the client to LinkedIn to get the person's
background and title. Salesforce also determines whether the contact is the right person in the organization for Erik to be speaking to and is viable as a potential customer.
This LinkedIn–Salesforce.com connection has allowed Erik and Pentaho to save time
by focusing on the right customer and has resulted in a dramatic improvement in the
company's sales process and its bottom line.

Let's Go Exploring

These are just some of the best examples of using LinkedIn to enhance your success. Now it's time to learn how to log into LinkedIn and use it, so let's proceed to
Chapter 2.

Signing In and Changing Your Account Settings

The Web site address for LinkedIn is easy to remember: http://www.linkedin.com. Opening the LinkedIn site for the first time, you see the LinkedIn home page as shown in Figure 2-1. The home page contains two links for you to join LinkedIn right away. Click the Join Now link at the top right of the page, or click the yellow Join Now button near the bottom of the page. Above the Join Now button, LinkedIn invites you to type the name of your company and/or your school, then click the Join Now button to connect with them. You don't have to type the name of the company and/or school because this information is not passed to the Join Now page that appears when you click the Join Now button. You'll learn more about joining later in Chapter 2.

Figure 2-1. **The LinkedIn home page**

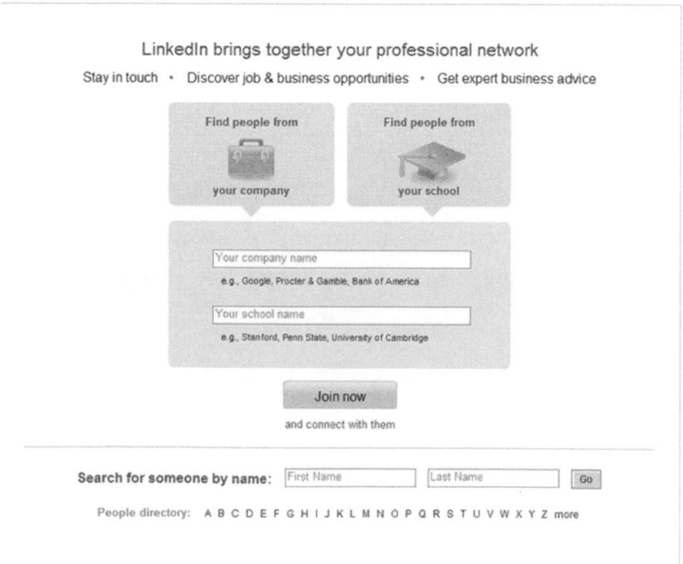

For now, let's turn our attention to the three links at the top right of the page. One of them is the Join Now link. To the right is a link for users to sign in. To the left is the What is LinkedIn? link, which, when clicked, opens the What is LinkedIn? page, as shown in Figure 2-2. You can click on one of the three boxes on the page to learn more about connecting with people, powering your career, and getting answers. If you want to join now, click the Join Now button. At the top of the page, the Home link appears so that you can go back to the home page if you want. The top of the page also contains the Sign In link if you already have an account.

Figure 2-2. **The What Is LinkedIn? page**

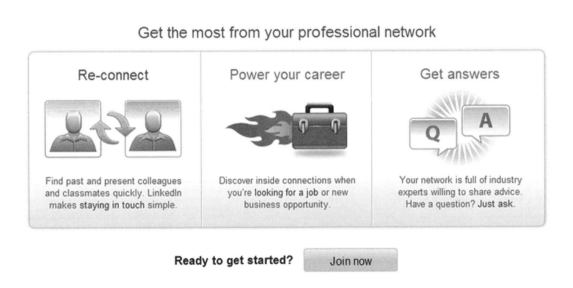

Find Someone Fast

To enable you to look for someone you believe is on LinkedIn, the home page offers two quick methods. Below the Join Now button, you can search for someone by name by typing the first name and last name in the First Name and Last Name boxes, respectively, and then clicking the Go button, as shown in Figure 2-3. If LinkedIn finds a match, it displays the public profile of the member in the public profile page. For example, when I search for my name, I find my public profile, as shown in Figure 2-4.

Figure 2-3. **The Search for Someone by Name boxes**

LinkedIn brings together your professional network

Stay in touch · Discover job & business opportunities · Get expert business advice

Find people from
your company

Find people from
your school

Your company name

e.g., Google, Procter & Gamble, Bank of America

Your school name

e.g., Stanford, Penn State, University of Cambridge

Join now

and connect with them

Search for someone by name: First Name | Last Name | Go

People directory: A B C D E F G H I J K L M N O P Q R S T U V W X Y Z more

Figure 2-4. **Eric's public profile**

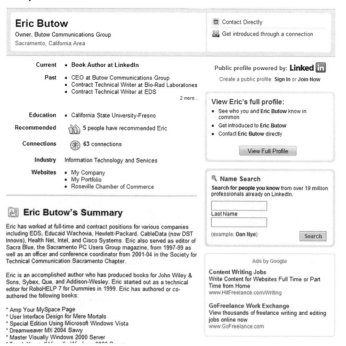

Eric Butow
Owner, Butow Communications Group
Sacramento, California Area

Contact Directly

Get introduced through a connection

Current • Book Author at LinkedIn

Past • CEO at Butow Communications Group
• Contract Technical Writer at Bio-Rad Laboratories
• Contract Technical Writer at EDS

2 more...

Education • California State University-Fresno

Recommended • 5 people have recommended Eric

Connections • 63 connections

Industry Information Technology and Services

Websites • My Company
• My Portfolio
• Roseville Chamber of Commerce

Public profile powered by: **Linked in**

Create a public profile: Sign In or Join Now

View Eric's full profile:
• See who you and **Eric Butow** know in common
• Get introduced to **Eric Butow**
• Contact **Eric Butow** directly

View Full Profile

Name Search
Search for people you know from over 19 million professionals already on LinkedIn.

Last Name

(example: **Dan Nye**) Search

Ads by Google

Content Writing Jobs
Write Content for Websites Full Time or Part Time from Home
www.HitFreelance.com/Writing

GoFreelance Work Exchange
View thousands of freelance writing and editing jobs online now
www.GoFreelance.com

Eric Butow's Summary

Eric has worked at full-time and contract positions for various companies including EDS, Educaid Wachovia, Hewlett-Packard, CableData (now DST Innovis), Health Net, Intel, and Cisco Systems. Eric also served as editor of Sacra Blue, the Sacramento PC Users Group magazine, from 1997-99 as well as an officer and conference coordinator from 2001-04 in the Society for Technical Communication Sacramento Chapter.

Eric is an accomplished author who has produced books for John Wiley & Sons, Sybex, Que, and Addison-Wesley. Eric started out as a technical editor for RoboHELP 7 for Dummies in 1999. Eric has authored and co-authored the following books:

* Amp Your MySpace Page
* User Interface Design for Mere Mortals
* Special Edition Using Microsoft Windows Vista
* Dreamweaver MX 2004 Savvy
* Master Visually Windows 2000 Server

Unfortunately, you can type only the exact first and last names. If you want to use a partial word search, you need to join LinkedIn to take advantage of its search tools. Also, the link to the home page may escape your attention. It's contained in the Public Profile Powered by LinkedIn logo in the upper right corner of the page. If you know that a person's last name starts with a certain letter but you're not sure of the spelling, you can use the People directory that appears below the Search for Someone by Name area.

Click the first letter of the last name. After you click the link, the LinkedIn directory appears with links to groups of users whose names start with that letter. For example, Figure 2-5 shows the LinkedIn directory for the letter "B." You may remember the card catalogs at your local library. Each card-filled drawer held a range of terms arranged alphabetically. LinkedIn uses the same principle. If you know the range of the desired contact's last name, click the link—that is, look in that drawer. LinkedIn drills down to the second level of name ranges.

From here you can refine your search by clicking on the appropriate name range link, or, to return to the top level of your search, click the letter link. For example, click the B link to return to the top search level for last names that start with

Figure 2-5. **The LinkedIn directory for the letter "B"**

B. If you want to go to the main directory page and search for names that start with a different letter, click the LinkedIn Directory link at the top of the page.

Unfortunately, using the LinkedIn Directory from the home page has two disadvantages. First, if you don't know the exact name of the LinkedIn member, you may spend a lot of time searching for the correct name. Second, because the link to the LinkedIn home page is embedded in the LinkedIn logo at the top of the page (i.e., there is no clear link saying "Home" or "Back to the Home Page"), how to get back to the home page isn't clear.

What's Happening?

Ten links sit at the bottom of the home page:

1. About LinkedIn
2. LinkedIn Blog
3. Privacy Policy
4. Copyright Policy
5. Help & FAQ
6. Advertising
7. LinkedIn Answers
8. LinkedIn Company Pages
9. LinkedIn Team
10. LinkedIn Updates

Of these, you might find six links of particular interest.

LinkedIn Blog

If you want to get the most out of LinkedIn by receiving tips and information from the people who manage the company, click the LinkedIn Blog link. The blog page is updated regularly and contains text, photos, video, and feedback from other LinkedIn company employees, as shown in Figure 2-6. Scroll down to read the blog entries and feedback from other LinkedIn members, to learn what's going on with the company, and to leave comments or questions for those employees. If you want to return to the LinkedIn.com home page, click the LinkedIn.com link at the top of the page.

↷ *Figure 2-6.* **The LinkedIn Blog page**

Help & FAQ

When you click the Help & FAQ (frequently asked questions) link, the Help & FAQ page appears. Figure 2-7 shows this page with the default topic: the top 10 questions users ask. When you click on the question, the answer appears below the question. You also can view answers for all the questions by clicking the Open All link in the upper right corner of the page. To get information about a different topic, click the link in the FAQ list. If you want to go back to the home page, click the LinkedIn icon.

LinkedIn Answers

LinkedIn users are constantly asking questions of other users to get information and opinions, and that makes LinkedIn a great information resource. Before you ask a question of other LinkedIn members, check to see whether anyone else has asked your question. You may also be interested in simply browsing the latest questions that have been asked to see whether you can learn something new today. If you want to know the questions LinkedIn users are asking, click the LinkedIn Answers link to view the list of most recently asked ones, as shown in Figure 2-8.

Figure 2-7. **The Help & FAQ page**

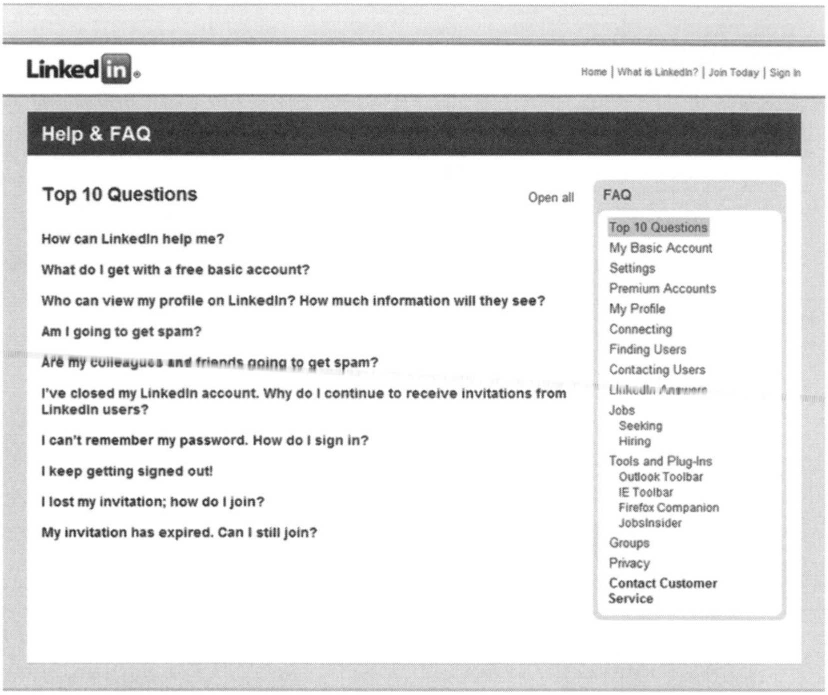

Figure 2-8. **The Answers page with a list of questions**

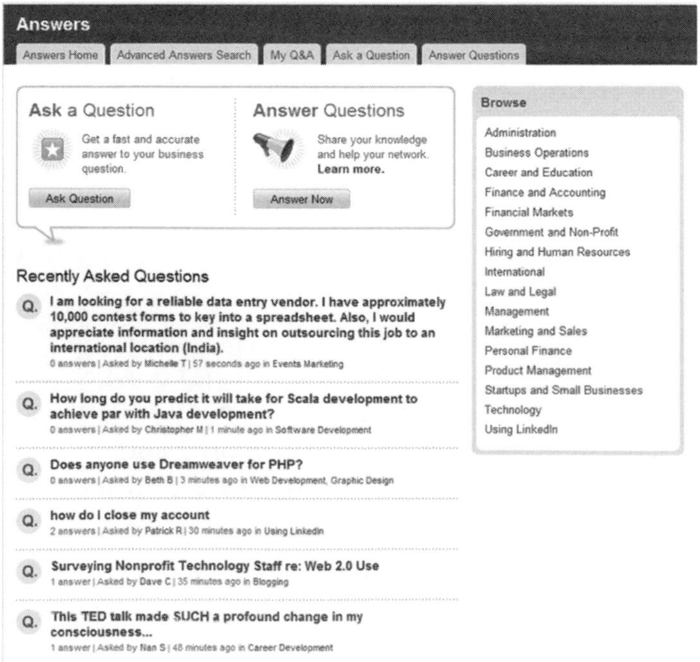

The browse area lets you look over questions according to categories, from business administration to how to use LinkedIn. Information underneath each question tells you the number of answers to the question, who asked the question, how long ago the member asked the question, and the question category. If you find a question that piques your interest, click it. LinkedIn lists ten questions on each page in order of how long ago members asked the questions. To see older questions, scroll down to the bottom of the page and click the Next link. If you want to ask or answer a question, click the Ask Question or Answer Now buttons, respectively, at the top of the page. If you're not a member, LinkedIn asks you to sign up.

You can return to the home page by clicking the Home tab at the top of the page.

LinkedIn Company Pages

Employees from many different companies are available on LinkedIn. If you want to know who's representing major companies on LinkedIn, click the LinkedIn Company Pages link. Figure 2-9 shows the list of nine company pages from major companies, including Apple, Dell, IBM, and Pfizer. Click on any of the links to see a list of LinkedIn members who are also employees of the company. For example, when you click the Apple link, the Apple company page appears, as shown in Figure 2-10. (Note: Though the company name hasn't changed on LinkedIn, the actual name of the company is Apple, Inc. and no longer Apple Computer.)

The company page contains all Apple employees who are currently members of LinkedIn. The employees are categorized into different areas, such as engineering and human resources. The contacts page lists only the first few contacts in each category. If you want to see more contacts, click the link at the bottom of the category list that tells you how many other company employees in that category are members of LinkedIn. (In some cases, hundreds or even thousands of other contacts are available at the company.) As with many other pages, go back to the home page by clicking the LinkedIn logo at the upper right corner of the page.

Go to Chapter 4 for more information about searching for companies in LinkedIn.

LinkedIn Team

Perhaps you want to know who the LinkedIn Team is. Or maybe you want to get connected with one or more people who worked at LinkedIn, in order to ask ques-

Figure 2-9. **The Company Pages page**

Figure 2-10. **The LinkedIn company page for Apple**

Employee Snapshot

Previous workplace:	Top Schools:	Average length of employment:
• Sun Microsystems	• San Jose State University	• 4.74 years
• Peoplesoft	• Stanford University	
• Adobe Systems	• University of California, Berkeley	**Years since graduation:**
• Sgi		• 12.46 years
• Cisco Systems		

Other company pages:

- Accenture
- AMD
- Apple
- Cisco Systems
- Dell
- IBM
- JP Morgan Chase
- Nortel
- Pfizer

See all

Find Contacts at Apple

My network only, Business Development, Consultant, Engineering, Human Resources, Information Technology, Marketing, Operations, Public Relations, Sales

Business Development

Michal Szklarz - Business Development Manager EMEA
Serge Robe - Business Development Manager
Simon Harper - Business Development Mgr Video
100+ more business development professionals at Apple

Consulting

John Whitehead - Consulting Engineer, Media & Entertainment
Morihide Tenpaku - Senior Consultant & Hardware Engineer
Todd Dailey - Senior Technical Solution Developer
Vin Agarwal - Consultant
100+ more consulting professionals at Apple

Engineering

Chris Emura - Engineering Manager
Jeff Calado - Engineering Manager
Jeffrey Kim - Developer Relations Manager
Mark Aitala - Field Service Worldwide Data Manager
1000+ more Engineering professionals at Apple

Human Resources

Dan Patel - Sr.Recruiter
Gilda Montesino - Senior Technical Recruiter
Patrick Burke - Staffing Manager/Recruiter, iPod Engineering
Purvi Patel, CIR - Recruiter/Research Sourcer
100+ more human resource professionals at Apple

tions, build your network, or give someone a well-deserved pat on the back. You can view the list by clicking the LinkedIn team link, which gives you the entire list of LinkedIn team members.

The LinkedIn team walks the walk, as they say, by making their profiles available for you to view and by giving you the opportunity to contact them if you have a question, comment, or suggestion. Click on a team member's name to see the profile and to learn more about the member and his or her background. If you want to contact the team member directly, click the Contact Directly link in the upper right corner of the profile page.

Who've Updated Their Profiles?

If you want to get the most out of LinkedIn, keep tabs on those who have been updating their profiles frequently so that you can determine whether there are any networking opportunities for you. You can get a quick view of members who have updated their profiles recently by clicking the LinkedIn Updates link. Figure 2-11 shows the list of recently updated profiles. The Recently Updated Profile page lists the latest 50 updated profiles, those with the most recently updated profiles listed at the top. The profiles include the names of the members, their titles, their locations, and their industries. If you want to see more profiles, scroll down to the bottom of the page and click the More Profile Updates link. You can view the user's full profile and do other things (like contact the user) by clicking the Full Profile button, but you have to sign up first before you can view the profile.

Create a New LinkedIn Account

Now that you've had a chance to see what you can do without signing up for LinkedIn, it's time to learn what you can do as a LinkedIn member. Signing up for LinkedIn is easy, and it's even easier after you sign up because, if you have cookies enabled in your Web browser, LinkedIn automatically remembers your login information and opens your home page when you sign in.

When you first log into LinkedIn, the home page invites you to type the name of your company or of your school, then click the Join Now button. Typing the information into the Your Company Name or Your School Name text boxes does you no good because this information isn't entered into the LinkedIn application form. So save yourself some time and skip typing in these boxes.

Figure 2-11. **The Recently Updated Profiles page**

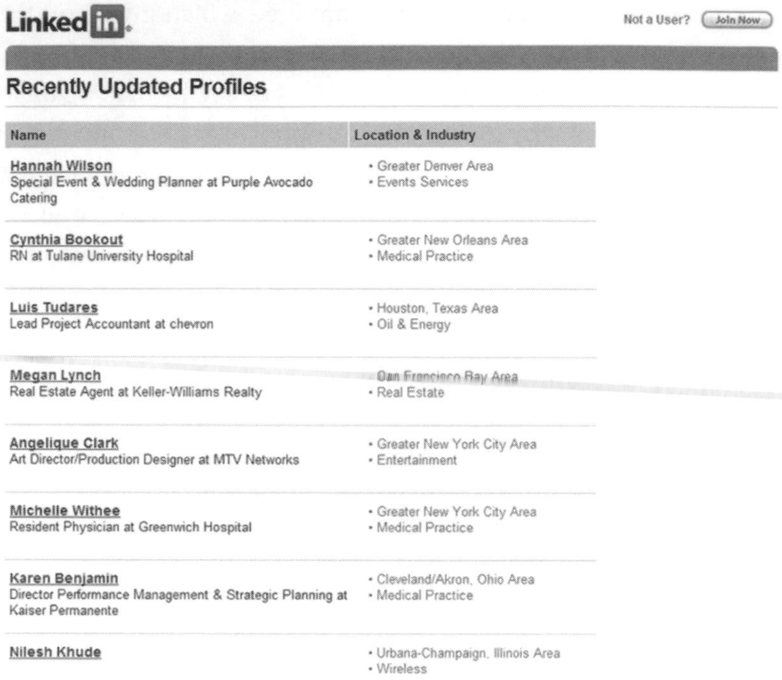

Instead, create a new LinkedIn account by clicking the Join Now link at the upper right corner of the home page or by clicking the yellow Join Now button. After you click the button or the link, the Join LinkedIn page appears, as shown in Figure 2-12.

The application form is divided into three sections: (1) your contact information at the top, (2) your employment information in the middle, and (3) your education information at the bottom.

Add Your Contact Information

In the top center, type (in the appropriate boxes) your first and last names, e-mail address, and your password (twice to verify it). Select your country, and then type in your postal code. Your password must be at least six alphanumeric characters, and the page notes that only your region will be visible for everyone to see so that you can maintain a level of privacy.

⌒ *Figure 2-12.* **The Join LinkedIn page**

Your Employment Status

In the middle section, the default button selection for your employment status is employed. If you have a different employment status, click one of the four other buttons, as shown in Figure 2-13.

You can select only one button; so consider which button to select. For example:

- If you're currently employed but looking for work, you may not want your boss to look at your profile and see that you're looking around. So you may want to state that you're currently employed and to conduct your new job search on LinkedIn discreetly.

- If you're currently employed, you can type the company name and your job title in the Company and Title boxes, respectively. If you click the business owner button, you can type your company name in the Company box. Then you can choose your industry from the Industry list.

Figure 2-13. **The employment status buttons**

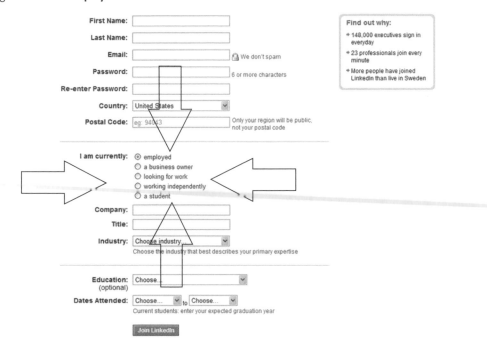

- If you're looking for work, working independently, or a student, you can choose only the industry you're in (or the area you're studying) from the Industry list.

Some Brief Educational Tidbits

In the bottom section, as shown in Figure 2-14, you must select the country in which you received or are receiving your education. Once you select a country, LinkedIn may ask you to select the state or province in which you received your education (from a state or province list). For example, if you select the United States, LinkedIn asks for the state (province in Canada). After you select the state, a new list box appears below the state list so that you can select your school. If your school isn't on the list, click Other at the bottom of the list. You can then type the name of your school in the box that appears below the school list.

In the Dates Attended area, you also can select the years you attended. Select the year you started from the left-hand Choose list and the date you completed or ex-

Figure 2-14. **The nation in which you received your education**

pect to complete your studies in the right-hand Choose list. Selecting the attendance dates is optional. You must add information in the rest of the boxes and lists. If you don't, after you click the Join LinkedIn button, the Join LinkedIn page reappears and tells you the information you need to enter before you can continue.

Note that, if you want to view the LinkedIn's user agreement and/or privacy policy, you can do so by clicking the appropriate link underneath the LinkedIn button. After you click one of these links, a new window opens and displays the information for your viewing pleasure.

Select Your Settings

Click the Join LinkedIn button to open the Contact Settings page, as shown in Figure 2-15. This page asks you how you intend to use LinkedIn to find people in your network as well as how you want other LinkedIn members to find you. Select the appropriate check boxes in the To Find and To Be Found areas. As you can see in Figure 2-15, several check boxes in each area are selected by default.

Figure 2-15. **The Contact Settings page**

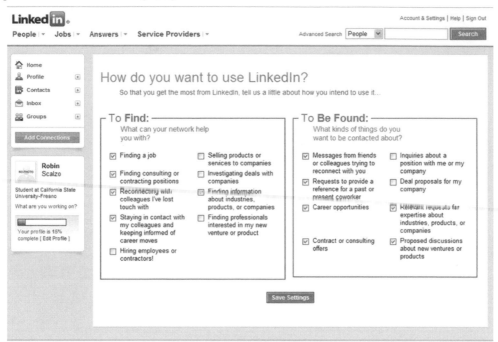

- In the *To Find* area, LinkedIn assumes you want to find a job, land consulting or contracting positions, reconnect with colleagues, stay in contact with colleagues, and obtain information about industries, products, or companies. However, if you have your own business or if you are happy in your current job, then you don't need to find a job or a consulting or contracting position, and you can clear those check boxes. However, you may want to sell products or services to companies and investigate deals with companies. In that case, select the appropriate check boxes.

- In the *To Be Found* area, LinkedIn assumes that you want to receive messages from friends or colleagues; accept requests to provide references; get information about career opportunities and about contract or consulting offers; receive requests from others for your expertise about industries, products, or companies; and discuss new venture or product proposals. If you have your own business, you're probably not looking for career opportunities; so you can clear that check box. However, if you have a company and you're looking for deals, you can select the Deal Proposals for My Company check box.

If you're looking for a job but you want to keep your search discreet, be sure to clear the check boxes about wanting to find a job and that you want to be contacted about career opportunities and/or contract or consulting offers.

When you're finished, click the Save Settings button. Now you see the LinkedIn member home page, as shown in Figure 2-16.

Figure 2-16. **The LinkedIn member home page**

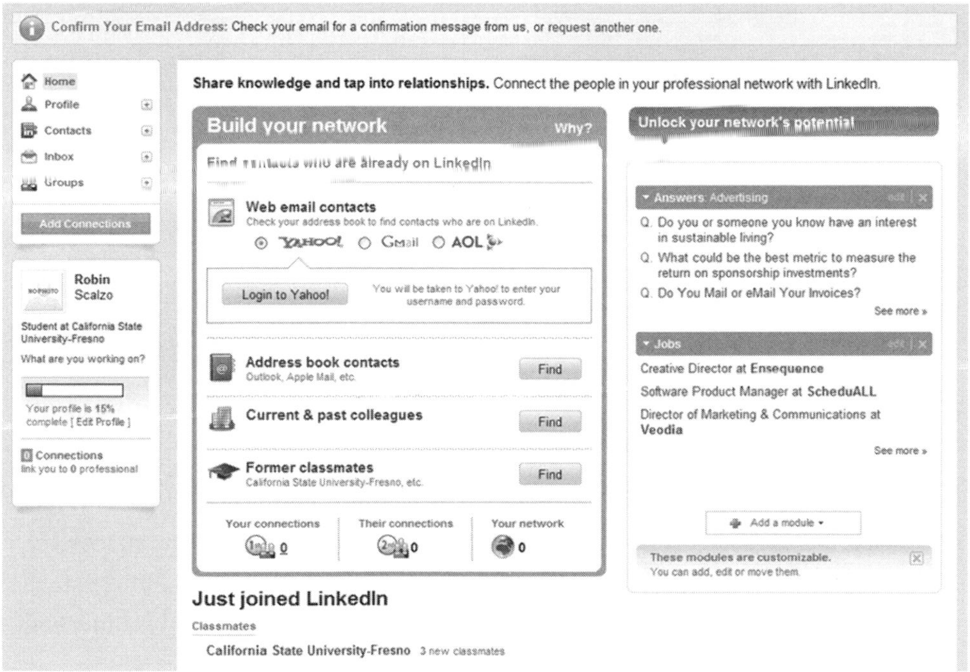

Congratulations! You have now set up your LinkedIn basic account. If you want to upgrade your account to a paid account, scroll down to the bottom of the page to see the available premium plans in the Upgrade area, as shown in Figure 2-17.

Upgrade Your Account

When you sign up on LinkedIn, you automatically receive a free account that lets you contact users in your network through the people you know (which LinkedIn calls introductions), send requests for introductions, and transmit private messages with business and career opportunities to any LinkedIn user. LinkedIn offers several different

Figure 2-17. **The Upgrade area**

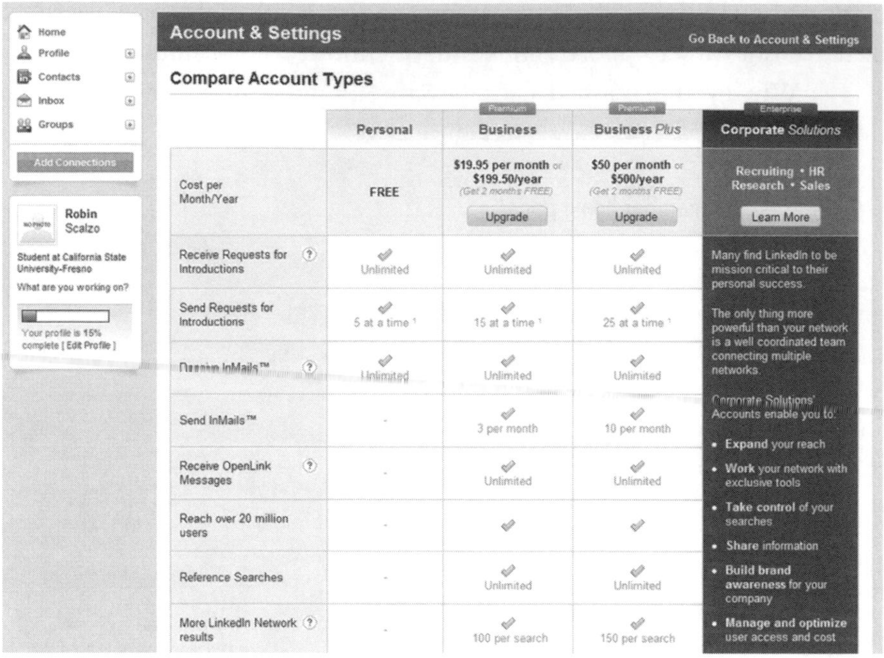

service packages with options to make your membership more successful and re-warding—at a price. For example, paid accounts allow you to send InMail messages to other users. InMail messages are private messages that let you send business and career opportunities directly to any LinkedIn user.

In the Compare Account Types table, you can select from one of three premium account types: Business, Business Plus, and Pro.

Business Account

When you click the Upgrade button in the Business column, the Account Options upgrade page for Business accounts appears, as shown in Figure 2-18.

The selected column shows the cost per month, the number of introduction requests you can receive at one time, how many InMail messages you can send per month, and how many LinkedIn Network results you can retrieve per search. If you want to see more features of the plan, click the Show Additional Features link underneath the table. At the bottom of the page you can choose to prepay for one year

Figure 2-18. **The Account Options page to upgrade to a Business account**

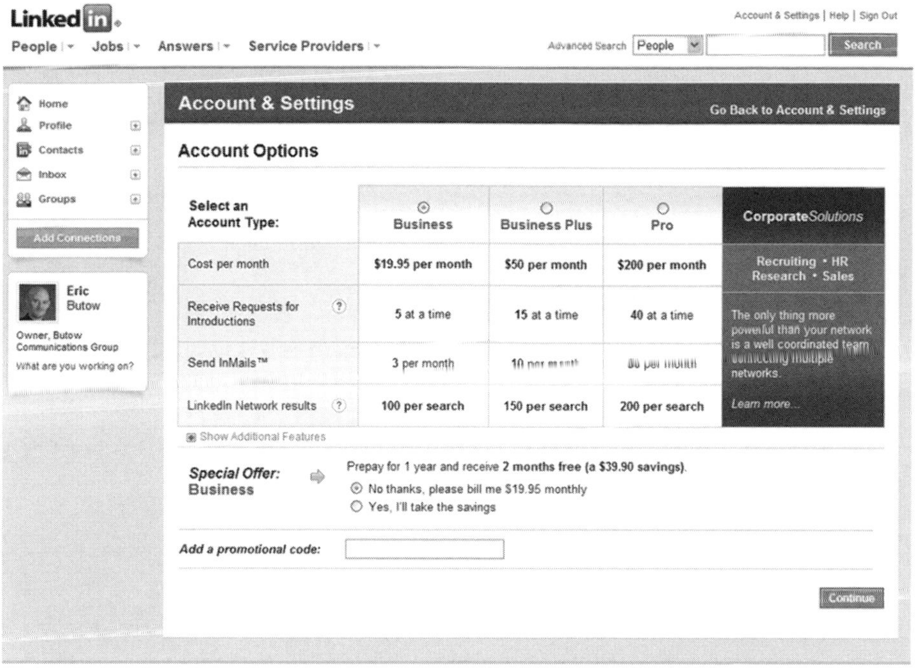

or billing at $19.95 per month (as of this writing). Note that with the Business, Business Plus, and Pro plans you can prepay for one year. LinkedIn knocks 20 percent off the price of the one-year payment, which is the equivalent of two months of service for free.

If you have a promotional code, which acts as a coupon for a discount on LinkedIn services, type the code in the Add a Promotional Code box.

Business Plus Account

Click the Business Plus button to highlight information about the Business Plus plan, as shown in Figure 2-19.

Pro Account

Click the Pro button to highlight information about the Pro plan, as shown in Figure 2-20.

Figure 2-19. **The Business Plus plan**

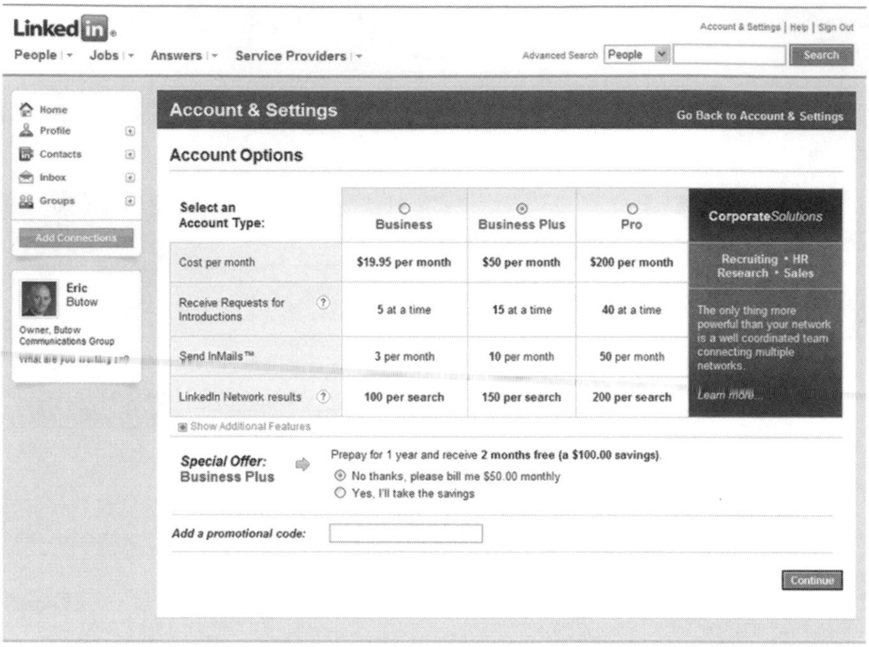

Figure 2-20. **The Pro plan**

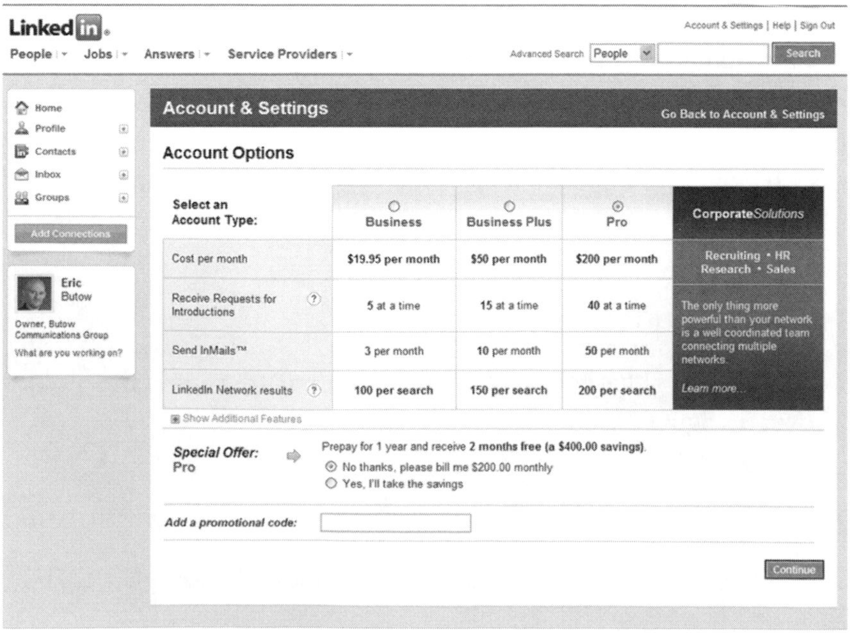

The far right column in the table contains information about the CorporateSolutions plan, which is primarily geared to recruiters, human resource personnel, and salespeople. You can get more information about this plan by clicking anywhere in this column. LinkedIn then asks you to fill out a form so that a representative can contact you right away.

After clicking the button in the table column for the plan you want to order and telling LinkedIn how you want to pay for the plan, click the Continue button to continue the order process.

Which Account Should I Select?

If you're not sure which plan suits your needs, click the Help & FAQ link in the Company area at the bottom of the LinkedIn home page. Then in the Help & FAQ page, click Premium Accounts in the FAQ list. Figure 2-21 shows the Premium Accounts FAQ page and lists the questions with answers. Just click the link to view the answer underneath the question.

Customer Service

If you need to contact LinkedIn about an issue or problem with the system, it's easy to contact LinkedIn Customer Service and write them a quick note. Access customer service by scrolling down to the bottom of the member home page and then clicking the Customer Service link, as shown in Figure 2-22. When you click the link, the Contact Customer Service page appears, as shown in Figure 2-23.

You can choose a topic that best describes your issue by clicking the appropriate button, or you can click the None of the Above button if none of the topics applies. If you want to type a description of the problem, type the message in the box. When you're finished, click the Contact Customer service button.

Sign Out and Sign Back In

LinkedIn saves all your information. So, if you close your browser tab or window and open it again, LinkedIn remembers who you are, and you can pick up where you left off. However, if someone else uses your computer or if you feel more secure by

Figure 2-21. **The Premium Accounts FAQ page**

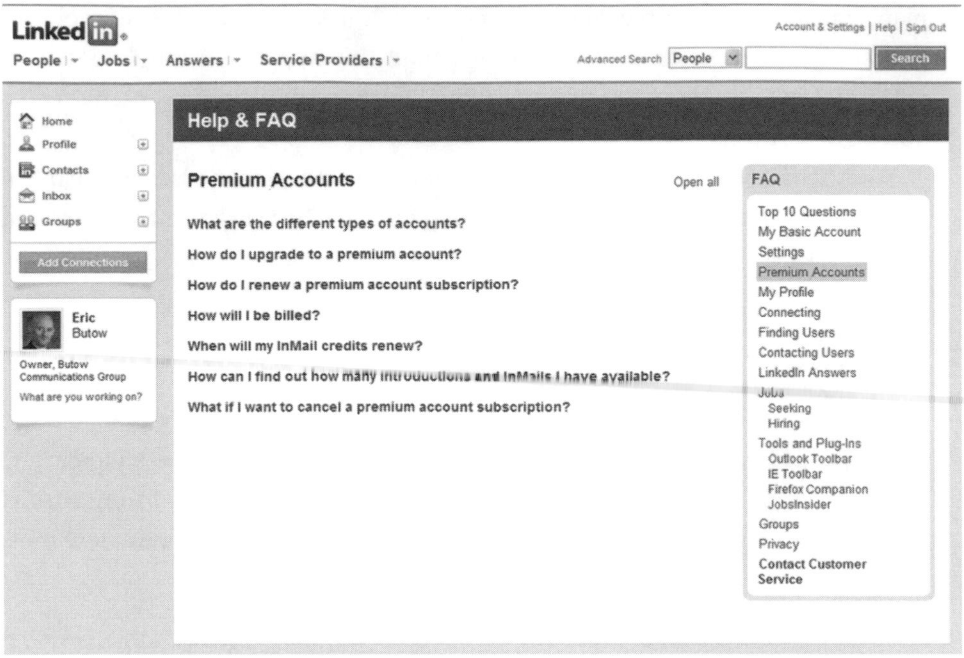

Figure 2-22. **The Customer Service link**

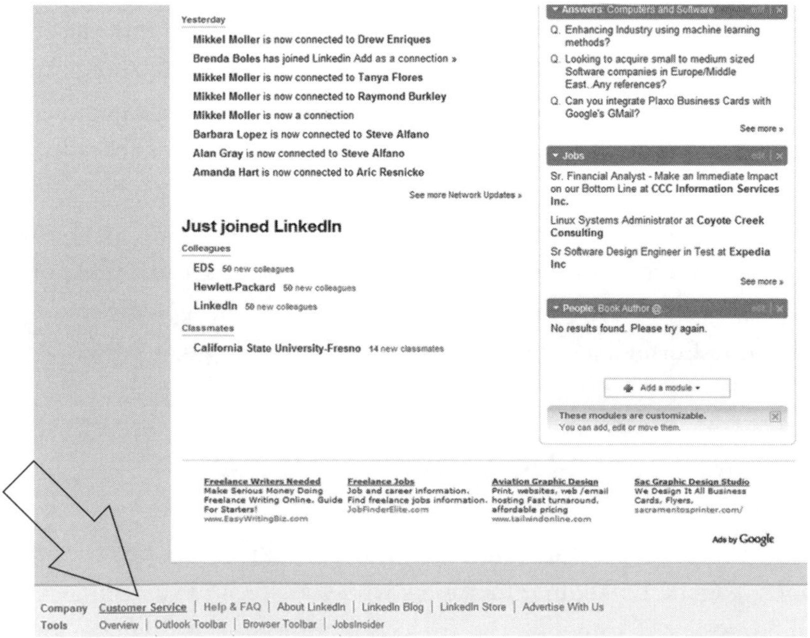

Figure 2-23. **The Contact Customer Service page**

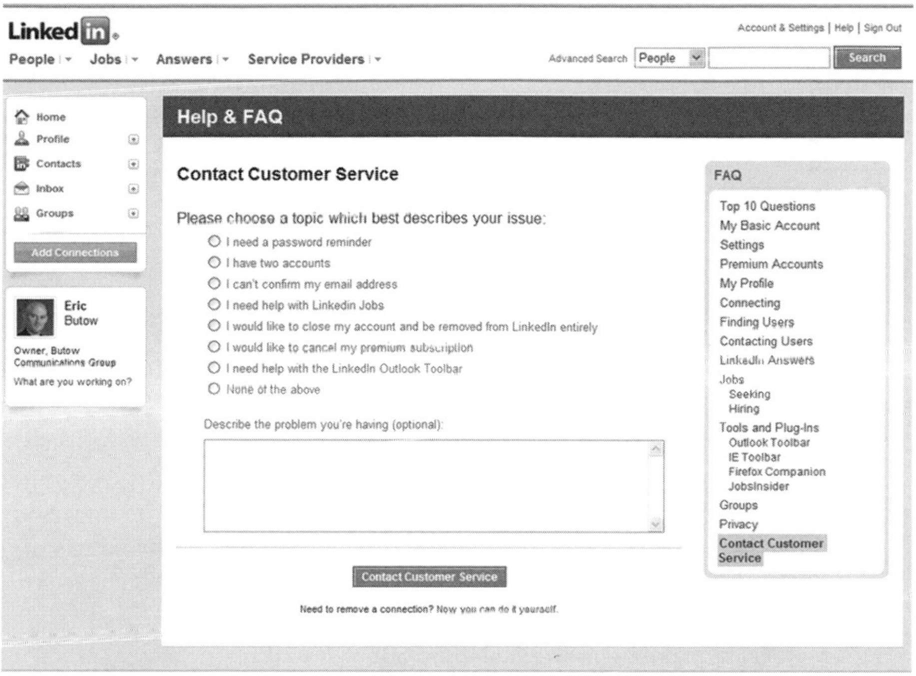

signing off, you can do so by clicking the Sign Out link at the top of the page (see Figure 2-24).

After you sign out, the Signed Out page appears. If your Web browser has cookies enabled, LinkedIn accesses the cookie file the next time you sign in and takes you immediately to your home page. You don't have to enter your user name and password.

If you want to sign out completely and don't mind typing your user name and password to log back in, click the Sign Out Completely button. If someone else uses or will be using your computer, it's a good idea to sign out completely, so that no one else can use your account. When you click the Sign Out Completely button, the LinkedIn member home page closes, and the standard LinkedIn member home page appears.

Sign back in by clicking the Sign In link in the upper right-hand corner of the page. Type your e-mail address in the E-mail Address box and the password in the Password box. If you forgot your password, click the Forgot password link and LinkedIn will ask you for your e-mail address to send you a link to reset the password.

Figure 2-24. **The Sign Out link**

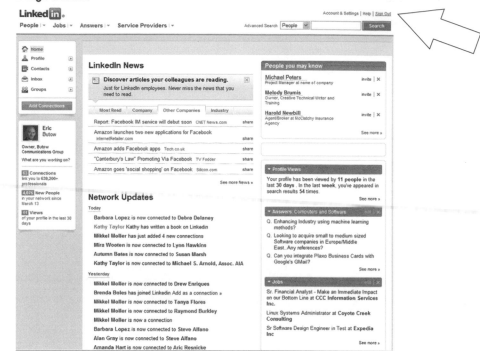

After you type your e-mail address and password, click the Sign In button. If the e-mail and password combination is incorrect, a message appears above the E-mail Address box informing you that the combination is incorrect and that you need to reenter your e-mail address, your password, or both. After you sign in successfully, your LinkedIn member home page appears.

Now that you've signed in, let's proceed to Chapter 3 to build your home page with current information about you and your successes.

3.

Creating Your Profile

When you sign in to LinkedIn for the first time, you see that the LinkedIn member home page is the "launch pad" for connecting with LinkedIn members, for building your profile, and for letting LinkedIn members know what you want them to know about you. LinkedIn provides the tools you need to build a profile that sells you (and your business if you have one) to the millions of LinkedIn members—many of whom are looking for someone just like you to share interests and information. LinkedIn also lets you know what information should be in your profile to make it as visible as possible to members. Once you complete your profile, you can make it visible only to certain LinkedIn members or to anyone on the Web.

The Sign In Page

If you skipped Chapter 2 or need a refresher, get started by accessing LinkedIn and then clicking the Sign In link in the upper right corner of the main LinkedIn page, as shown in Figure 3-1. After you click the link, Figure 3-2 shows the Sign In page that appears.

Type your e-mail address in the Email Address box, then type your password in the Password box. If you forgot the password, click the Forgot Password link so that LinkedIn can send a password reset link to your e-mail address. When you're ready to sign in, click the Sign In button.

When you use LinkedIn for the first time, the member home page appears as shown in Figure 3-3.

Figure 3-1. **The Sign In link on the main LinkedIn page**

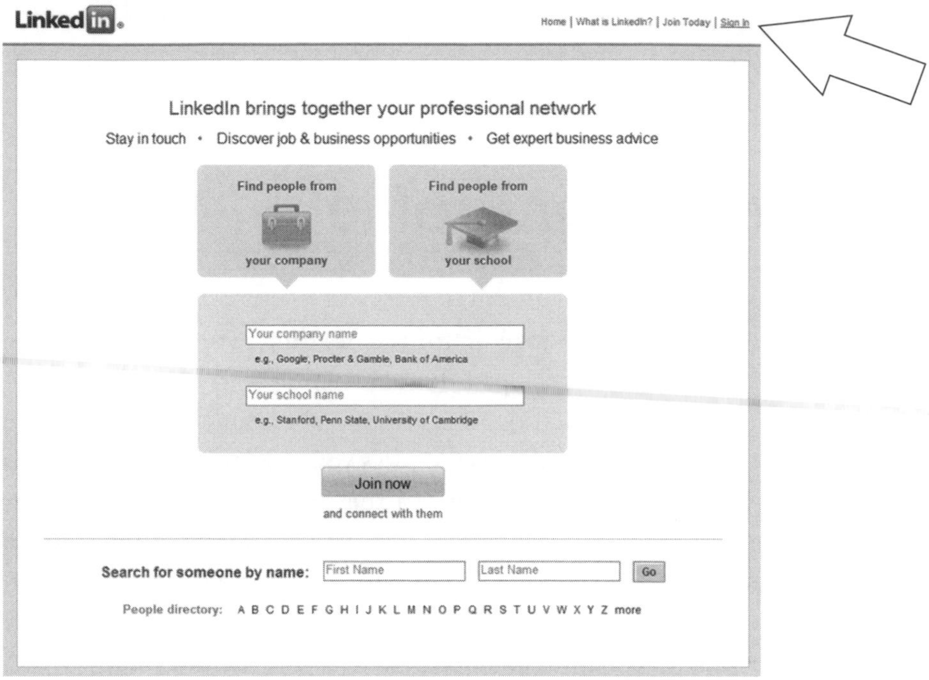

Figure 3-2. **The Sign In page**

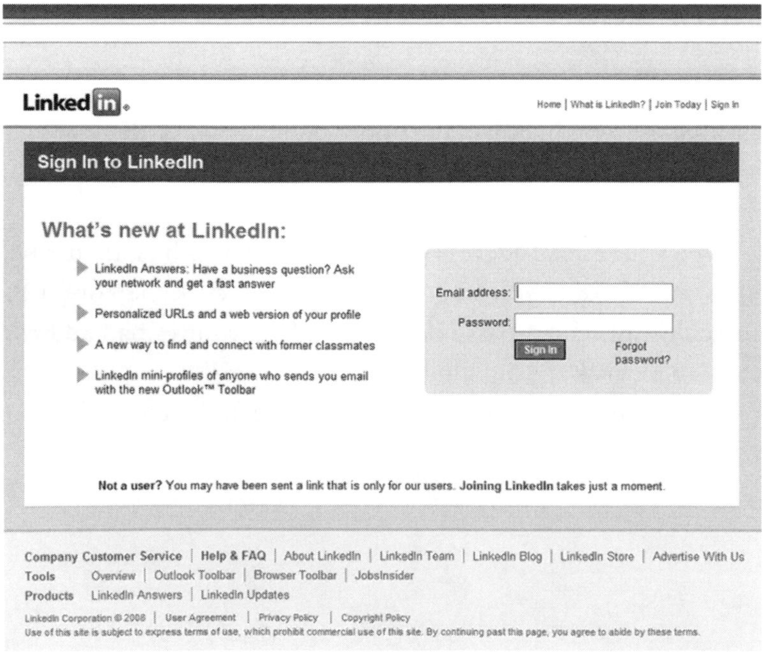

◯ *Figure 3-3.* **The LinkedIn member home page**

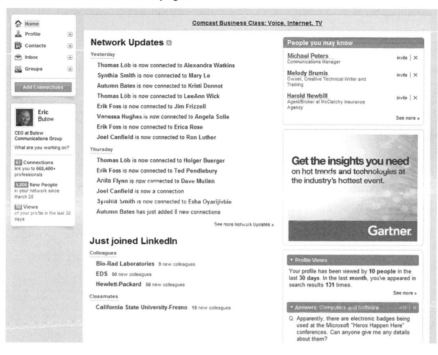

The Member Home Page

The member home page is broken up into four main areas:

1. The top area.
2. The Information box on the left side.
3. The Navigation and Profile boxes on the left side.
4. The Information area at the bottom of the page.

The Top Area

The top of the page contains links to other LinkedIn areas and functionalities, as well as your account settings. At the left are links to four areas of LinkedIn:

1. People.
2. Jobs.
3. Answers.
4. Service Providers.

As you click on each link name, LinkedIn opens the main page for that link. For example, if you click the People page, LinkedIn opens the main People page so that you can search for other LinkedIn members.

If you click on the down arrow to the right of each link a menu appears underneath the link with additional options. Figure 3-4 shows a list of options available under the Answers link. Click on one of these additional options to open the appropriate page. For example, if you click the My Q&A link, LinkedIn opens the Messages page so that you can view questions you have asked.

Figure 3-4. **The options under the Answers link**

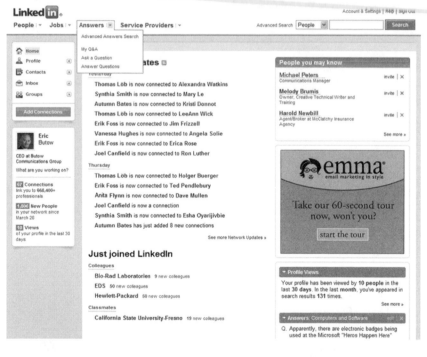

The Search box, at the right side of the area, enables you to search for people, jobs, and answers. (You'll learn more about searching starting in Chapter 4.) LinkedIn searches for people by default.

Three links appear above the Search box. These links, from left to right, allow you to change your account settings, get help, and sign out.

The Information Box

The large Information box contains news articles that may be of interest to you, information about your network updates, and whether anyone has just joined LinkedIn. This box appears on the left side of the LinkedIn member home page, as shown in Figure 3-5.

Figure 3-5. **The Information box**

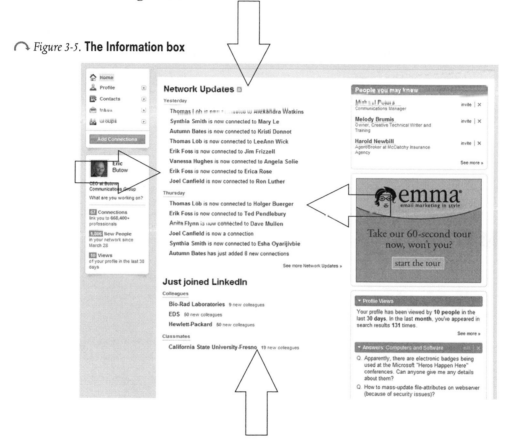

The sections you see at the top of the Information box depend on two factors. If you haven't built your network, then the Build Your Network section appears so that you can start building your connections list. If you have inbox messages, the Inbox section appears at the top of the page (or underneath the Build Your Network section) and lists the most recent inbox messages you've received.

If you have already built your network and have no inbox messages, the LinkedIn News section appears at the top of the page. Note that, as of this writing, this section is not available for all users because LinkedIn gradually introduces this feature to its membership. This section contains five articles, taken from Web news sites, about your competition. If you want to read the article, click the article title.,

If you don't see the news section, the Network Updates section appears, as shown in Figure 3-6. Network Updates information is categorized by date, with the most recent updates at the top of the list. You can click on the names of LinkedIn members to get the update about them, such as members who have new connections. Underneath the Network Updates section is the Just Joined LinkedIn sections that lists new colleagues from current and past employers as well as current and past schools who have joined LinkedIn since you last logged on.

Figure 3-6. **The Network Updates and Just Joined LinkedIn sections**

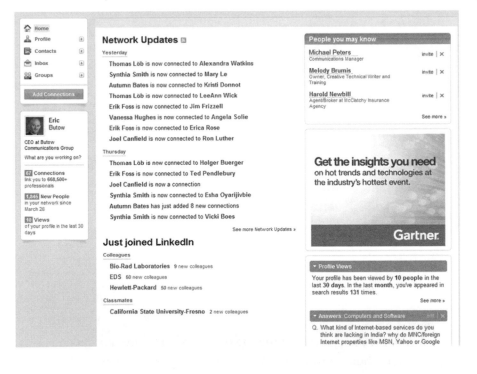

Modules

On the right side of the box, a list of LinkedIn members you may know appears, as shown in Figure 3-7. If you want to invite someone to join your list of connections, click the Invite link. (You'll learn how to invite other LinkedIn members in Chapter

5.) You can remove a person from the list by clicking the "X" to the right of the contact name. If you want to see more potential invitees than the three listed in the module, click the See More link.

Figure 3-7. **The People You May Know module**

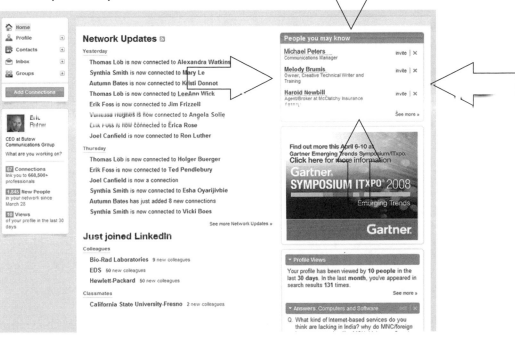

Underneath the advertisement, the Profile Views module tells you how many people have viewed your profile and have searched for you. If you want to get more information about who's been looking you up, click the See More link at the bottom of the module. The Who's Viewed My Profile page appears, as shown in Figure 3-8.

Underneath the Profile Views module, three modules display a list of answers, a list of jobs that may be of interest to you based on your current job title, and a list of people who may be of interest to you, as shown in Figure 3-9. These modules are customizable areas that you can add, edit, hide, move, or delete. Each module heading is in a blue bar, and the module information appears below the heading. The module information lists the first three summaries, such as the first

Figure 3-8. **The Who's Viewed My Profile page**

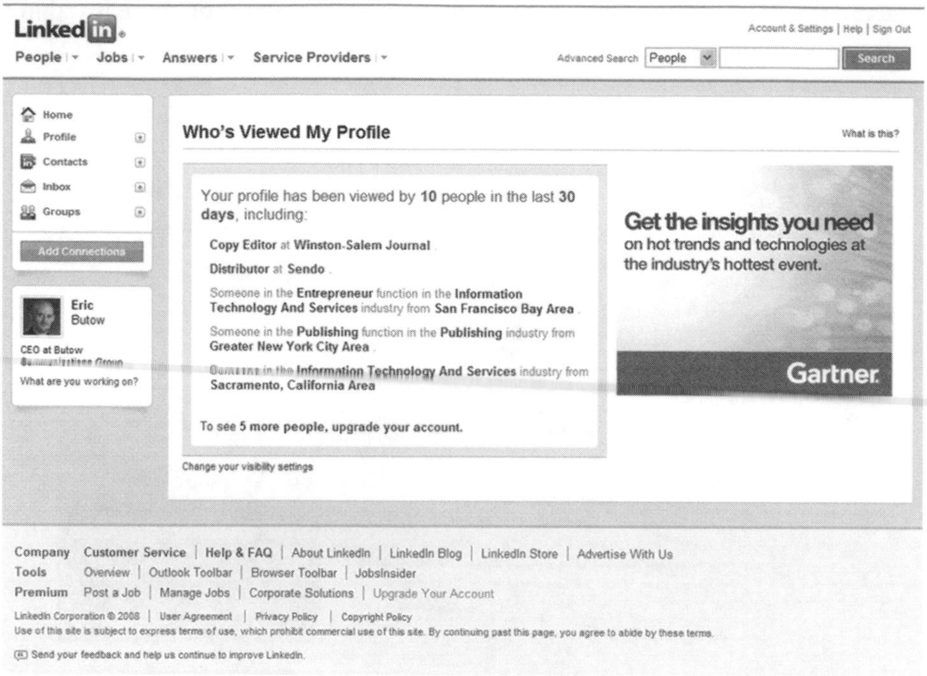

three answers and the first three jobs. If there is more to see, such as more answers, click on the See More link at the bottom of the module. You can also hide each module by clicking the down arrow to the left of each module name in the heading bar. If you want to delete a module, click the X button at the right side of the heading bar.

Editing a Module

If you don't like what you see in a module, its content is often editable. To edit the module, click the Edit link in the heading bar. You can then change how LinkedIn searches for information in the module. For example, in Figure 3-10 you can click the Edit link in the Answers module to search for answers in a category other than the default, Computers and Software. When you select a new answer category, click the Save button, and the module lists the first three answers it finds in the new category in the module. If you would rather keep the category you have, click the Cancel link.

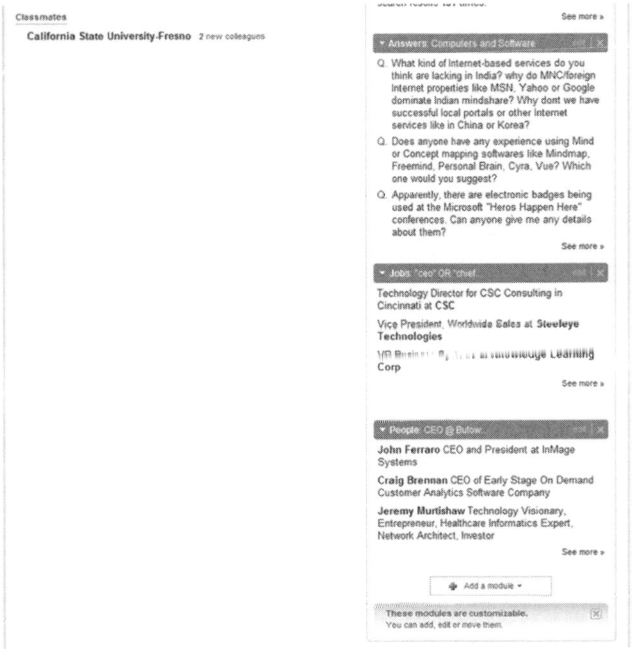

Figure 3-9. **Answers, Jobs, and People modules**

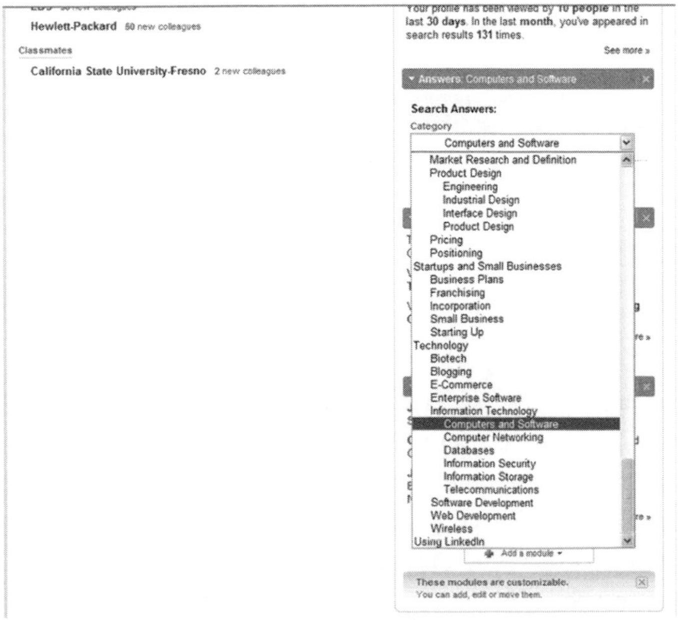

Figure 3-10. **Changing the answers in the Answers module**

Adding a Module

If you want to add a module, move the mouse pointer over the Add a Module button below the Jobs module. A list of available modules appears below the mouse pointer, and by default you can add one of three modules: (1) the People Search module and copies of the (2) Job Search and (3) Answers modules. When you add a module, it appears below the Jobs module. For example, if you add a People module, the new module appears as shown in Figure 3-11.

Figure 3-11. **The new People module**

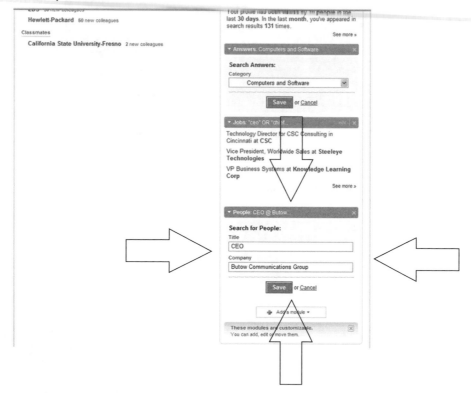

You can type a person's title and/or company name in the Title and Company Name boxes, respectively, and click the Save button. Then LinkedIn finds the first three people who meet the criteria, such as the first three people who work at LinkedIn. If LinkedIn finds more people, you can click the See More link at the bottom of the module to open the People Search Results page and view more people who match your search criteria.

The Navigation and Profile Boxes

To the left of the Information box are two smaller boxes. On the top is the Navigation box, as shown in Figure 3-12. This box contains quick links to common LinkedIn areas: Home, Profile, Contacts, Inbox, and Groups. When you click one of the links, LinkedIn opens the related page. For example, when you click the Inbox link, LinkedIn opens the Inbox page so that you can send a message to another LinkedIn member. (If you're impatient to learn more about sending invitations, refer to Chapter 5.)

Figure 3-12. **The Navigation box**

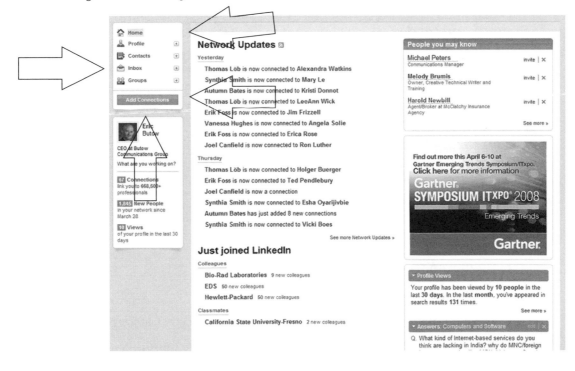

Click the small box with the plus sign to the right of the link name to view other options related to the link, as shown in Figure 3-13. The options appear underneath the link. Click the link options to open the associated pages. For example, in Figure 3-13, if you click the Network Statistics link under the Contacts link, LinkedIn opens the Your Network page so that you can view your network statistics.

Figure 3-13. **Contact link options**

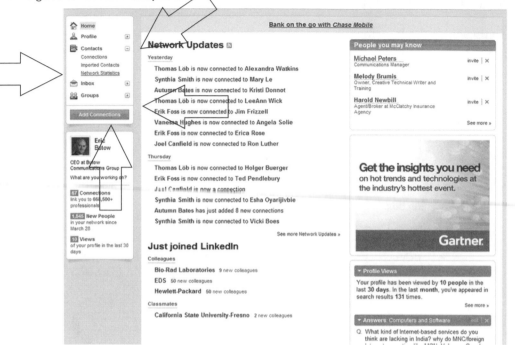

Underneath the navigation box, the Profile box shows a summary of your profile information, including:

- Your photo (if you have one).

- Your name and title.

- The number of connections you have.

- The number of new people in your network since you last logged in.

- How many other LinkedIn members have viewed your profile in the last three months.

If you want to see more information, click the Connections, New People, or Views link. For example, if you click the New People link, LinkedIn opens the Search Results page, as shown in Figure 3-14, so that you can see new people who have joined your network through your connections since the last time you logged on.

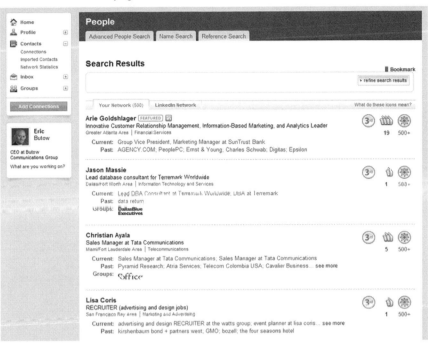

Figure 3-14. **The Search Results page**

Other LinkedIn members who have viewed your profile recently may be interested in you and/or your business; so you may also want to check them out to find out whether there is a mutual connection. If so, you may want to add them to your network and/or contact them to talk more about working together.

And the Bottom Area

When you scroll down to the bottom of the page, three link rows appear, as shown in Figure 3-15. These rows are categorized from top to bottom starting with Company links at the top for information about LinkedIn, including:

- Getting customer service, which you learned about in Chapter 1.

- Getting help and answers to frequently asked questions, which you also learned about in Chapter 1.

- Learning more about LinkedIn.

- Viewing the LinkedIn blog, which is updated regularly by the good people at LinkedIn.

- Buying LinkedIn merchandise like T-shirts and knickknacks.

- Learning about advertising your company on LinkedIn.

Figure 3-15. **The bottom area of the member home page**

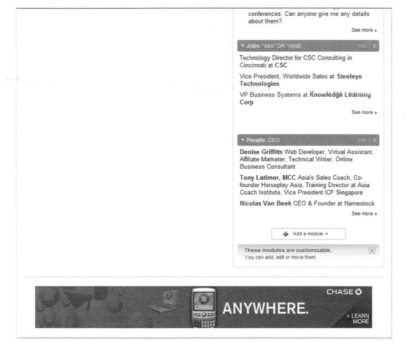

Below the Company links are Tools links for downloading plug-in tools. These tools enable you to get more information from LinkedIn more quickly than with the method described in Chapter 2. At the bottom, the Upgrade links let you upgrade to the Personal Plus, Business, or Pro Accounts, which you also learned about in Chapter 2.

Editing Your Profile

Now that you're familiar with the LinkedIn home page, it's time to update your profile and personalize it to your needs. At the top of the home page, click the My

Profile link in the Navigation box. Figure 3-16 shows the Edit My Profile page. In the upper right area of the page is a green box that tells you how complete your profile is. The status bar in Figure 3-16 shows that the profile is only 15 percent complete. What makes for a complete profile? You need to include the following:

- Your current position as well as two past positions.
- Your education information.
- Your profile summary that includes a photo.
- Your specialties.
- At least three recommendations from other LinkedIn users.

Figure 3-16. **The Edit My Profile page**

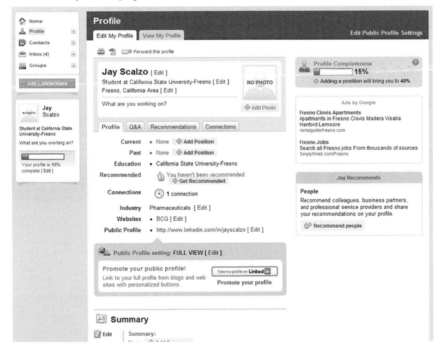

The information requested for the LinkedIn profile is based on LinkedIn's research, which shows that, if you have all this information, you're 40 times more likely to receive opportunities through LinkedIn for your career and/or your business. After all, people are going to feel more like they know you and will want to contact you if they know as much as possible about you, if they know others like you and what you do, and if they can see from a photo that you're a real person.

In the Recommends box that appears underneath the Profile Completeness box (not counting the ad between the boxes), you can also recommend other LinkedIn users by clicking the Recommend People link.

To the left of the green Profile Completeness box is a summary of your profile that displays your name, your position, and your location. To help protect your privacy, the location is specific only to the ZIP code area you live in, or at least the one you gave LinkedIn when you signed up. If you want to edit any of this information, click the Edit link to the right of each line. For example, click the Edit link to the right of the name to change your name and your location in the Account & Settings page.

You can add a photo by clicking the yellow Add Photo button. Figure 3-17 shows the Add Photo page where you can browse for your photo on your computer and then upload it by clicking the Upload Photo button. The file size limit is 4 megabytes (MB). If you're not sure of your photo's file size, open the appropriate folder and check the size in the file details. If the size is too big, open the file in your favorite photo editor and resize the photo accordingly to get it under the size limit.

Figure 3-17. **The Add Photo page**

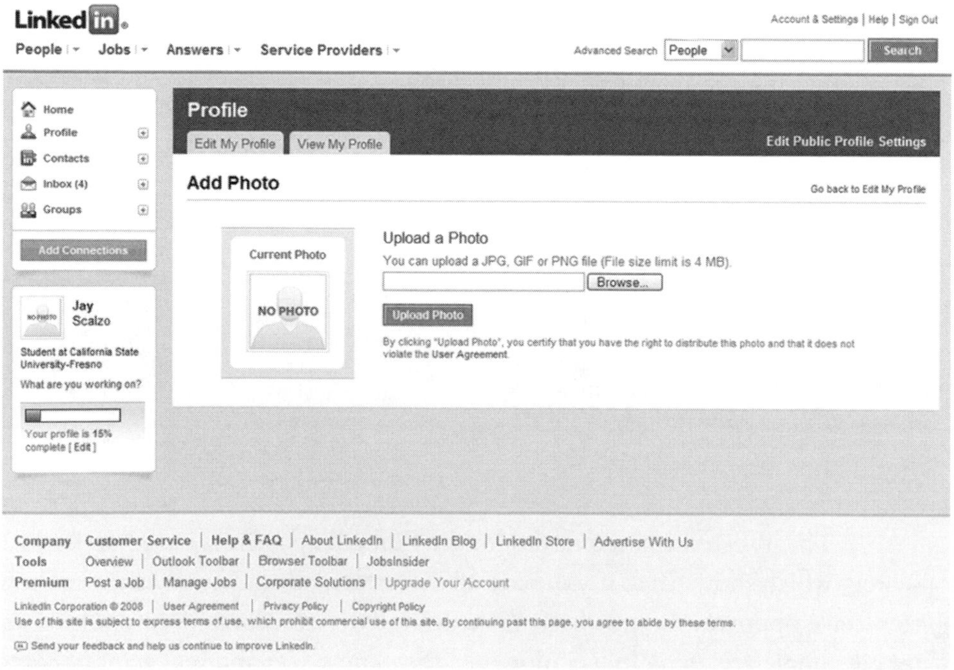

If you'd rather not upload a photo right now, click the Go Back to Edit My Profile link to the right of the My Profile/Add Photo headline. LinkedIn continues to use a silhouette of a photo in place of your real photo until you add one.

Underneath your name, position, location, and photo information is a set of four tabs: Profile, Q&A, Recommendations, and Connections. The Profile tab is selected by default. (Don't worry about the other tabs for now; we'll cover those in other chapters.) The top of the Profile tab lists a summary of the information available in your profile, including your current and past information, education, recommendations, connections, the industry you're in, Web sites you have, and a link. This tab enables you to see what your profile looks like to LinkedIn visitors and LinkedIn members. As you scroll down the page, you see information about your summary, experience, education, other LinkedIn members who have recommended you, any additional information about you, and contact settings (how you want to be contacted).

LinkedIn identifies areas that are lacking information and prompts you to add it via links. With a link having a yellow background and a green plus sign, you can add a photo, or, by clicking a green button with a green plus sign, you can add a professional position to your list of past positions.

One good way to make yourself more interesting is to click the Add Information button. When you click the button, the Additional Information page appears, as shown in Figure 3-18. In this page, you can not only add information that makes your profile more interesting, you're more likely to meet people with similar interests with whom you can network and perhaps meet. For example, it might be someone who belongs to the same organization as you do but never knew until she saw your LinkedIn profile. Adding your personal interests and hobbies helps connect you to potential contacts, but be sure not to add any sensitive personal information about yourself (such as banking information), which people don't need to know about. When you seem more real and other LinkedIn members feel that they know you, they'll be more interested in connecting with you.

You can add your Web sites, blogs, RSS feeds, and other online resources that you want people to see to the Additional Information section of your profile. For example, you may like Google News, and you can type its Web site address in the URL box. ("URL" stands for uniform resource locator, which also is known as a Web address.)

Type your interests in the Interests box, and separate the interests with commas. If you want to see examples of interests, click the See More Examples link above the Interests box.

Figure 3-18. **The Additional Information page**

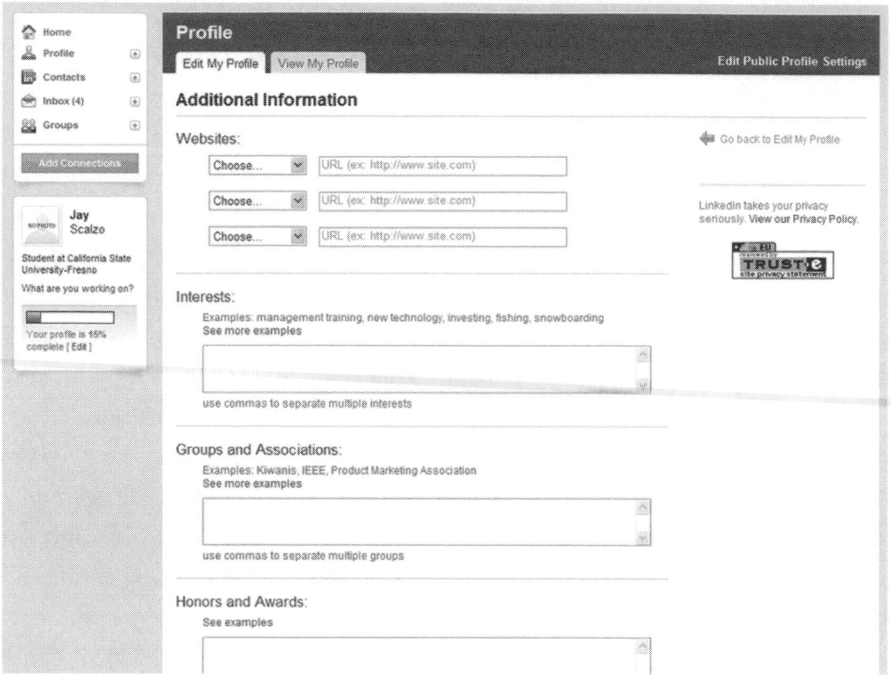

If you belong to any groups or organizations, such as a local chamber of commerce, type the groups or organizations in the Groups and Associations box. Separate groups with commas.

If you have received awards and honors related to your job that you want LinkedIn members to know about, add them in the Honors and Awards box. Include the name of the award and when you won it. Even if you won a volunteer award, you can add it if it's related to your professional experience and growth. For example, I won a president's award from the Society for Technical Communication a few years ago for coordinating a one-day conference that attendees found to be valuable. Because I'm a technical writer, that's an award I want to promote.

When you're finished adding your information, click the Save Changes button. The information you added appears in the Profile tab. For example, when I add my Web site to the list, it appears in the Websites category in the Additional Information section, as shown in Figure 3-19.

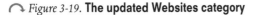

Figure 3-19. **The updated Websites category**

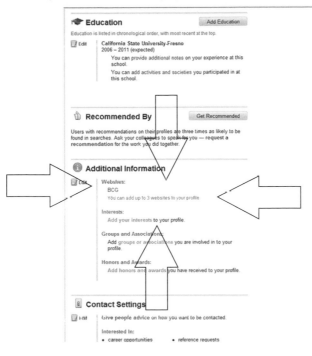

Your interests, the groups you belong to, and your honors and awards don't stay the same over time. Therefore, it's important to keep updating your profile regularly to show LinkedIn members that you continue to grow and excel.

Making Your Profile Public

LinkedIn members aren't the only ones who can see your profile. The general Web viewing public can see it; all they need is the correct URL. LinkedIn automatically provides a URL for your profile, but you can change it to something a bit more friendly, For example, it's better to have a recognizable URL, such as www .linkedin.com/in/mycompany, rather than www.linkedin.com/in/2458678.

To change the URL, start by clicking the Edit My Public Profile link. The Edit My Profile page is shown in Figure 3-20. To change the URL in the Your Public Profile URL box at the top of the page, type the new name after the www.linkedin.com/in/

portion of the URL in the Customize This Address box. For example, I can type "ebutow" as part of the new URL name and then send the completed URL, "http://www.linkedin.com/in/ebutow," to anyone who wants to see my Web site online and put the link on my Web site. (Note: Your name must be between 5 and 30 alphanumeric characters, and you can't use spaces, symbols, or any special characters.) After you type the new URL name, click the Set Address button. The new URL appears in the Your Current URL line.

Figure 3-20. **The Edit My Profile page**

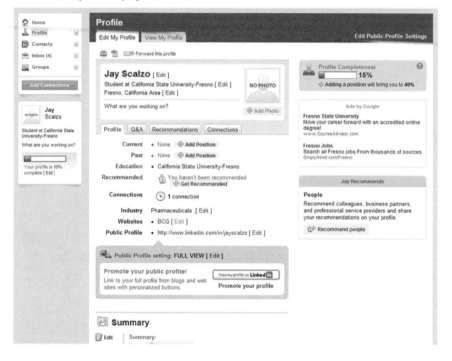

You may also want to set which features of your profile to make visible to the public. For example, if you're concerned that someone will use your photo and some of your information for nefarious purposes, perhaps in a scam, you may not want to have the photo and that information posted on your profile. So you can change what people can see in the public profile in the Public Profile box. By default, all information in the profile is included except for the picture. If you have uploaded a picture and you want to include it in your profile, select the Picture check box. You also can make your profile private—viewable by LinkedIn members only—by clicking the

None button. When you're finished making changes, click the Save Changes button. The page refreshes, and a green bar appears at the top of the page saying the changes have been saved.

If you want to see what your profile looks like to the public, click the View My Public Profile as Others See Itlink. When you click the link, a new browser window or tab opens (depending on your type of browser) and displays the public page, as shown in Figure 3-21.

Figure 3-21. **The Public Profile page**

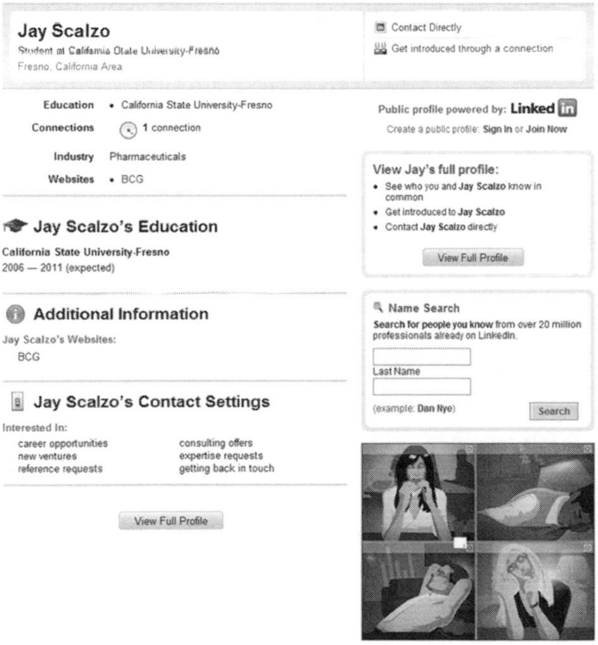

Close the public page by closing the tab or the browser window. If, after viewing the public page, you want to make changes to what people see on the Web site, make the changes in the Public Profile box. You also can change your profile information by clicking the Edit My Profile link at the top of the page.

Now let's move on to Chapter 4 and discuss how to do one of the central tasks of LinkedIn: finding other LinkedIn members and connecting with them so that you can share information.

4

Searching for People

When you're searching for people on LinkedIn, you need to use the tricks you learned as a child when you went on scavenger hunts. There are many different ways of finding a person, so you need to take some time to think about how to find the person you're looking for.

One obvious method is to search by name. If the name isn't common, finding someone is much easier than if the name is common. For example, when I search for John Smith in LinkedIn, there are 500 matches. So you may need additional information about the person, such as the company she works for, the type of work she does, or the area where she lives. You also have to spell someone's name accurately when searching this way.

The name search is the basic type of search, but LinkedIn also lets you search by a variety of criteria other than the person's name. Before you begin, be sure that cookies are enabled in your Web browser. If you don't like cookies on your system, you can change your browser settings to accept cookies only from LinkedIn. If you choose not to enable cookies at all, you won't be able to use LinkedIn's search functionality. Begin the search by logging into LinkedIn. (See Chapter 2 if you need a refresher on logging in.) Click the People link at the top of the page. The People page appears, as shown in Figure 4-1. In this page, you can search by name, or you can perform an advanced search using a number of criteria.

Search By Name

To search by name, type at least the last name of the person. Unfortunately, you can't search by using wildcard characters, such as an asterisk to signify all characters. After you type the last and any other names of the person, click the Search button. For

Figure 4-1. **The People page**

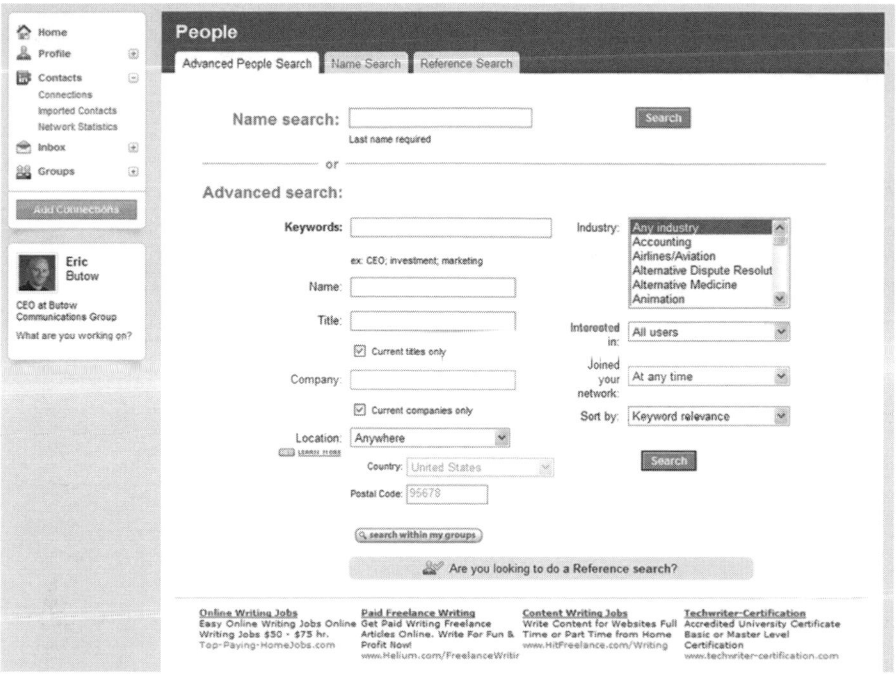

example, when I type the name "Butow" in the box and search for it, the search returns the name matches shown in Figure 4-2.

The number of matches LinkedIn has found appears at the top of the page. If you want to refine your search, click the Refine Search Results button above the first name in the list. Additional search criteria boxes appear, as shown in Figure 4-3. You can type or select additional criteria, including the person's employer, location, country, and ZIP code. If you need to look up the postal code, click the Lookup link to the right of the Postal Code box and search for the ZIP code in the GeoNames Web site that opens in a new browser tab or window. When you're finished refining your search, click the Search button to display the list of names that match your criteria. If you want to view the name of the person in the list, click the name of that person.

Advanced Search

You also can search by name as one of several criteria in the Advanced Search area.

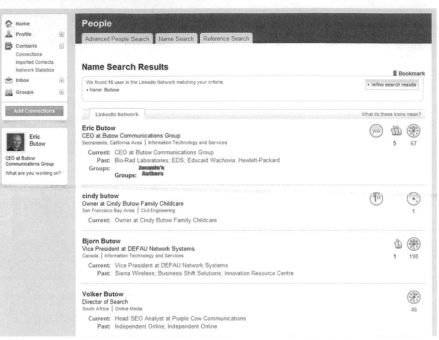

↺ *Figure 4-2.* **The search results for the name "Butow"**

↺ *Figure 4-3.* **Additional name search criteria**

Search by Keywords

If you want to perform a more advanced search than a name search, click the Advanced People Search tab. The Advanced People Search page appears, as shown in Figure 4-4.

Figure 4-4. **The Advanced People Search page**

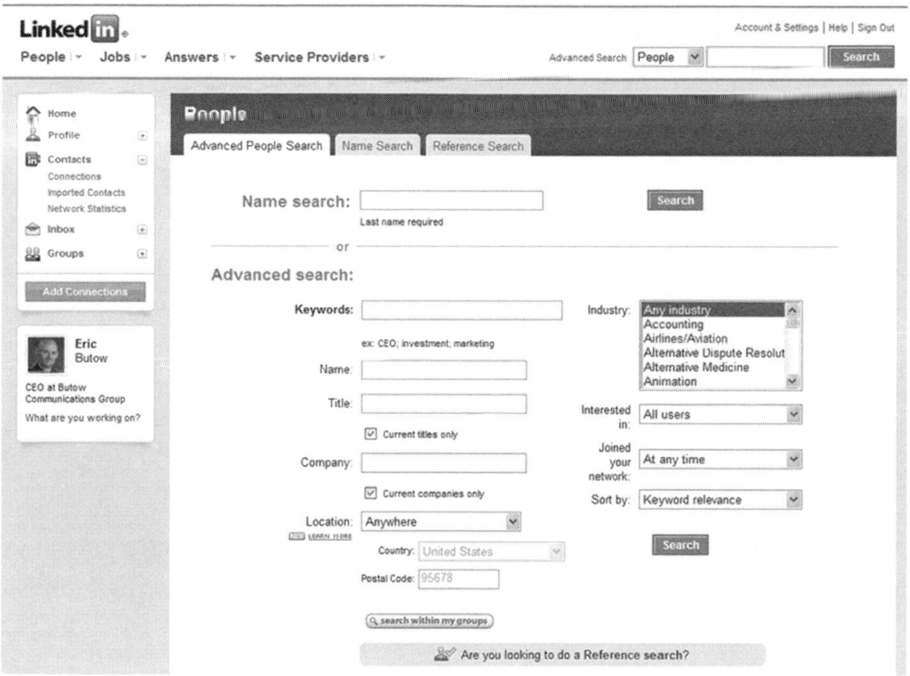

If you want to search for one or more keywords, type the keyword in the Keywords box. If you have multiple keywords, separate them with semicolons. For example, if you are a recruiter looking for a marketing person to work at an e-commerce company, then you would type "marketing; e-commerce" in the Keywords box.

Search by Title, Company, and/or Industry

You can search for someone by the person's current title or any past title by typing the title name in the Title box. By default, the Current Titles Only check box is selected, but, if you want to search a title that the person held previously, just clear this check box.

You can also search for the person by the company he currently works for. However, if you want to search for the person by a company he previously worked for, then clear the Current Companies Only check box, which is selected by default.

You also can select the industry that the person works in from the Industry list. Any industry is selected by default, but you can browse through the list and select the industry that more accurately reflects what the person does. However, if you can't find a good match, leave Any industry selected.

Search by Location

The default location for your search is Anywhere. If you want to zero in on the person's geographic area, then select Located In or Near in the Location list. When you do, LinkedIn enables the Country and Postal Code boxes so that you can select the country and type in the ZIP or postal code of the person, respectively.

As with searching for a name by postal code, click the Lookup link to open a new browser tab or window, then search for the postal code on GeoNames.

Search by Interest

If you're looking for someone who has a specific interest, such as a person who wants to be hired by another company, select one of the six options in the Interested In list.

The options available are:

1. Potential Employees
2. Consultants or Contractors
3. Entrepreneurs
4. Hiring Managers
5. Industry Experts
6. Deal Making Contacts

Select the interest that best matches the LinkedIn members you're looking for. For example, if you are searching for people who want to be hired, select Potential Employees in the list, and LinkedIn returns all results from people who are interested in finding work. However, if you don't see an interest that matches what you're looking for, leave the default All Users option selected.

Search by Connections

You can search by other LinkedIn members who have connected with you within a specific period of time. For example, if you believe that the person you're looking for joined in the last three months, you can select In the Last Three Months from the list. You can select from one of seven time criteria—the member may have joined:

- (1) At any time (the default).
- (2) Since you last logged into LinkedIn.
- In the last (3) day, (4) week, (5) two weeks, (6) month, or (7) three months.

If you aren't sure when the member joined your network, leave the default At Any Time option selected.

Sorting the Search Results

You can sort your search results in the Sort By list in four different ways, as shown in Figure 4-5:

1. By keyword relevance.
2. By degrees and recommendations.
3. By degrees away from you.
4. By number of connections.

The default is keyword relevance, meaning that members with profiles that match your keywords are listed first.

However, if you don't have any keywords or would like to sort by other different criteria, you can select one of three other options.

1. You can sort by the *number of connections* each member has by selecting Number of Connections in the list. LinkedIn displays all results, starting with the member with the most connections.

Figure 4-5. **Sort by list criteria**

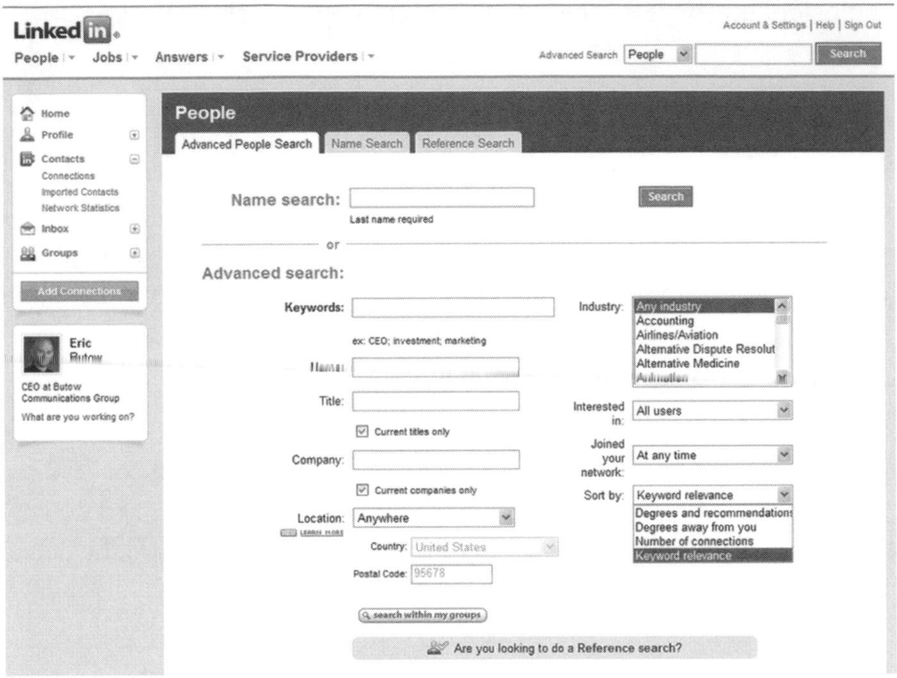

2. You can sort by the *number of degrees away from* you by selecting Degrees Away from You. LinkedIn displays results starting with the members who are in your network, then all members who are connections of those people in your network, and then all connections of those connections.

3. You also can sort by the *degrees away from you and the number of recommendations* by selecting Degrees and Recommendations. LinkedIn displays results starting with people who have the most recommendations and who are in your network or closest to it. For example, one of the connections of people in your network may have 23 recommendations, and the connection with the second highest number of recommendations, 18, is in your network. LinkedIn lists the connection with 23 recommendations first and the connection in your network with 18 recommendations second.

Ready to Search

When you have set all your search criteria in the Advanced Search area, click the Search button below the Sort By list. LinkedIn displays the results in the People Search Results page, as shown in Figure 4-6.

Figure 4-6. **The People Search Results page**

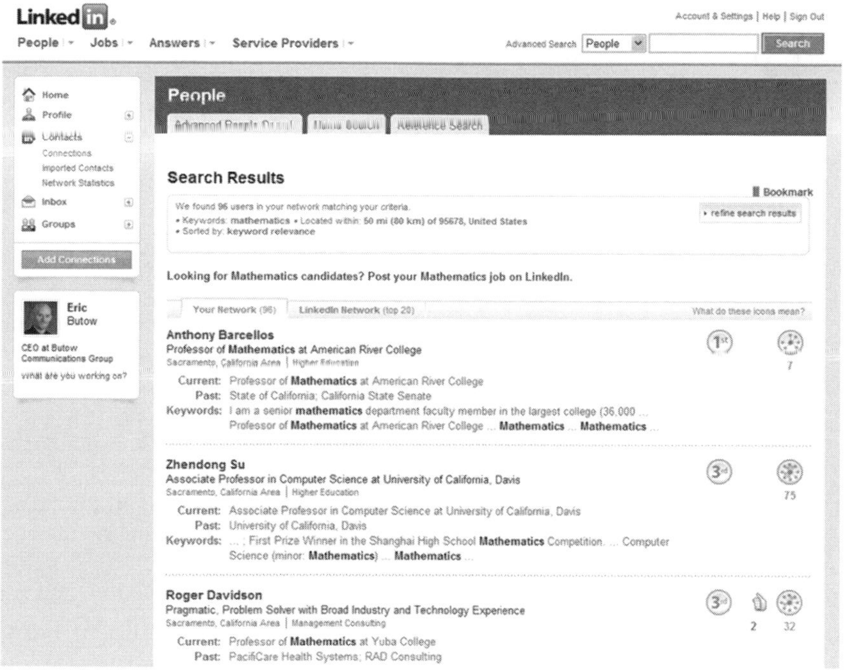

If LinkedIn can't find any members who meet your criteria, the People Search Results page displays a search form as shown in Figure 4-7 so that you can adjust your criteria or start a new search.

A Search Example

Recruiters are good examples of people who use LinkedIn's search feature to find people they're looking for to fill their open positions. They start by searching by keyword for names that match the keyword. Recruiters should try to keep their initial

↷ *Figure 4-7.* **The People Search Results page for adjusting your search criteria**

search as narrow as possible so that they can zero in on those who have as many skills as possible related to the vacant position.

For example, ABC Corporation, a business-to-consumer (B2C) company, is looking for a senior director of product management. The list of names might be quite small to begin with as the recruiter focuses on all the skills needed for this role, but, as the search goes on, the list grows and other keywords present themselves as ways to search for this talent. As a result of reaching out to people for this role, the recruiter's database grows with referrals and new contacts.

The search might begin this way:

- Keywords: Consumer, ecommerce, e-commerce, marketing.

- Title: Director of Marketing.

- Location: In or near a specific ZIP code within the United States.

Note the two different spellings of the word "e-commerce" because not all people spell the word with a hyphen (between the first "e" and the first "c") in their profiles. The same is true for other technical terms. For example, some people use "website," others "Website," and still others "Web site." On the other hand, if someone can't spell a nontechnical term (such as "marketing"), then it's probably better that you find someone else anyway.

Searching by Reference

On average, recruiters find that a keyword search gives them about 50 percent of the population they are seeking. The rest come from:

- Expanding the search parameters.

- Including researching by contacts, companies, titles, and industries.

- Sending compelling e-mail messages to potential candidates and/or clients (which you'll learn about in Chapter 6).

- Checking references informally through their network. (LinkedIn provides reference checking of clients when you click Reference Search underneath the tabs at the top of the screen.)

Figure 4-8 shows the Reference Search page that appears when you click the Reference Search tab. This page lets you enter the companies the person worked for (or currently works for) and the years the person worked there. If the candidate is still with the company, type the current year in the right-hand Year box (the one on the right side of the word "to"). When you click the Search button, LinkedIn finds people in your network who can provide professional references for the person you're thinking of hiring. Unfortunately, with a standard personal account, all you can get is this basic information about the search results. To contact those people directly using LinkedIn's e-mail service, you have to upgrade to a Business or Pro account. To do that, click the Upgrade Now button.

In this example, a search for people who worked at Hewlett-Packard from the years 2003 through 2004 resulted in 16 friends of connections and 484 third-degree contacts, as shown in Figure 4-9.

Figure 4-8. **The Reference Search page**

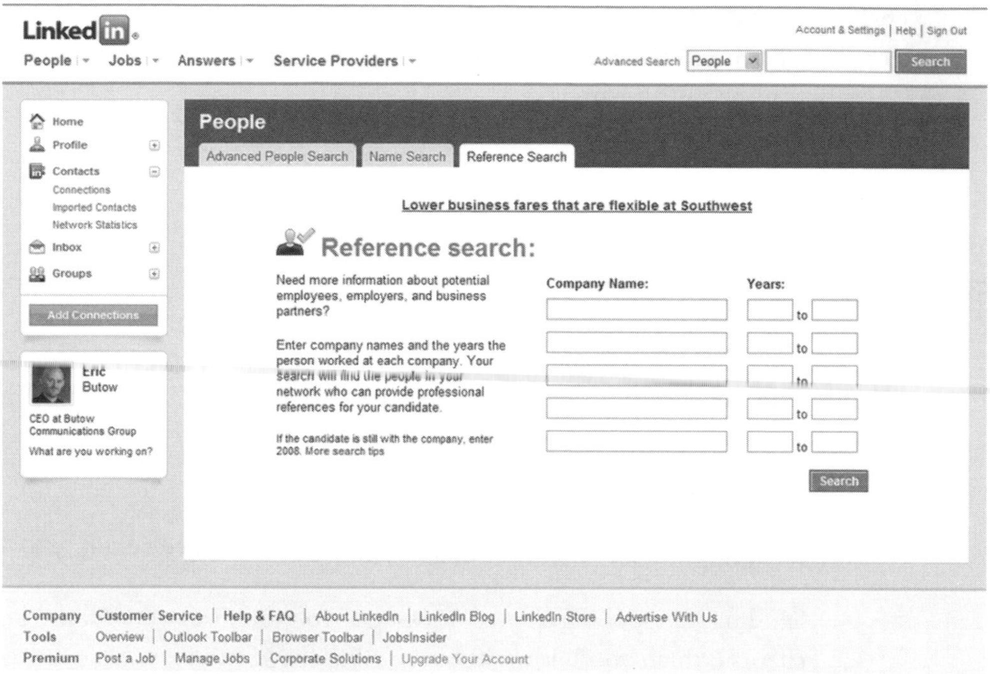

Figure 4-9. **The Reference results page**

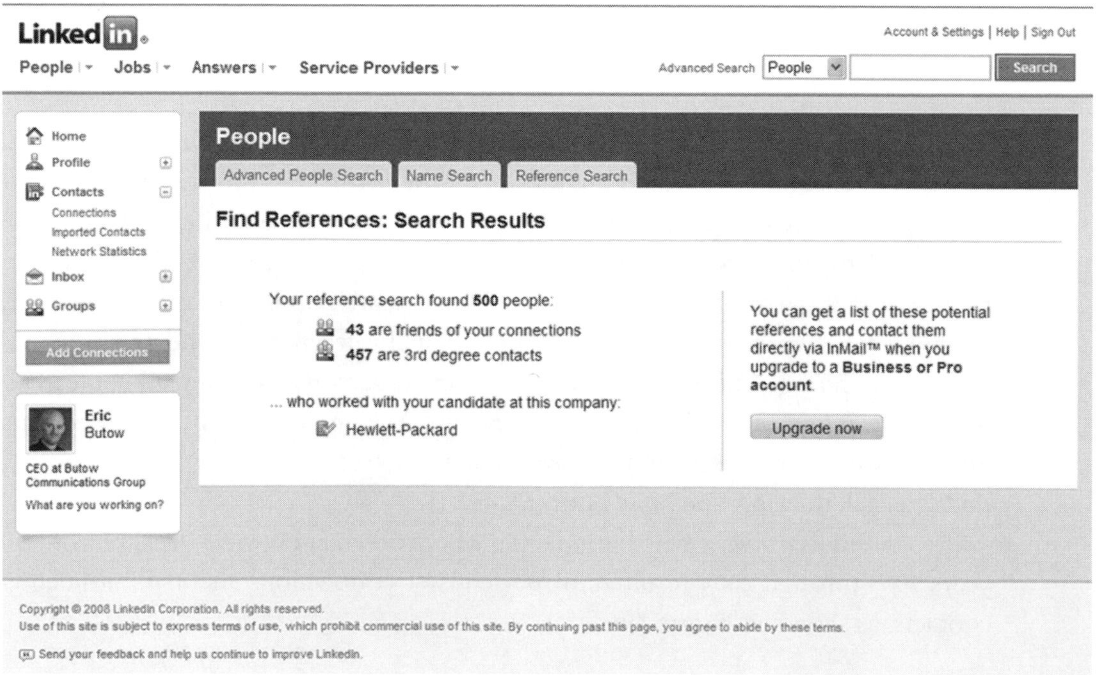

Using Complex Searching Techniques

When you use keywords to search for people, jobs, or anything else, you can type special search criteria to help LinkedIn zero in on exactly what you're looking for. You may be familiar with some of these functions from other searches you have performed in the past on the Web or when searching a database.

- If you want to search for an exact phrase, enclose it in quotation marks (e.g., "Web designer").

- You can exclude a search term from the list of keywords by typing a hyphen (or a minus sign) before the term. For example, many sales jobs also include marketing. If you want to search for only straight sales jobs, insert a hyphen before the word "marketing": sales -marketing. LinkedIn looks for sales job postings that don't have the word "marketing" in them.

- Use the Boolean operator "OR" between keywords to search for jobs that have just one of two or more terms (e.g., Web OR graphics OR advertising). LinkedIn finds job postings that include at least one of these words.

- You also can use the Boolean operator "AND" to include two or more terms. However, the word "AND" is superfluous when searching because, if you search for more than one keyword, LinkedIn automatically presumes there is an "AND" between keywords.

- LinkedIn also uses parentheses to do complex searches. For example, to find either a Web design job or a marketing and advertising job, you can try this: Web design OR (marketing advertising). LinkedIn then looks for jobs or candidates with listings that include the words "Web design" only and listings that include the words "marketing" and "advertising" only.

Now that you know how to search for other members in LinkedIn, it's time to add them as contacts in your network. Chapter 5 shows you how to add contacts and manage them in your contact database.

5

Adding and Managing Contacts

LinkedIn is only as effective as your contact list is. Your effort to reach out to as many *appropriate* people as possible to grow your connections is the path to success in growing your own profile and your own business. The key word, however, is "appropriate." Your LinkedIn connections could very easily have no rhyme or reason to them if you randomly invite everyone you come across. Be selective about whom you invite into your network so that your list of connections has value and will return that value to you. By randomly inviting people you don't know, you quickly pollute your network .

The best way to start growing your contact list is by adding people who know you and trust you. These are the people who will refer you to others first for business. You can encourage them to grow their own base by recommending them to others within your network for business opportunities. This encourages and excites them to grow their own connections lists.

Good Connection Practices

When people you know and trust are acting as a conduit to someone you are trying to reach, make sure to include a thank-you note to them for their effort in passing the message along and to ask whether you can do anything for them. Doing so provides a good foundation for you to grow your connections. It's recommended that you make your connections visible to everyone who views your profile because your connections are evidence of the quality of your contacts and of your desire to help others.

Improve your connectability by having high-value connections; that is, have as many decision makers and people who can help you. If you are looking for a job, connect with recruiters in your area. If you have a business, connect with CEOs, venture capitalists, and vice presidents in both small and large corporations. To date, all 500 of the Fortune 500 companies are represented on LinkedIn, and LinkedIn research says that at least 499 of these companies have the title of director or higher. If this is the world you want to be connected to, make every effort to have your connections comparable in value.

Most new users put only their current company in their profile. By doing so, they severely limit their ability to connect with people. You should fill out your profile as though it were an executive biography. Include past companies, education, affiliations, and activities in your profile. (Remember that we discussed adding this information and more in Chapter 4.) You also can include a link to your profile as part of an e-mail signature that enables people to see all your credentials as an attachment.

Make Your Connection the Right One

Stay focused on who you are and what you do when building your contacts. As tempting as it might be to invite your favorite auntie into your connections list, it might not be the best idea. Your goal is to grow the number of contacts that are relevant to your work—those who will help you find your next job, assignment, and/or business opportunity. This means constantly growing your network in a targeted way.

When do you invite someone whom you have just met or just connected with? A good rule of thumb is to speak with the contact on the phone at least once so that you can hear in his voice a sense of ease in getting to know more about you. You also may want to think about other questions to ask during a phone call in order to gauge the contact's receptiveness. For example, if you're a recruiter, some questions might be:

- Did you respond to my LinkedIn email about a position I was recruiting for?

- Did you reach out to me in some other fashion and are interested in keeping a dialogue going for future opportunities?

- Is there familiarity between us because we know quite a few of the same people?

These are just a few ways to get comfortable with people whom you may or may not know very well before inviting them into your network. If you don't feel some sort of connection, extending an invitation may not be appropriate at that point.

Adding a Connection

LinkedIn makes it easy for you to add a connection to another LinkedIn member. Start by signing in to LinkedIn if you haven't done so already. (See Chapter 2 if you need a refresher.) Then click the Contacts link in the Navigation box, as shown in Figure 5-1.

Figure 5-1. **The Contacts link**

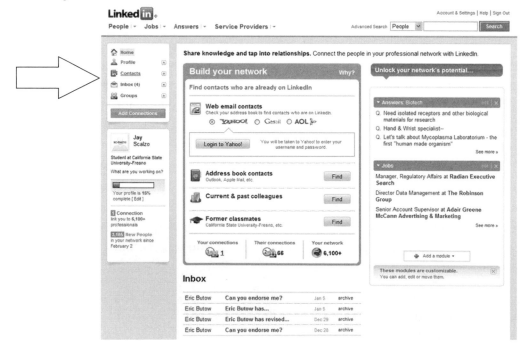

If you haven't built your network yet, then the Start Building Your Network link appears, as Figure 5-2 shows. Click the Start Building Your Network link. In the Find Contacts Already on LinkedIn page that appears, as shown in Figure 5-3,

◠ *Figure 5-2.* **The Start Building Your Network link**

◠ *Figure 5-3.* **The Find Contacts Already on LinkedIn page**

you have three options for adding friends and colleagues to your contact list. You can:

1. Search outlook.
2. Search Webmail contacts.
3. Use a few other tools, including address books.

Import Outlook Connections

If you use Outlook for e-mail, click the Check Outlook button. LinkedIn communicates with Outlook, and after a couple of minutes it identifies potential connections in your Outlook address book that you may want to add to LinkedIn. Figure 5-4 shows an example of the results of the Outlook address book search.

Figure 5-4. **The results of the Outlook address book search**

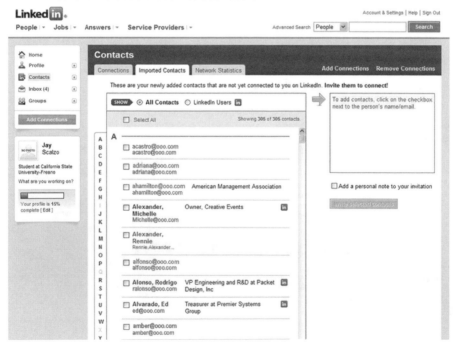

You can add contacts by selecting the check box to the left of the e-mail address in the list. The added name appears in the box to the right of the address list. If you want to invite the selected contacts, click the Invite Selected Contacts list.

Import Webmail Connections

If you have an account from an online mail service such as Yahoo Mail, Gmail, or Hotmail, you can check your service address books to see if any of them are on LinkedIn by clicking the Check Webmail Contacts button. At the Import Webmail Contacts page, shown in Figure 5-5, you can select your Webmail service, log in, and find out which of your Webmail contacts are already on LinkedIn.

Figure 5-5. **The Import Webmail Contacts page**

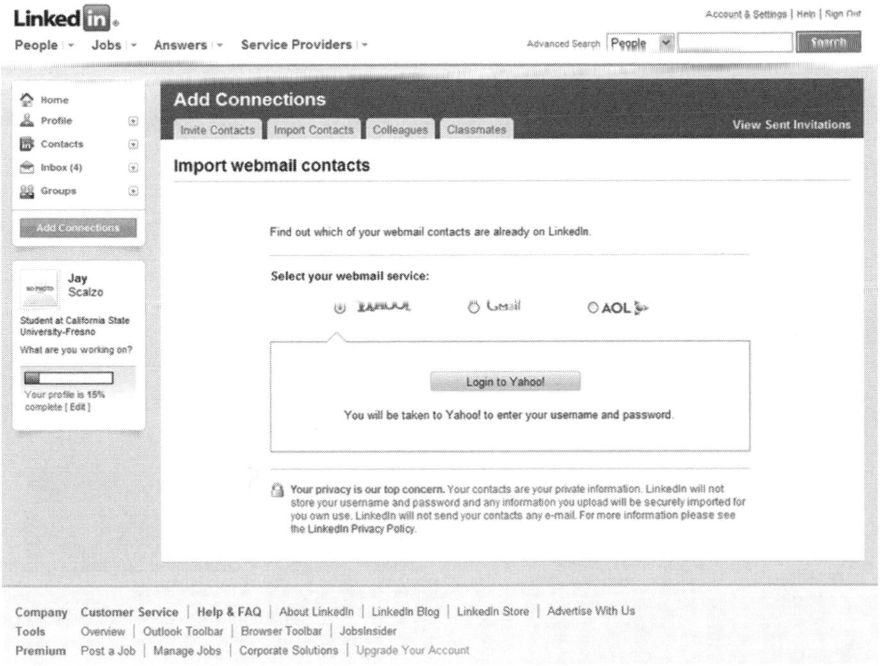

Add Contacts Manually

You also can add your contacts manually by clicking the Enter Contacts Manually button. Click this button to open the Add Contacts page, as shown in Figure 5-6. Type the e-mail address in the box, or copy it from an e-mail message and paste it in the box. If you have multiple e-mail addresses, separate them with commas: for example, name-1@address-1.com, name-2@address-2.com, ... After you type in all the names, click the Search button. If LinkedIn finds the contact associated with the e-mail address, the system automatically adds the name to your contacts list in the Newly Added Contacts page, as shown in Figure 5-7.

Figure 5-6. **The Add Contacts page**

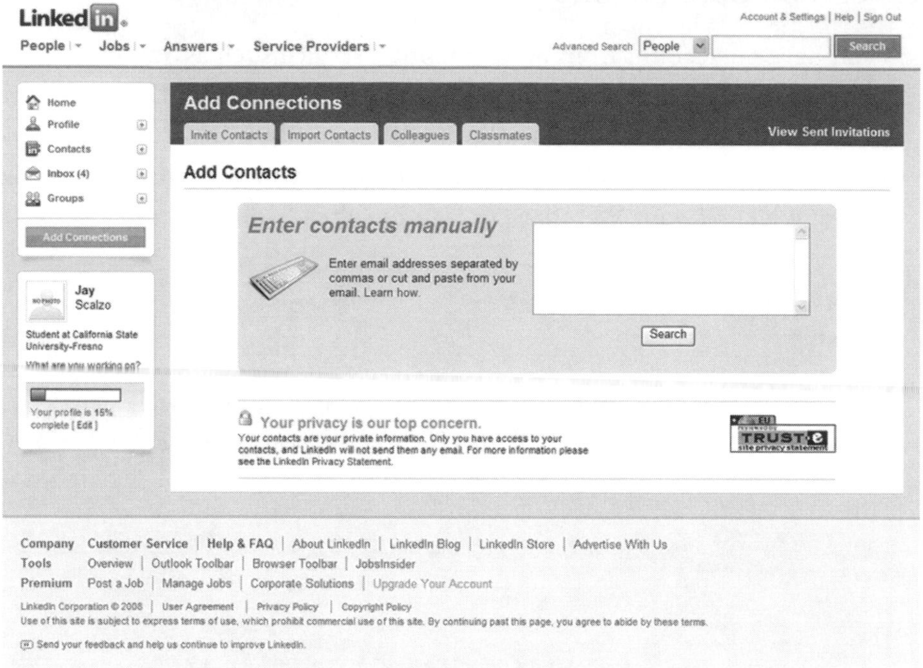

Figure 5-7. **The Newly Added Contacts page**

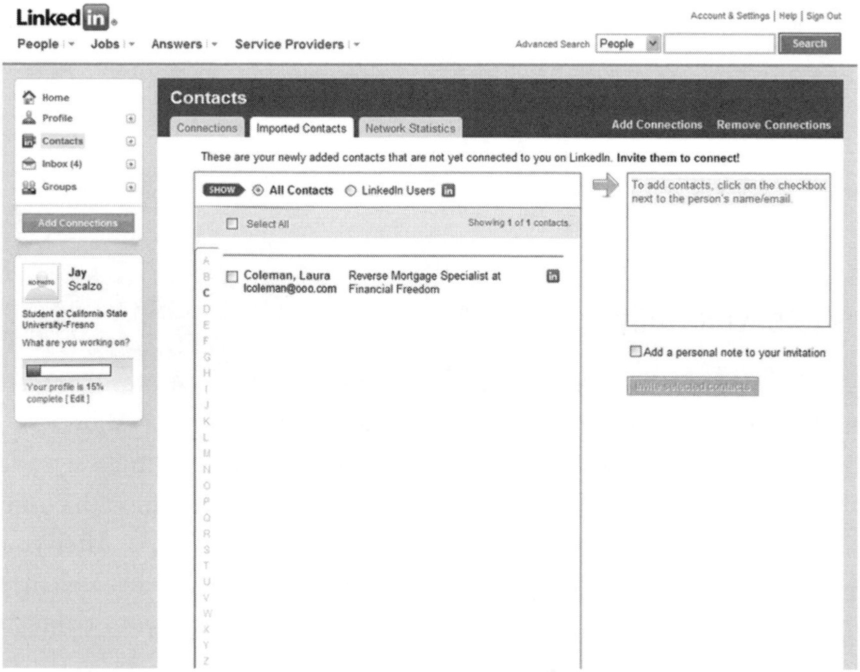

Inviting Your Contact to Connect

Now that you've added a contact to your list, you need to invite her to connect with you. Select the check box next to the contact name that you want to invite, and the name appears in the connection list.

If you want to add a personal note to your invitation, select the Add a Personal Note to Your Invitation check box. A box appears underneath the check box, as shown in Figure 5-8. You can use the default personal note or change it by deleting it and typing a new one. When you finish typing the personal note, click the Invite selected contacts button. The Other Contacts page appears and tells you that an invitation has been sent.

↷ *Figure 5-8.* **The Personal Note box**

You can add more contacts to your contact list by clicking the Add More Contacts link below the list. If you want to see the invitations you have sent out and the status of each, click the Connections tab at the top of the page, and then click the sent invitations link above the list. The Invitations Sent page appears, as shown in Figure

5-9. By default, the Invitations Sent list shows you all the invitations you have sent to other LinkedIn members. The status of each invitation appears in the Status column. If there is no status, the invitee hasn't responded to the e-mailed invitation yet. You can view all invitations you have received by clicking the Received link above the Invitations Sent list, and you can also view all blocked invitations by clicking the Blocked link.

Figure 5-9. **The Invitations Sent page**

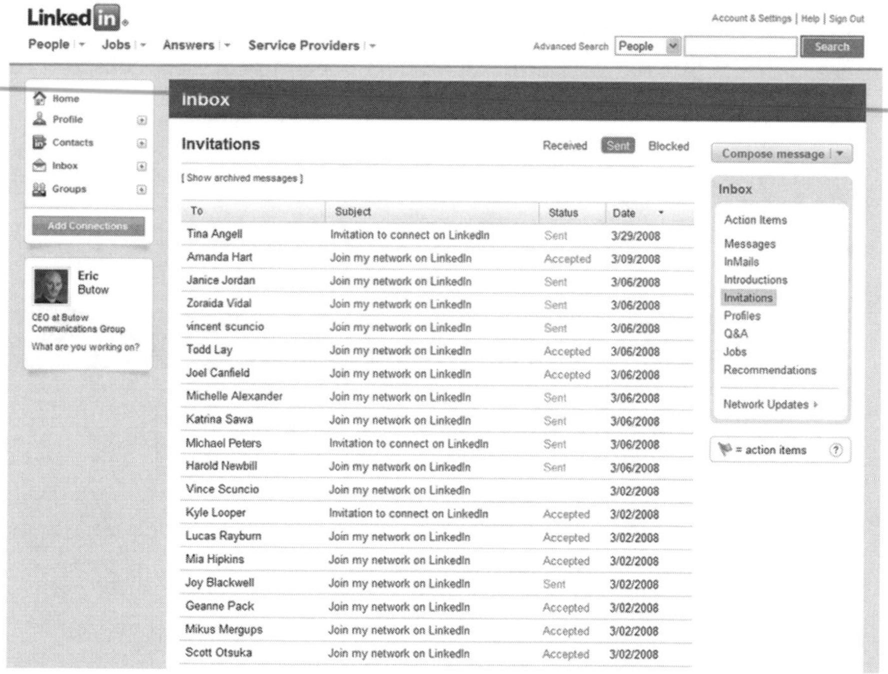

If you want to add more contacts, click the Contacts link in the Navigation box. The invitation you sent earlier doesn't appear in your connections list in the My Connections page because the invitation hasn't been accepted yet. However, the top of the list shows how many outstanding sent invitations you have. If you click the sent invitations link at the top of the list, the Invitations page in Figure 5-10 shows 10 of those 17 outstanding sent invitations.

You can click the Invitations Sent link to view your invitations. After your invitee accepts your invitation to connect, LinkedIn refreshes the My Connections page with your new contact in the list, as shown in Figure 5-11.

⌢ *Figure 5-10.* **A list that contains 10 outstanding sent invitations**

⌢ *Figure 5-11.* **Amanda Hart is the new contact in the list**

Filtering the Connections List

As you add new connections, your list of connections will grow. You may want to filter your connections list to show only those that meet your criteria, such as connections in a certain geographic area. LinkedIn offers three filter options. You can show:

1. Only the contacts that have new connections.
2. Only your connections by location.
3. Only your connections by information technology and services.

Click the Advanced Options link at the top of the My Connections list to open the Advanced Options tab that you see in Figure 5-12. You can show contacts with new connections by selecting the Show Contacts with New Connections check box. You can filter the list by location to show connections in a specific locale (such as one in your area) in the Filter by Location list. And you can filter the list by industry (such as your connections in the biotechnology industry) in the Filter by Industry list. Note that if you want to refine your search by looking for an industry in a particular location, select

Figure 5-12. **The Advanced Options tab**

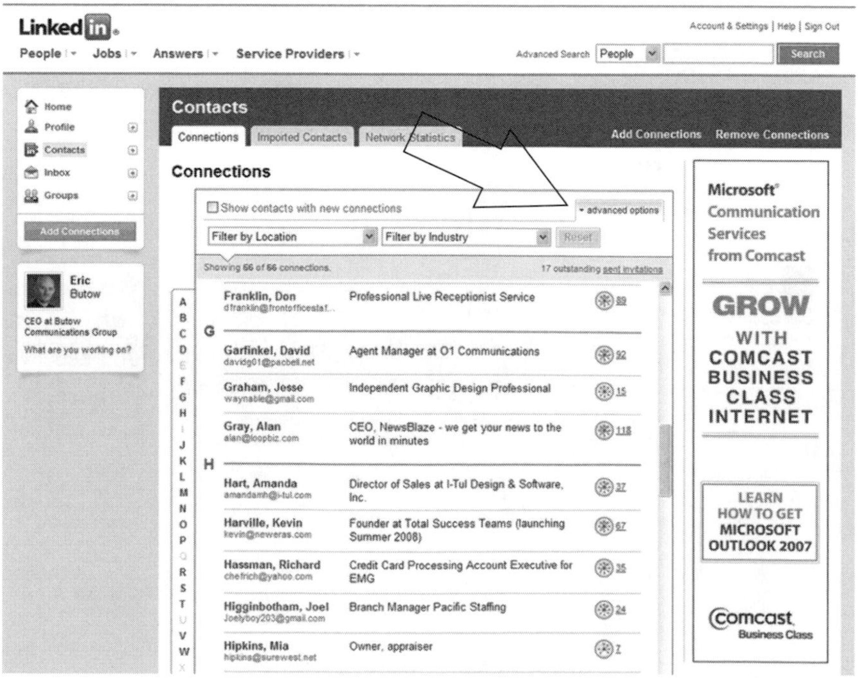

the location in the Filter by Location list, then filter the list by industry in the Filter by Industry list. If you want to reset the filter, click the Reset button.

Removing a Connection

From time to time, one of your connections is no longer needed, such as if the connection no longer works with the company you're working with on a project. In that case, you can remove a connection from your list by clicking the Remove Connections link above the connections list and to the right of the Add Connections link. When you click the Remove Connections link, the Remove Connections page appears, as shown in Figure 5-13.

Figure 5-13. **The Remove Connections link**

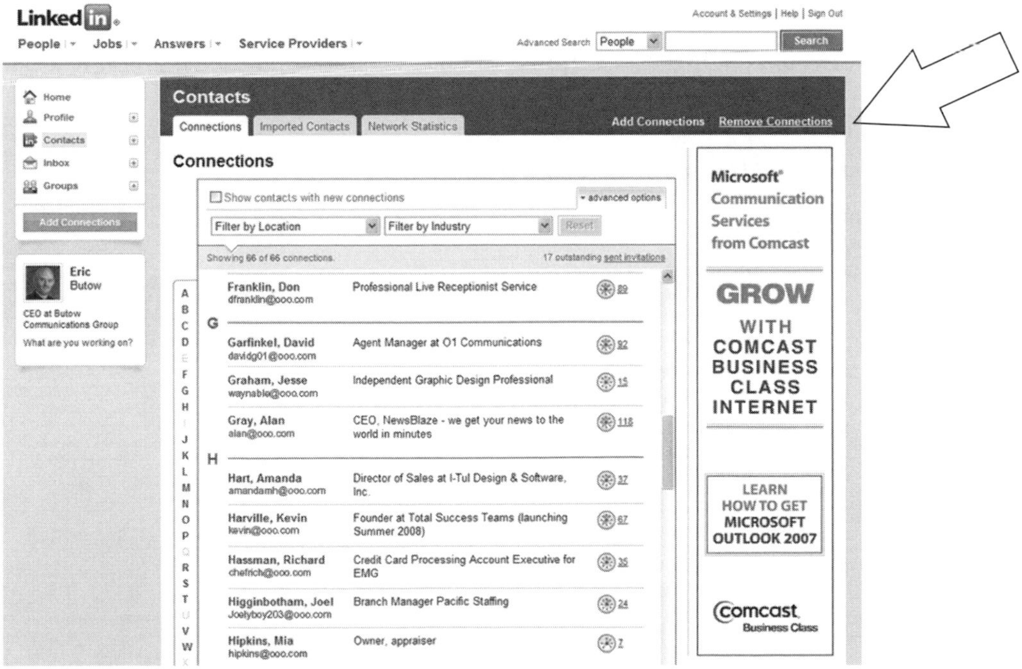

Removing the connection is simple: Select the check box next to the name of each contact you want to remove and then click the Remove Connections button. A Confirm Your Request dialog box appears that asks whether you're sure you want to remove the connection because the action cannot be undone. (Though you can't restore the connection, you can reinvite the contact to join your network again at a later time.) If you want to remove the connection, click Yes. If you change your mind, click the Cancel link. After you remove a connection, the My Connections page appears and the connections list no longer includes the removed connections. If you have removed all your connections, the list includes a link to start building your network.

Adding Anyone to Your Invitation List

You can invite other connections you already have, such as someone in your e-mail address book, to join LinkedIn and your LinkedIn connections. Doing so keeps all your connections in one location and introduces your connections to more opportunities through LinkedIn.

You can invite a non–LinkedIn member quickly and easily by clicking the Add Connections button in the Navigation box. The Add friends or colleagues to your network? page appears, as shown in Figure 5-14. Type the first and last names of the

Figure 5-14. **The Add friends or colleagues to your network? page**

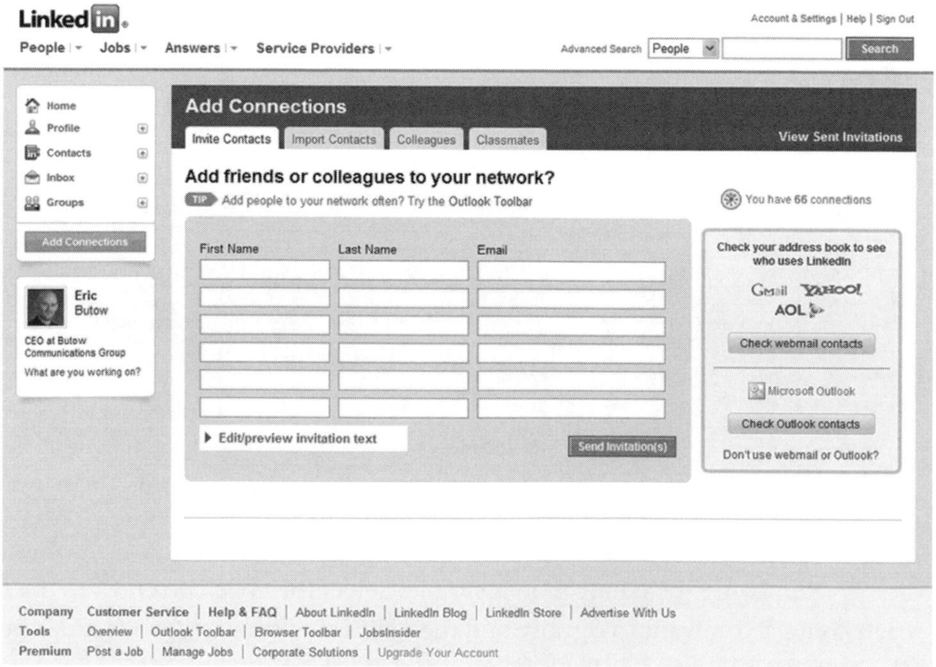

invitee in the First Name and Last Name boxes, respectively. Then type the e-mail address of the recipient in the Email box. You can preview the invitation text by clicking the Edit/Preview Invitation Text button. The text of the message appears at the bottom of the page, as shown in Figure 5-15.

Figure 5-15. **The invitation message information**

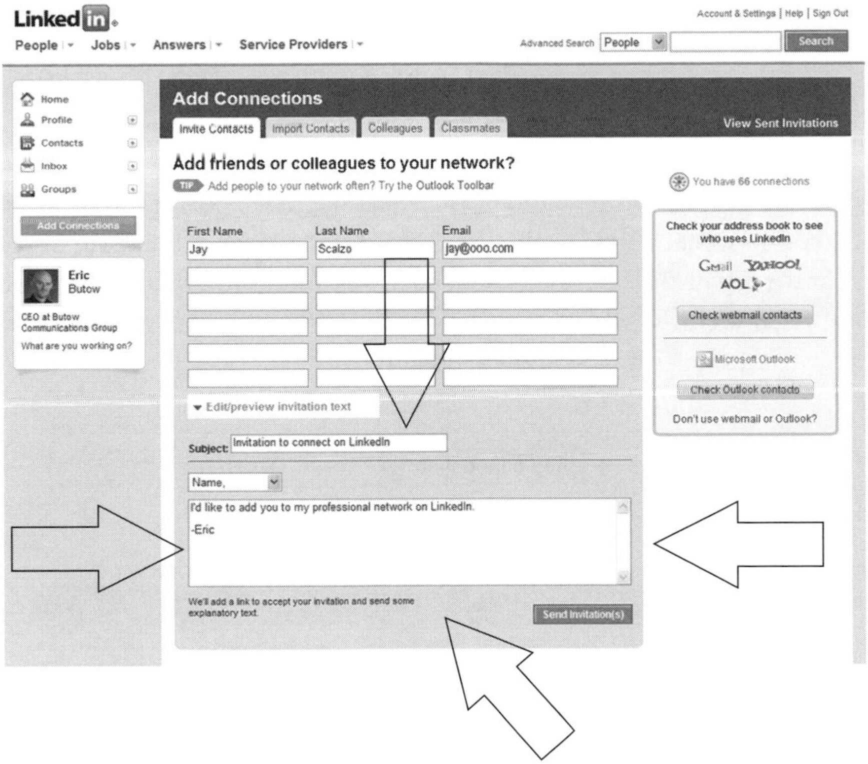

You can change the message information:

- Change the default subject text in the Subject box.
- Change the salutation from the Salutation list. You can keep the default salutation, choose one of two other salutations, or select no salutation.
- You also can change the default invitation text by typing a new message in the message box.

When you're finished making changes to your invitation, click the Send Invitation(s) button.

Archive Invitations

Note that removing a connection doesn't affect the status of any invitations that have been accepted or rejected. They still appear in the Invitations list. You can archive your received, sent, and blocked invitations so that you don't have those old invitations cluttering up the page. Archiving also gives you a record of the invitations in case you need to confirm that you sent an invitation at some point (for example, if you haven't received a response from the person to whom you sent the invitation).

Start the archival process by clicking the Inbox link in the Navigation box, then click the Invitations link. When you click the Invitations link, the Invitations page appears. In the example shown in Figure 5-16, the invitation for an accepted connection appears in the invitations list. Select the check box next to the name of each invitee you want to archive, then click the Archive button. LinkedIn displays a green bar at the top of the Invitations Sent page, informing you that the selected messages have been archived. If you want to view the archived messages, click the Show Archived Messages link, as shown in Figure 5-17.

Figure 5-16. **The invitation for an accepted connection**

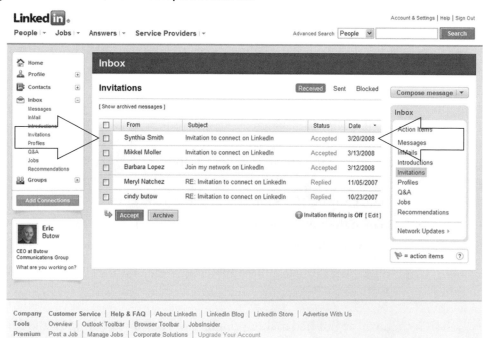

Figure 5-17. **The Show Archived Messages link**

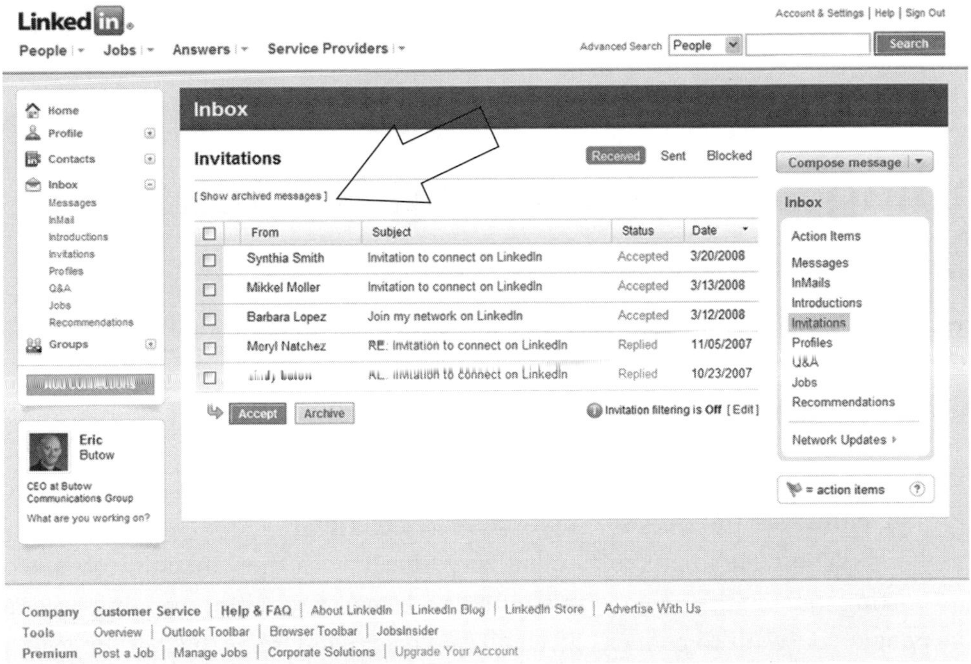

You also can archive received and blocked invitations by clicking the Received or Blocked link and repeating the archival process for any invitations you want to archive.

Now that you've set up your contacts list, it's time to start exploring LinkedIn. If you're looking for jobs or if you want to recruit for jobs, either as a recruiter or for your own business, go on to Chapter 6. If you own your own business and want to become a service provider, or if you want to search for a service provider, turn to Chapter 7. You can also learn more about making and asking for recommendations in Chapter 8.

6

Finding and Recruiting for Jobs

LinkedIn is a valuable resource for finding jobs as well as for finding qualified people to fill open positions. Your ability to find or fill a job depends on taking full advantage of the tools that LinkedIn offers. The first and most important step is to create a compelling profile, and we explained how to do that in Chapter 3. Without a profile that effectively sells you and what you do, people won't be interested in working with you, either as a prospective employee or as a recruiter.

The next step is to familiarize yourself with the LinkedIn job search and posting tools so that you can customize your search to target the companies and/or people you want to contact. (If you haven't signed in, refer to Chapter 2.) If you're a job seeker or a recruiter, click the Jobs link on the member home page. The Jobs home page appears as shown in Figure 6-1. The Jobs home page shows the Find Jobs tab by default. You also can search jobs in the Search box above the Find Jobs tab. This box is one of several ways you can search for a job that's posted on LinkedIn; others are employing JobsInsider, finding jobs through your network, and using the Search box.

Getting JobsInsider and Other Tips

In Figure 6-1, notice the large box titled Tips for finding jobs with LinkedIn. At the bottom of the box, there is a link to download LinkedIn tools for job seekers. LinkedIn may add more job-seeking tools over time, but for now the only tool available is JobsInsider. When you click the Get JobsInsider link on the page, the JobsInsider page appears, as shown in Figure 6-2, so that you can get more information about this tool. JobsInsider is a toolbar for Internet Explorer or Firefox that works with major job sites, including Dice, Monster, and Craigslist. When you view a job in one of these Web sites, JobsInsider checks the ad to see if anyone in your network

Figure 6-1. **The Jobs Home page**

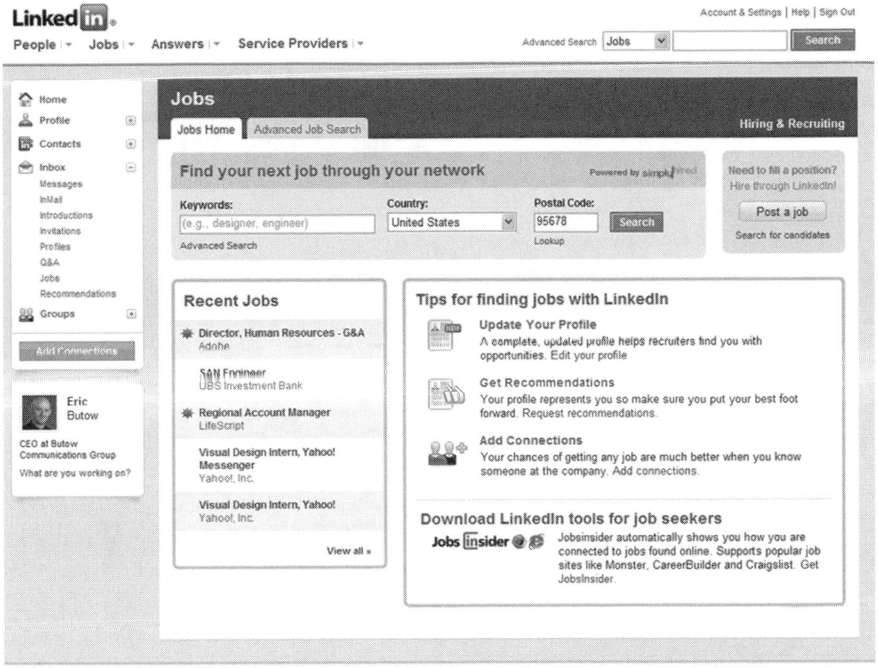

works for the hiring company. You can then use LinkedIn to get more information about the company and get your resume to the right person. The JobsInsider toolbar is part of the LinkedIn Browser Toolbar; so you can search LinkedIn from anywhere.

You can download the toolbar by clicking the appropriate Download it now button for your browser. Note that the Internet Explorer version of JobsInsider is for Windows only, but you can use the Firefox version for Windows and Mac OS. If you're in the JobsInsider page, you can return to the Jobs Home page by clicking the Jobs & Hiring page.

Viewing Recently Posted Jobs

To the left of the box showing Tips for Finding Jobs, LinkedIn lists the five most recently posted jobs on the system in the Recent Jobs list on the left-hand side of the page. If you want more information about the job, click the job title in the list. If the

Figure 6-2. **The JobsInsider page**

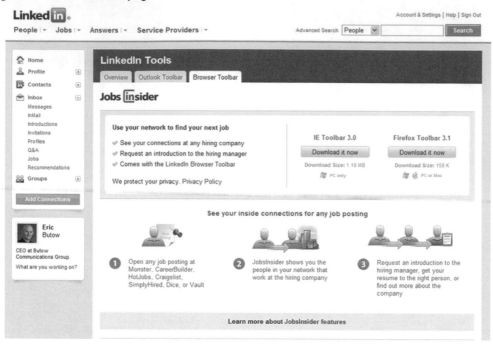

job is exclusive to LinkedIn, you'll see a blue star to the left of the job title. You can view all recent jobs by clicking the View All link at the bottom of the list. Figure 6-3 shows the Job Search Results page that appears after you click the link. The Job Search Results page displays the LinkedIn Jobs tab that lists the 10 most recent jobs posted to LinkedIn. Above the list you'll see the total number of jobs that match your search criteria, which in Figure 6-3 is 500 matches.

Information about each job is organized into five columns from left to right. The first column is the job title, followed by the company looking for an employee, the job location, the date the job was posted, and the job poster name. You can sort the results alphabetically by title, company, location, or the job poster by clicking the Title, Company, Location, or Posted By column titles, respectively.

If you don't see a job you want, you can scroll down the page to view the page number index, as shown in Figure 6-4. Each page contains 10 job listings, and the default sort order for the list is from newest to oldest. Therefore, page 2 contains job listings that are older than listings on page 1, page 3 contains job listings that are older than those on page 2, and so on. The page index lists the first 50 pages. To go to the

Figure 6-3. **The Job Search Results page**

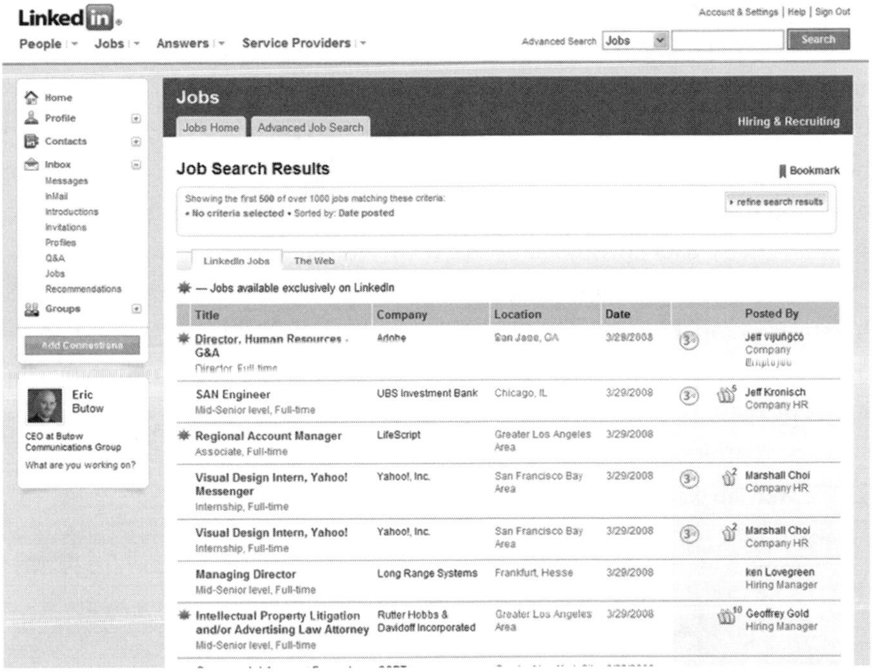

Figure 6-4. **The page number index**

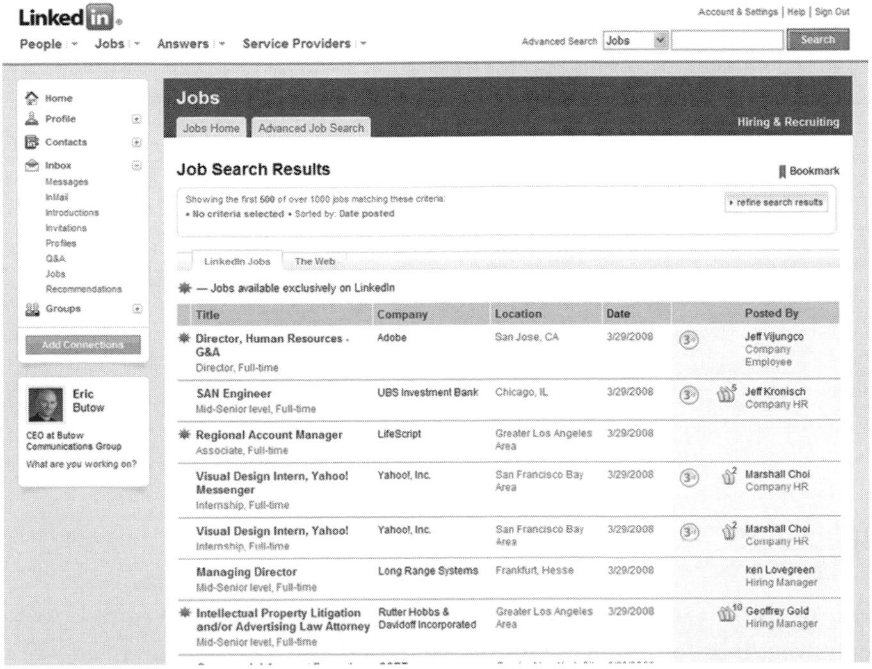

next page, click the Next link. If you're on a page other than page 1, click the Previous link to go to the previous page.

If you change the sort order of the list, the information on each page changes to match your sort order. For example, if you sort the list by title, then page 1 shows the first 10 titles that start with special characters such as a quote, the pound sign (#), the dollar sign, the left parenthesis, the asterisk, and the period. As you move to the following pages, you'll see that LinkedIn continues listing entries in numerical order and eventually lists entries that start with a letter.

If you don't find what you want in the LinkedIn Jobs tab, you can search the Web by clicking The Web tab. LinkedIn displays all the jobs it can find on the Web that match your search criteria. If LinkedIn can't find any matches, the tab asks you to refine your search or check the job listings from a major city, as shown in Figure 6-5.

Figure 6-5. **The Web tab that returns no results**

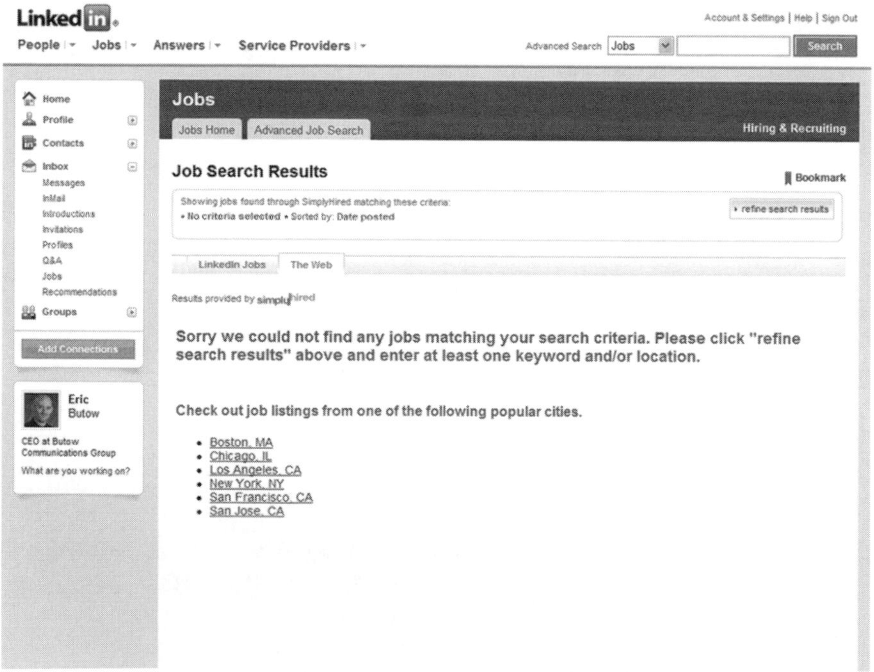

Finding Jobs

So how do you search effectively for jobs in LinkedIn? The system provides four different methods for refining your search to find exactly what you need—or to give you some comfort in knowing that currently there aren't any jobs with the parameters you selected.

If you're not in the Jobs Home page, go there by clicking the Jobs & Hiring tab. The Jobs & Hiring Home page provides links to all three methods of refining your search:

1. Searching by keyword, company, or job title.

2. Finding a job through your network.

3. Performing an advanced search by clicking the Advanced Search link that appears in the Find Your Next Job through your network box and to the right of the Search box.

Searching by Keyword, Company, or Job Title

The Search box at the top of the page, as shown in Figure 6-6, allows you to find job openings quickly by typing one or more keywords, a company you want to work for, or the title of the job you want. If you type multiple keywords, separate them with

Figure 6-6. **The Search box**

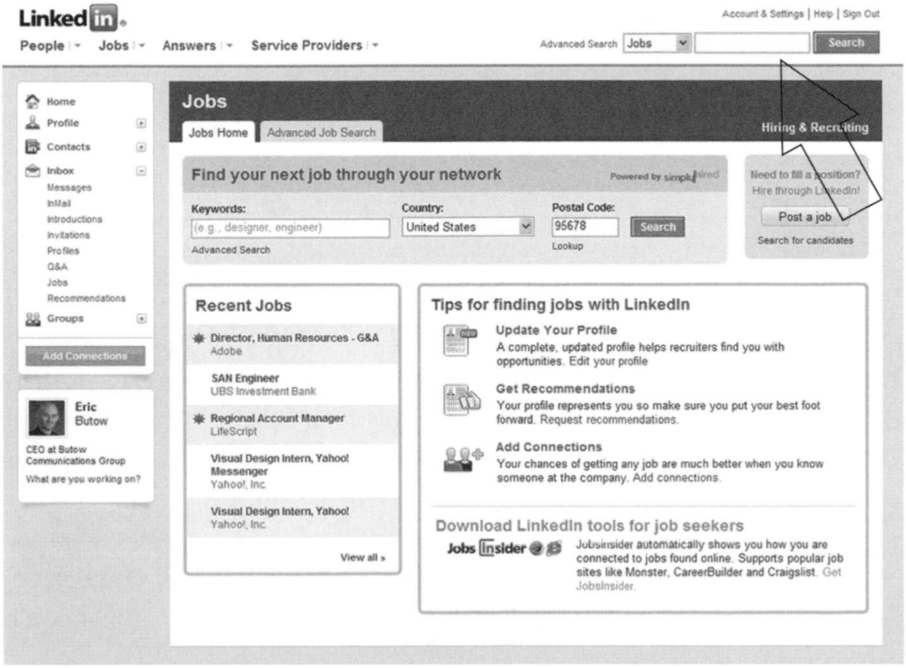

spaces, commas, or semicolons. When you're finished typing your search criteria in the box, click the Go button. The Job Search Results page appears. For example, I typed "technical writer," and Figure 6-7 shows all technical writing jobs and when they were posted.

Figure 6-7. **The Job Search Results page for technical writing jobs**

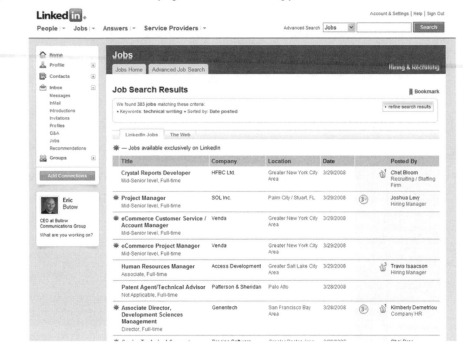

Refining Your Search

If the search results don't give you what you're looking for, especially if there are a lot of matches to search through, you can refine the search by clicking the Refine Search Results button. When you click this button, the Refine Search Results tab appears, as shown in Figure 6-8. The tab is divided into three columns:

- In the left column, the keywords I entered for this example appear in the Keywords box. Here I can type the job title and/or company, select the ex-

Figure 6-8. **The Refine Search Results tab**

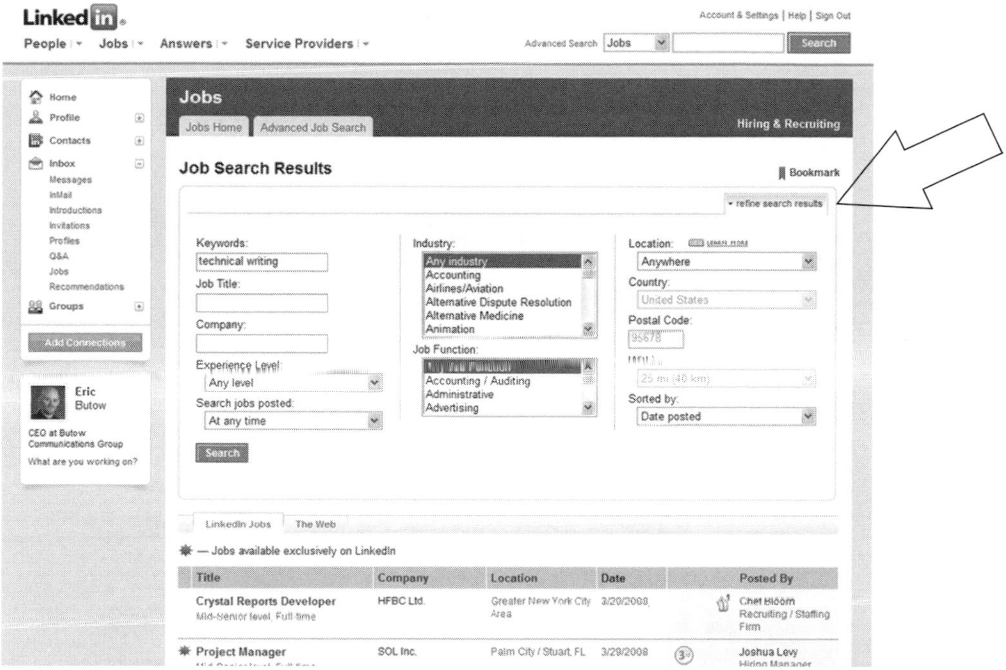

perience level for the job, and search jobs that were posted within a certain time period.

- In the middle column, I can search for the industry and/or any job function. If you don't see the industry and/or job function in the Industry and Job Function lists, leave the default Any Industry and Any Job Function options selected.

- In the right column, the default location is Anywhere. If you select Located In or Near in the Location list, the other lists and boxes become active. In these boxes you can specify a country, postal code, or distance from your location, and you can sort the list by title, company, location, or the job poster. You also can look up postal codes in the GeoNames site by clicking the Lookup tab to the right of the Postal Code box, then searching for the information in a new browser tab or window.

When you finish refining your search, click the Search button. The Job Search Results page refreshes with your refined results Above the list, you see the number of jobs and the search criteria LinkedIn used. You also can click The Web tab to see more jobs that match your criteria as shown in Figure 6-9.

Figure 6-9. **The Web tab that lists jobs that meet your criteria**

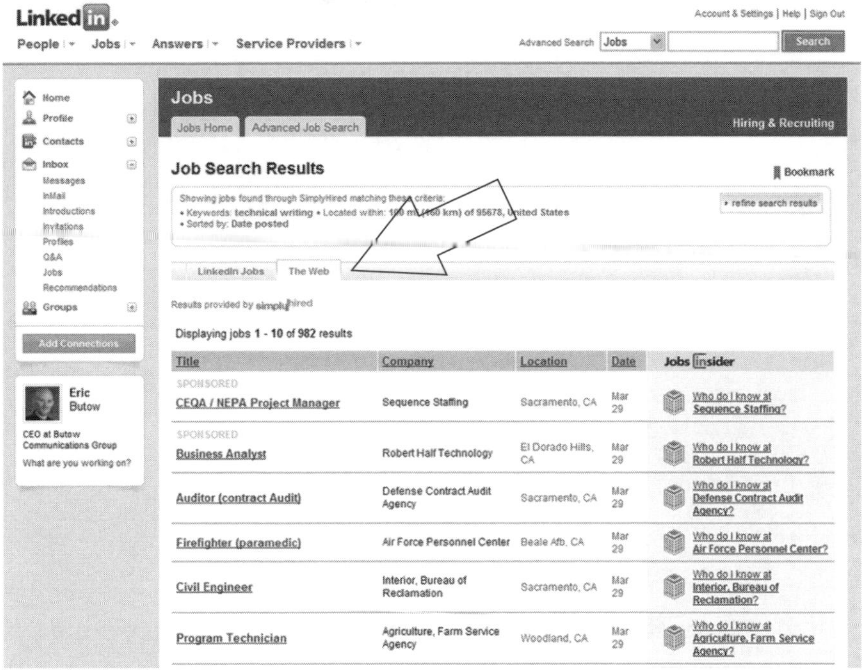

If the company is connected with JobsInsider, the JobsInsider column provides links so that you can find out whether you know of anyone who works for that company. If you do, you can contact him and get what LinkedIn refers to as an inside connection to get that job.

Searching for a Job

You can find a job through your network in the blue Find Your Next Job link, which appears near the top of the Jobs home page.

Finding a job in LinkedIn is simple. Start by typing your keyword or keywords in the Keywords box. Then select the country in which you want to search from the Country list. And then type the postal code where you want to look for work. The default postal code is your own, but if you need another postal code, click the Lookup link underneath the Postal Code box to search for a postal code in the GeoNames Web site.

When you're finished, click the Search button. If LinkedIn finds any jobs in your network, the system lists the files in the Job Search Results page LinkedIn tab. If LinkedIn can't find any connections in your network, it searches the Web for jobs that meet your criteria.

Performing an Advanced Search

You can access LinkedIn's advanced job searching tool by clicking the Advanced Search link below the Keywords box in the Find your next job through your network box at the top of the page as shown in Figure 6-10, or by clicking the Advanced Job Search tab.

Figure 6-10. **The Advanced Search link in the Jobs Home page**

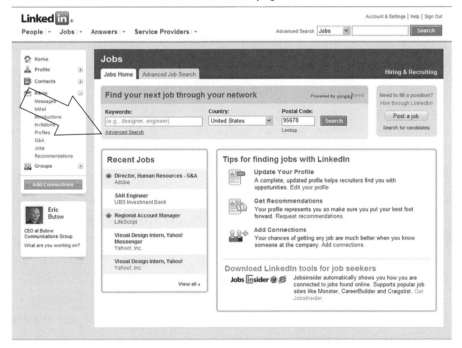

When you click the Advanced Search link, the Job Search page appears as shown in Figure 6-11. This page contains the Advanced Job Search box for refining your search with up to 11 different criteria. You can search by keyword by typing the keyword or keywords in the Search For box. Separate keywords with spaces. If you want to search only by keywords, click the Search button to the right of the Search for box.

Figure 6-11. **The Jobs page with the Advanced Job Search box**

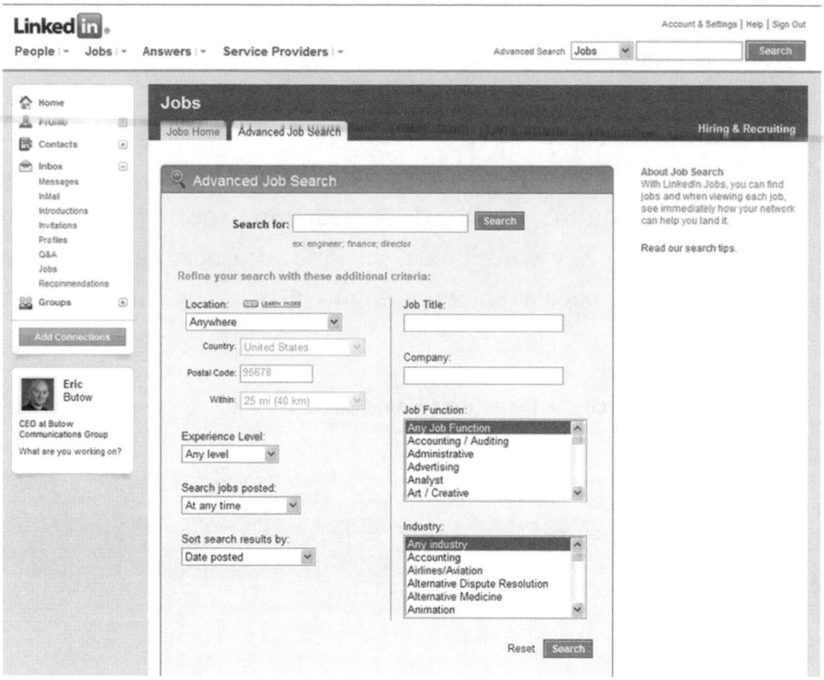

If you want to refine your search, the search criteria are split into two columns. In the left column, you can search anywhere (the default) or in a particular country, postal zone, and within a certain distance around your location. You can also specify experience level, a specific time period when the job was posted, and how to sort the search results. In the right column, you can type the job title and/or company, search by job function, and search by industry.

If you decide you want to clear all the search criteria you entered and start over, click the Reset button at the bottom of the box. Otherwise, click the Search button to have LinkedIn search for jobs that meet your criteria and display those results in the Job Search Results page.

Applying for a Job

Once you locate a job, how do you apply for it? LinkedIn provides two ways to get the job poster's attention.

1. You can use the standard method of sending a cover letter and uploading your resume to LinkedIn, and the system sends the information to the job poster. That's something you should always do so that the job poster knows that you're interested in the job.

2. However, to make sure the job poster knows you're a candidate who goes the extra mile to get the job, LinkedIn encourages you to build inside connections with people who work at the poster's company.

Figure 6-12 shows an example of a job posting. You can apply by clicking the Apply Now button to the right of the job title.

Figure 6-12. **The Apply Now button in the job listing**

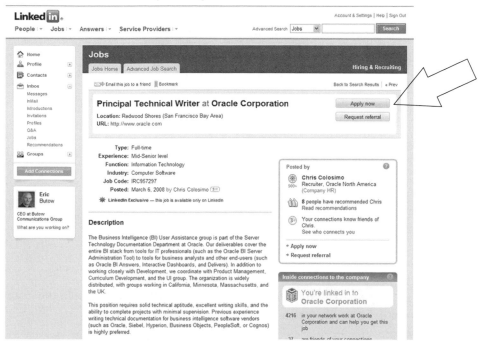

When you click the Apply Now button, the Apply for this Job page appears, as shown in Figure 6-13. In this page you can write your cover letter, enter your contact information, and upload your resume. The first step is to write a cover letter to the poster in the Write Cover Letter box. Though the cover letter is Web-based and has no fancy formatting, write the letter as if you were printing it out on nice stationery and mailing it to the employer. If you're not sure about how to write your cover letter, click the See Tips link to the right of the Write Cover Letter box. A new browser window opens that contains useful information for writing an effective cover letter, including writing a strong opening paragraph that demonstrates how your experience and strengths apply directly to the job and proofreading carefully.

Figure 6-13. **The Apply for this Job page**

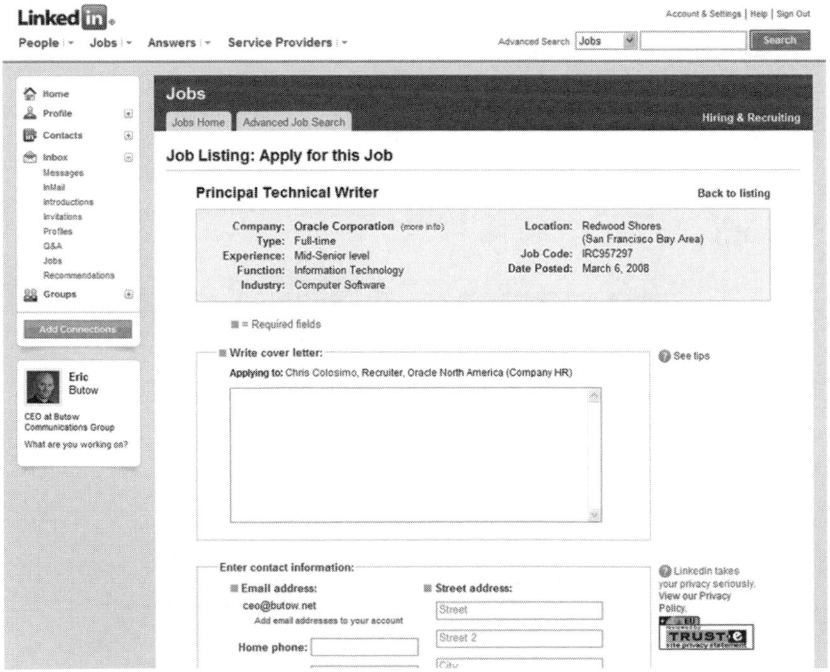

Scroll down the page to add your contact information in the Enter Contact Information area, as shown in Figure 6-14.

Figure 6-14. **The Enter Contact Information area**

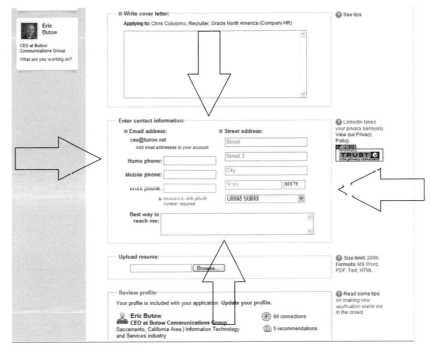

In this area you can add your home, work, and mobile phone numbers, your street address, and the best way to reach you.

In the Upload Resume area, click the Browse button to open a window so that you can navigate to the folder containing your resume and then select your resume file to upload. LinkedIn accepts files in text, HTML, Microsoft Word, and PDF formats. However, the maximum size LinkedIn can handle is 200 kilobytes (KB), so check the size of your resume file before you upload it. (My two-page text resume is only 39 KB.)

At the bottom of the page, you can review your profile in the Review Profile area. You can make changes to the profile by clicking the name and then making the profile changes in a new browser tab or window.

If the poster prefers applicants to have recommendations, LinkedIn includes that information at the bottom of the area. You can get recommendations by clicking the Get Recommendations link. If you don't have recommendations, you can still

Figure 6-15. **The Confirm Application page**

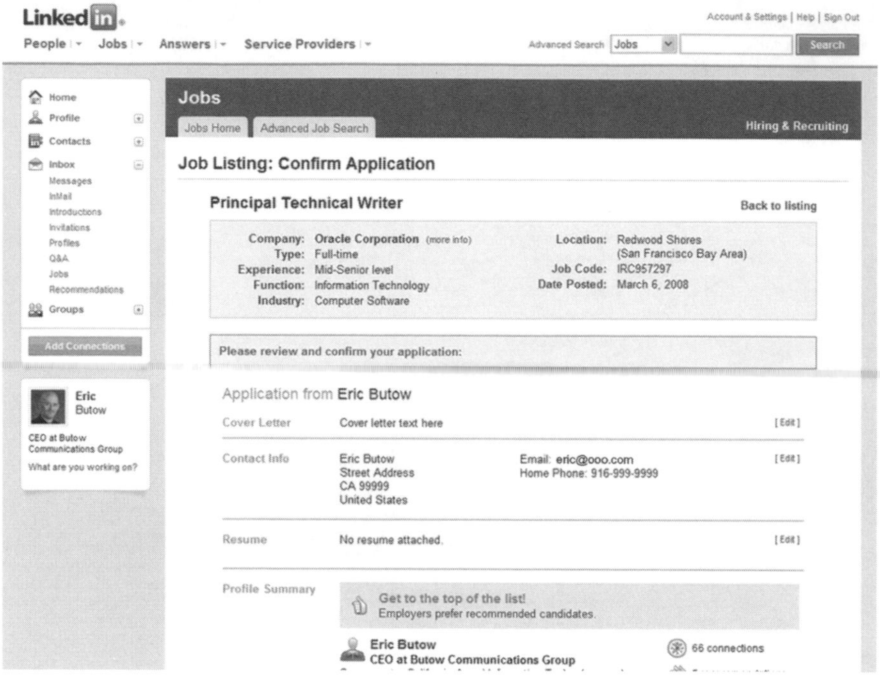

submit your application, but, unless your skills blow away the job poster, it's highly likely that your application won't be considered.

When you're finished entering information, click the Next button to review and confirm your application in the Confirm Application page, as shown in Figure 6-15. Click the Edit link to the right of each area of information to make any further changes. When you're satisfied, click the Submit Application button. You also can go back to the listing by clicking the Back to Listing link to the right of the job title near the top of the page.

In the listing page, the poster information appears on the right-hand side of the page in the Posted By box. The information in this box tells you the name of the poster and how many recommendations she has. A blue box below the Posted By box invites you to make inside connections to the company advertising the job, as shown in Figure 6-16.

LinkedIn also invites you to build your network to find an inside connection to the poster and to add connections to find people at the company. How do you do that? The best way is by clicking the poster name in the Posted By box to see the

Figure 6-16. **The Posted By and Inside Connections to the company boxes**

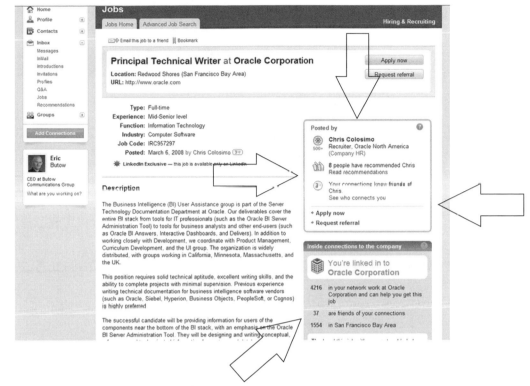

poster's profile, which normally includes recommendations from others—and many of them are likely to be from the poster's company. (The absence of any recommendations from coworkers at the poster's company could be a bad sign.) Then you can view the profile of the LinkedIn member who recommended the poster and create an inside connection by adding that member to your network.

Hiring and Recruiting

If you're a recruiter, the Jobs Home page includes the Hiring and Recruiting tab that enables you to search LinkedIn to find the best candidate. Open the Hiring and Recruiting tab by clicking the down arrow to the right of the Jobs link at the top of the page and then clicking Hiring Home. The Hiring Home page appears and displays the Hiring tab, as shown in Figure 6-17. The home page contains information about what hiring on LinkedIn can do for your company and provides links if you want

Figure 6-17. **The Hiring Home page**

more information, including how to sign up. On the right-hand side of the page are three small boxes:

1. Search Candidates.

2. Post a Job.

3. Find Independent References.

Search for Candidates

The top box lets you type keywords in the Search Candidates box to search quickly for any profiles containing experience with a particular type of job. For example, if I type "Web design" in the box and click the Go button, the top 20 results appear in the People Search Results page, as shown in Figure 6-18.

Figure 6-18. **The People Search results page**

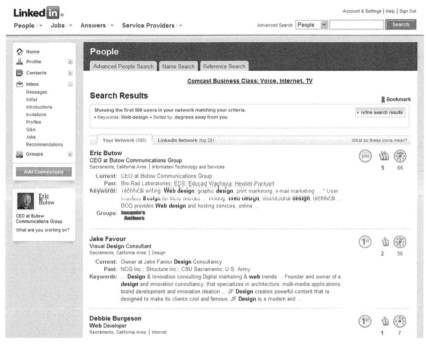

If you want to refine your search, you can do so in the same way as you did with job search results (as explained earlier in this chapter). Click the Refine Search Results button to open the Refine Search Results tab, as shown in Figure 6-19.

- In the left column of the tab, your keywords appear in the Keywords box, and you can delete them and type new ones if you want. You also can type the name, title, and company the person works for. If you want to see only the person's current title and/or the current company, select the Current Titles Only and Current Company Only check boxes, respectively.

- In the middle column, you can search by the user type (for example, if you're looking for a consultant or contractor), when the person joined, and the industry in which the person works.

- In the right column, you can search for the person by a specific country and/or postal code.

Figure 6-19. **The Refine Search Results tab**

The search results include a summary of the member's profile, specifying the number of her connections and recommendations.

Post a Job

If you're interested in posting a job, all you have to do is click the Post a Job tab. The Compose Job page appears, as shown in Figure 6-20. At the top of the page, the company name appears in the Company Information area. You can change the name in the Company Name box and add the company Web site in the Company URL box.

The Job Information area, shown in Figure 6-21, lets you add information about the job, including the title, the job function and type, the industry, the experience level needed, optional salary and job code information, and the job description. At the bottom of the page, as shown in Figure 6-22, the Location Information, Additional Information, and Promote Your Job areas allow you to specify where the job is and what you prefer from candidates and to have LinkedIn promote your job if the job is available exclusively on LinkedIn.

Figure 6-20. **The Compose Job page**

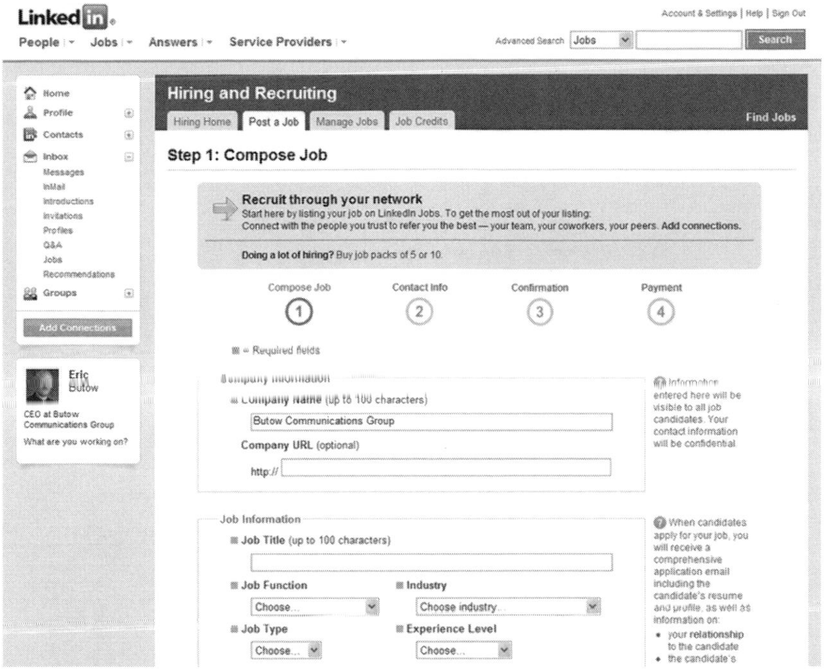

Figure 6-21. **The Job Information area**

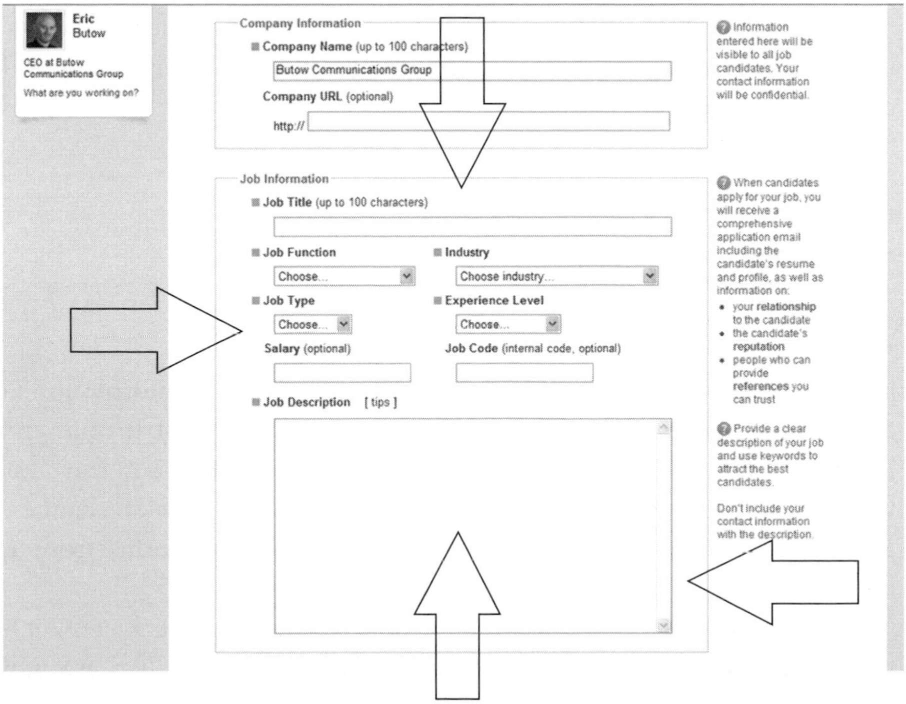

Figure 6-22. **The Location Information, Additional Information, and Promote Your Job areas**

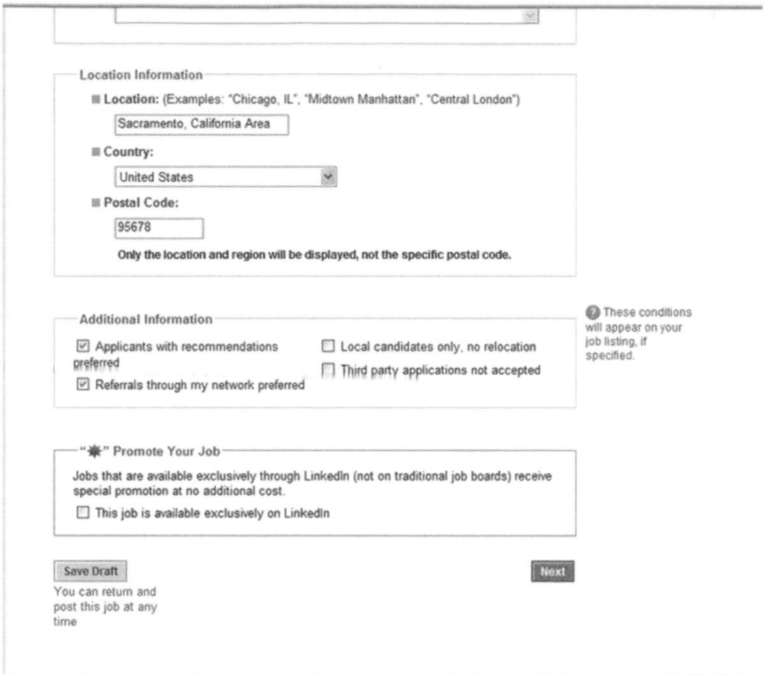

In addition to composing the job, there are three other steps in the job posting process, and on every page you can save the draft of your job and post it later by clicking the Save Draft button:

1. Entering contact information.

2. Confirming the posting.

3. Paying for the posting.

Click the Next button to go to the next step, the Contact Information Step page, as shown in Figure 6-23. This page contains your default profile and contact information, as well as your role in hiring for this position. You can show or hide your profile on the job listing (the default is to show the profile), change your role, and specify a different e-mail address to receive applications from interested applicants.

In each area of the Confirmation Step page, you can click the Edit link if you need to change the post and/or the posting information. When everything looks

Figure 6-23. **The Contact Information Step page**

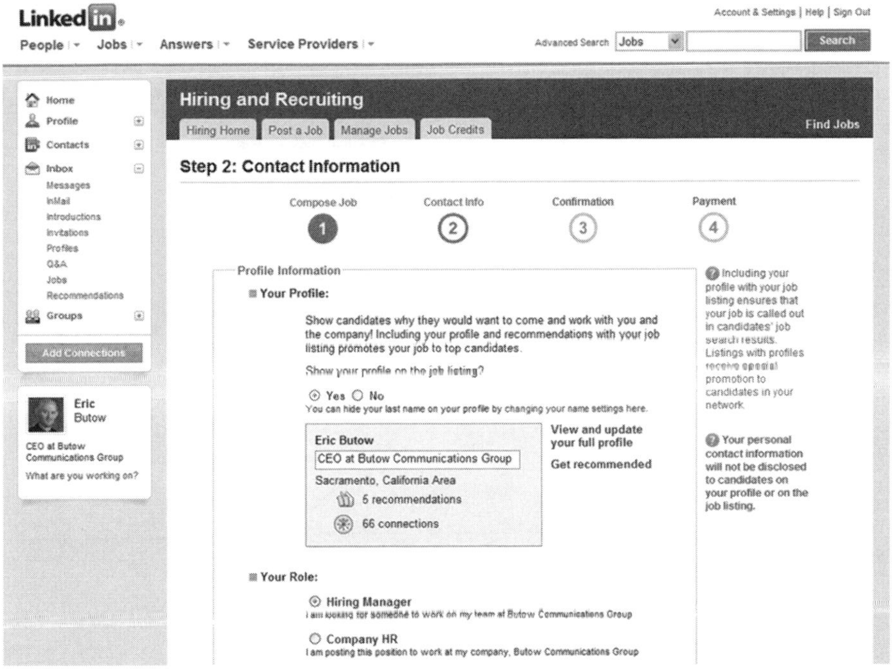

good, scroll down to the bottom of the page and click the Post This Job button to go to the final step: the payment page.

The cost for posting a single job is $145, though, if you have more postings, LinkedIn offers 5- or 10-job posting credits for a discounted price-per-job posting. You can learn more about purchasing credits and managing your job credits by clicking the Job Credits tab. When you click the link, the Job Credit Summary page appears, as shown in Figure 6-24. If you haven't purchased any job credits, click the Purchase credits button. After you use your credits, you can view information about those credits by clicking the Used/Expired Credits tab.

Manage Jobs

If you've posted jobs or simply created a draft to work on later, you can view a summary of the jobs you've posted, jobs that have expired, and draft jobs by clicking the down arrow to the right of the Jobs link and then clicking Manage Jobs. Clicking the link opens the Manage Jobs page, as shown in Figure 6-25. Each tab tells you how many open jobs, past jobs, and draft jobs you have. If you haven't posted any jobs or

Figure 6-24. **The Job Credit Summary page**

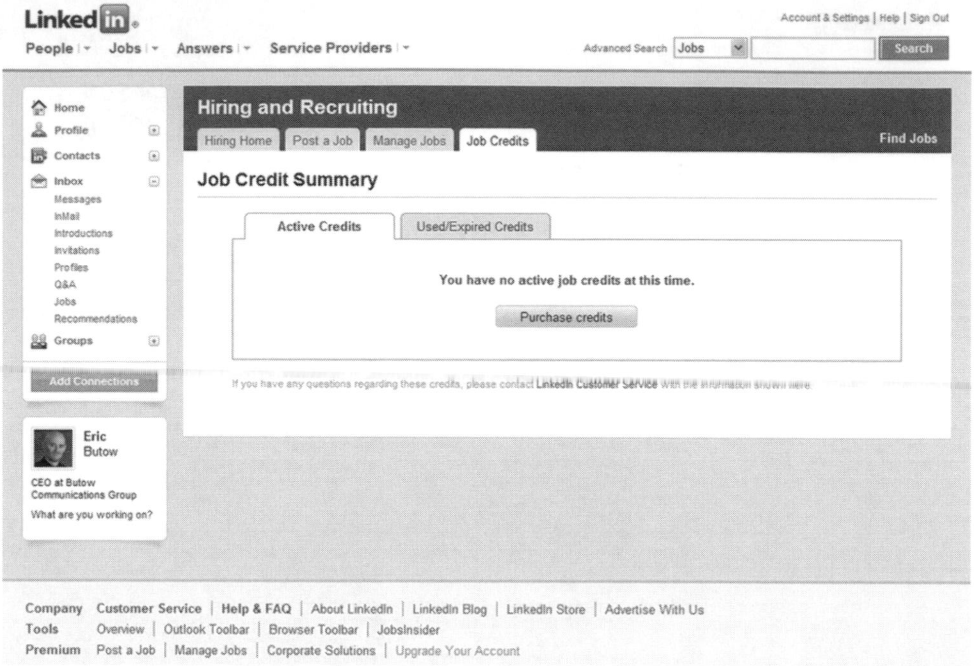

Figure 6-25. **The Manage Jobs page**

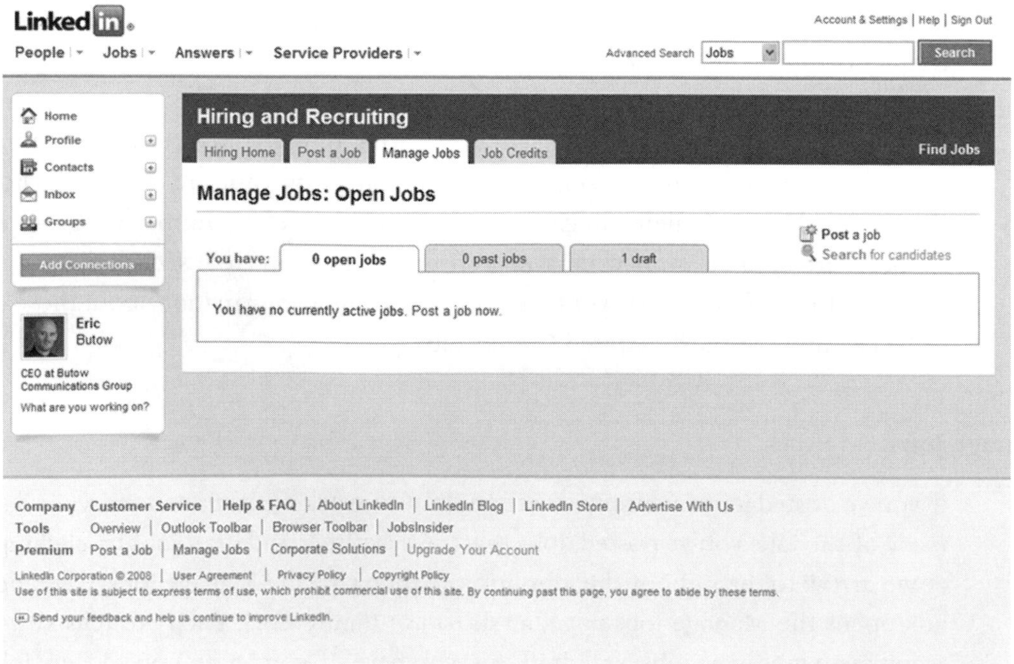

if you have no expired jobs, LinkedIn invites you to click the Post a Job Now link to post one.

If you have saved a draft of a job, click the Draft tab to view the draft summary, as shown in Figure 6-26. The draft summary shows the job title, the date the job was last updated, and the state of the job.

Figure 6-26. **The draft summary**

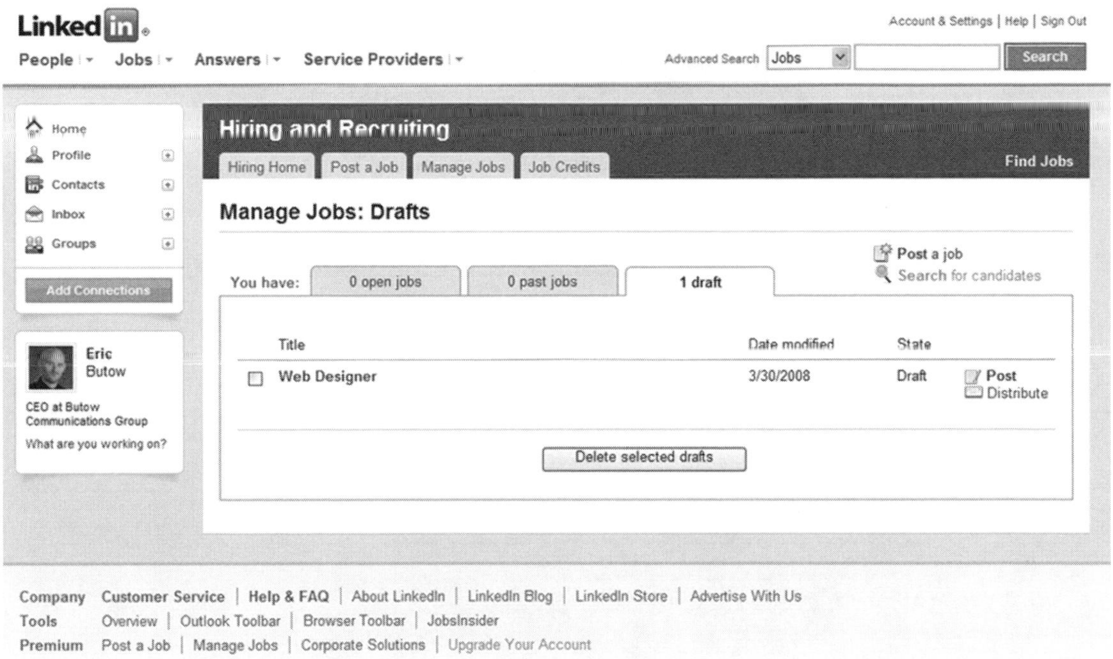

- If you want to post the draft job, click the Post link.
- You can also work on the draft further by clicking the title of the job.
- If you decide that you no longer want to post the job, such as when the job is removed by the powers that be, select the check box to the left of the job title and click the Delete selected drafts button. A dialog box appears and asks whether you want to delete the draft. Click the OK button to delete it. The Manage Jobs: Draft page refreshes, and a green bar appears at the top of the page to let you know that the drafts have been deleted successfully.

Find Independent References

If you go back to the Hiring Home page (click the Hiring Home tab), you see that under the Post a Job button there is a box, as shown in Figure 6-27, that invites you to find independent references by clicking the Go button.

Figure 6-27. **The Find Independent References box**

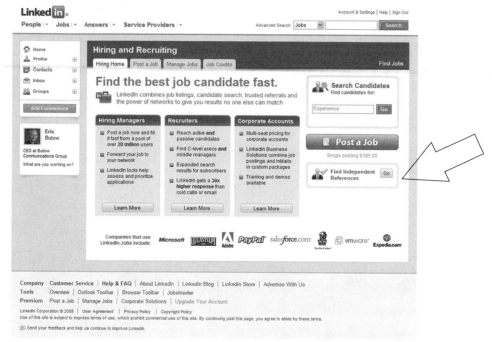

When you click the Go button, the Find References page appears as shown in Figure 6-28, so that you can search for LinkedIn members who can provide professional references for your candidate. You can type the company names that appear in the person's profile, as well as the start and end years of their employment in the Years boxes. Add the start and end years by typing the start year in the box to the left of the word "to" and then typing the end year in the box (or the current year if the candidate is still with the company) to the right of it. You can type up to five company names and their associated start and end dates. When you click the Search button, LinkedIn searches for people in your network who also worked with the applicant at the same time the applicant worked there—people who can give you quality references.

Figure 6-28. **The Find References page**

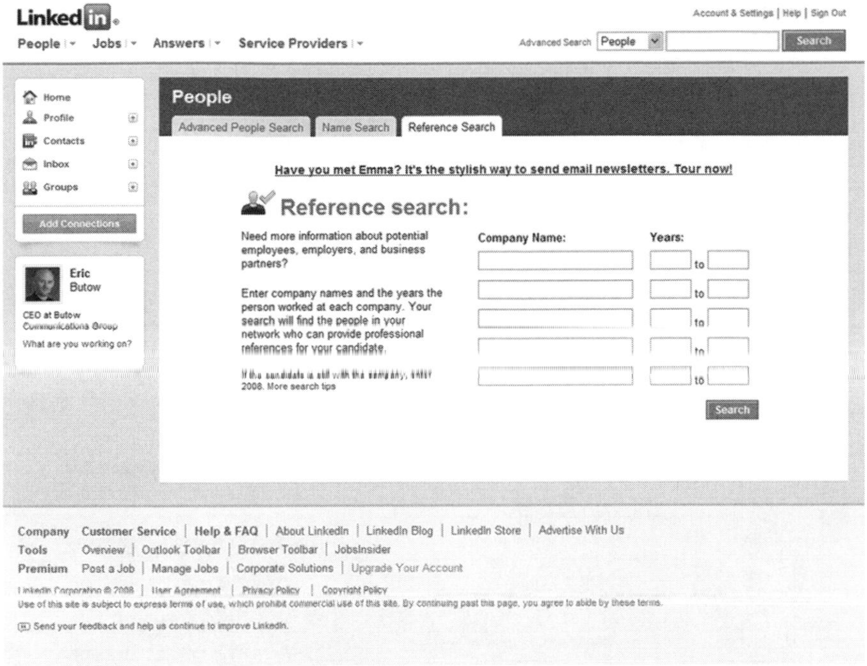

Leveraging Your Network to Find Candidates

Your network is a valuable resource. So, if you're trying to find a worthy candidate, take advantage of it! You can distribute a new job to connections in your network and ask them if they can forward your job information to anyone they think would be interested in the position.

Start in the home page by clicking the Inbox link in the Navigation box, as shown in Figure 6-29. In the Inbox: Action Items page, move the mouse pointer over the Compose Message button, then click the Send Job Notification link in the drop-down menu, as shown in Figure 6-30.

At the top of the Distribute New Job page that appears in Figure 6-31, you can view the default subject and message that you will send to your connections. You can also make changes to the subject and the message in the Subject and Message boxes, respectively.

Figure 6-29. **The Inbox link**

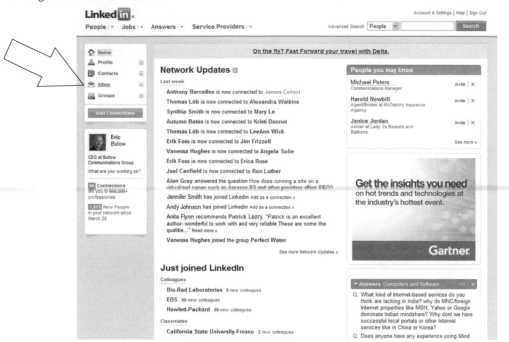

Figure 6-30. **The Send job notification link**

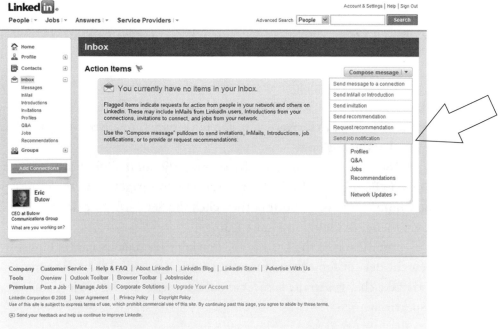

Figure 6-31. **The Distribute New Job page**

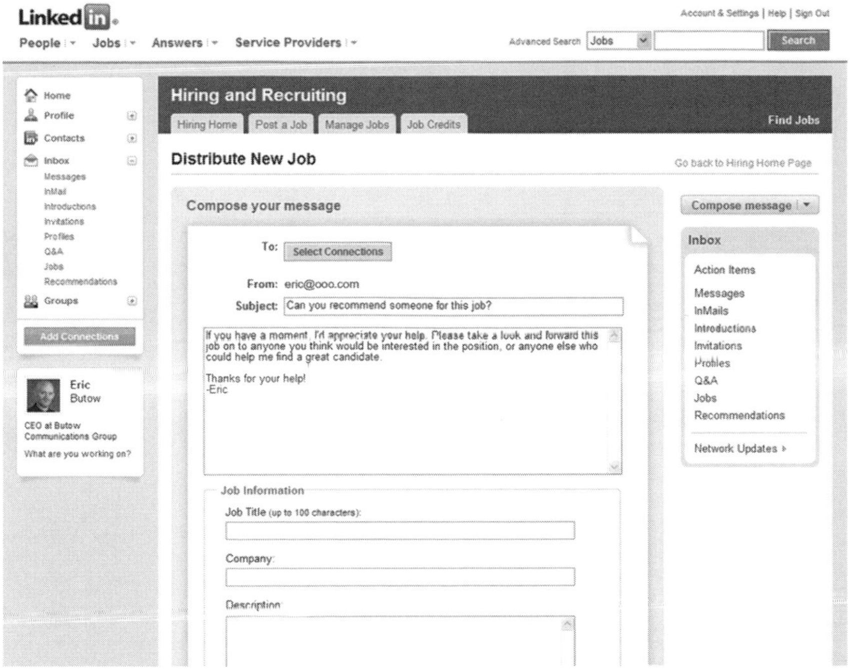

Select the members to whom you want to send the job posting by clicking the Select Connections button at the top of the window. When you click the button, the Narrow Your Connections box appears, as shown in Figure 6-32. Select members by scrolling down the list and selecting the check box to the left of each member's name. As you select each check box, the corresponding name appears in the connections box at the right side of the Narrow Your Connections box. You can add as many as 200 connections. When you're finished adding connections, click the Finished button. (You'll learn more about using the features of the Narrow Your Connections box in Chapter 8.)

In the Job Information area, type the job title (up to 100 characters) in the Job Title box, the company that's hiring in the Company box, and the job description in the Description box. If you want to receive a copy of your message in your e-mailbox, select the Send Me a Copy check box.

When you're finished preparing your message, click the Send button. LinkedIn sends each connection an individualized message asking for his or her help in finding great candidates for your job opening.

Figure 6-32. **The Narrow Your Connections box**

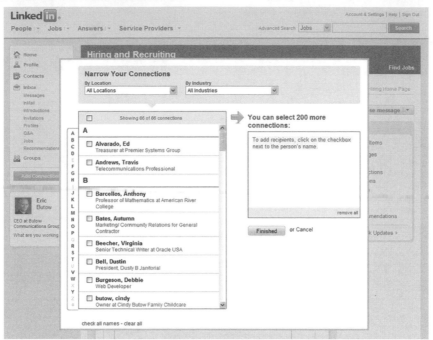

An Example of Searching for Talent

Let's say you're seeking a software product manager with skills in e-commerce software, focusing on the consumer market. There are more than 52,000 product managers on LinkedIn as of this writing; so the need to narrow the focus for the search is obvious. LinkedIn makes this easy by using the Advanced People Search function.

Access the Advanced People Search page from the home page by clicking the down arrow to the right of the People link at the top of the page. In the drop-down menu that appears, as shown in Figure 6-33, click the Advanced People Search link.

To find this talent, type the search criteria into the following boxes:

- Keywords: Consumer, ecommerce, e-commerce, product management
- Title: Product manager
- Company: (This may or may not be filled in.)

Figure 6-33. **The Advanced People Search link**

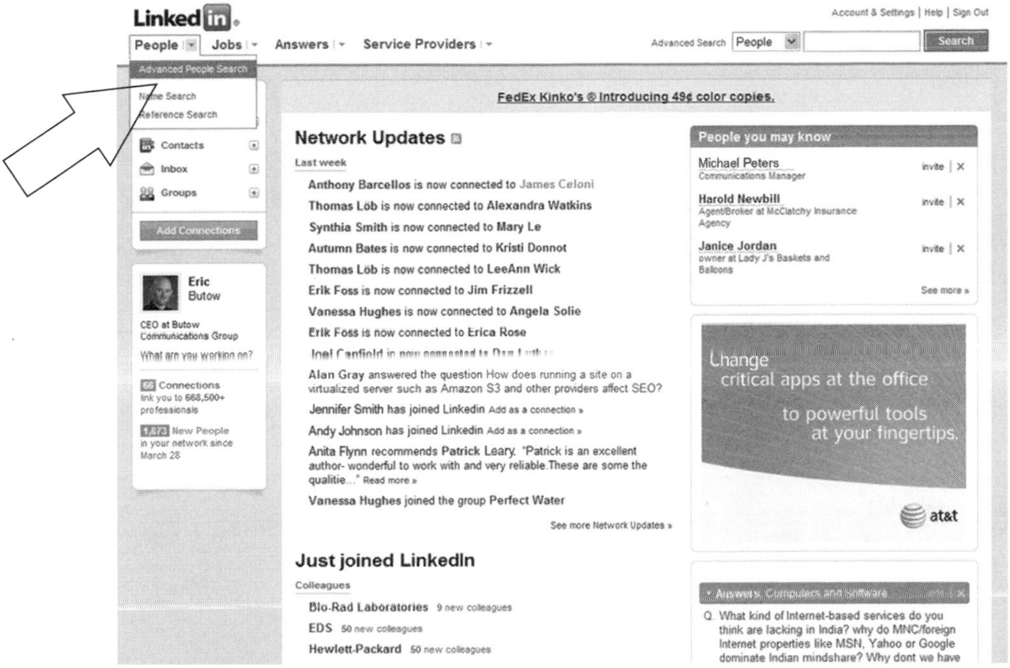

Note that in the keyword list, the term "e-commerce" is spelled two ways. People spell terms differently—especially newly coined terms—so you should take variant spellings (and even misspellings) into account when you type search criteria.

You also have the option of checking or unchecking current titles and current companies. This is, of course, a personal choice that really depends on how widely you want to cast your net.

LinkedIn allows you to narrow your universe by searching in and around a postal code, by keywords, or by your relationship with the LinkedIn network at-large. For example, you can sort by postal code 94118 and:

- Keyword relevance.

- Number of connections.

- Degrees away from you.

- Degrees and recommendations.

Figure 6-34. shows an example of narrowing your search accordingly.

Figure 6-34. **An example of narrowing your search**

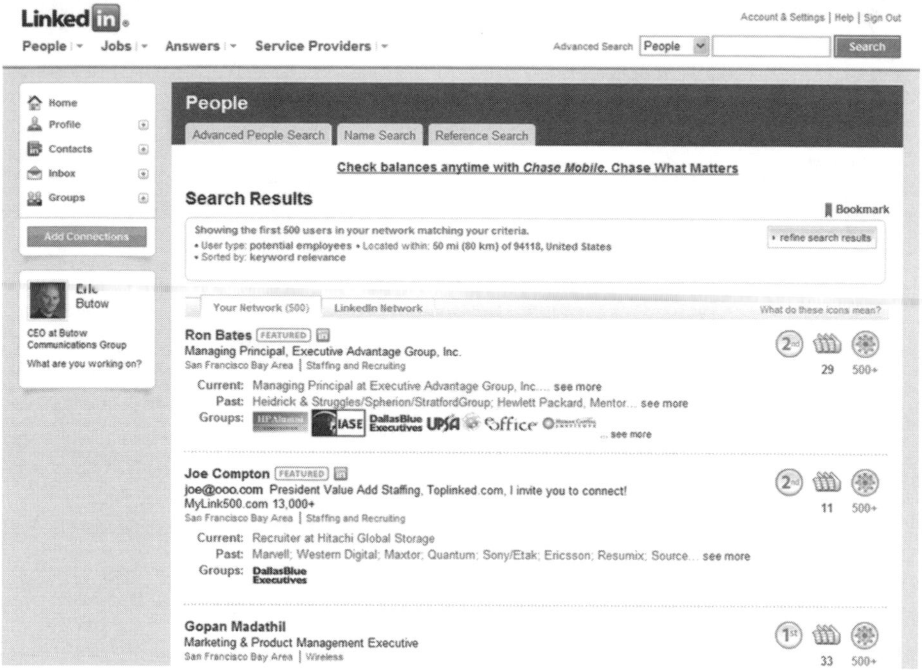

Now the task entails looking through the list of names that have come up for those whose credentials that best fit the opportunity. The search begins by the way it is sorted. For example, if Keyword Relevance was selected in the Sort By list, then the resulting names are sorted by those whose profiles contain all or most of the keywords. There is no across-the-board best way to do the search; there is only the way that best fits the individual search and searcher. If it is extremely important that the candidate is one or two degrees away, then it is important to sort by that relevance.

If the person's profile is properly built, you can peruse it to see whether there is a fit. If some of the talent looks interesting but there isn't enough information on the profile, you may have to look at their connections for further information about them. It is always good to check the candidate's connections to see whether you consider him a trusted adviser before making a decision whether to pursue this particular talent.

What's Next?

The next most important step is to find a good job provider if you're looking for a job or finding a good recruiter if you're looking to fill a job. Then you need to use your LinkedIn connections to get referrals from others who work at the company where you want to work, as well as recommendations from as many connections as possible. Many potential employers and recruiters require that profiles include recommendations, and the more potential employers or employees see that you are well thought of by others, the more interested they become in working with you. You'll learn more about getting referrals and recommendations in Chapter 8. Once you receive endorsements from others, you'll learn how to connect with those clients appropriately in Chapter 10.

For now, turn to Chapter 7 to learn about how to find the best job provider and/or recruiter for you.

7

Looking for and Becoming a Service Provider

How do you go about finding a good plumber when you have a leaky faucet? If you want to find someone you can depend on, you can call a neighbor, friend, or colleague who may be able to recommend someone. However, if that's not an option or you can't get a recommendation, as a LinkedIn member you don't have to go to the paper or online Yellow Pages and take your chances with someone. You can use LinkedIn to view service provider recommendations to learn who else has used services in your area that you need and what those members think of the providers. LinkedIn also allows you to share your recommendations with other LinkedIn members.

Open the Service Providers page by clicking the Service Providers link on the home page. When you click the link, the Service Providers page appears with the Services tab active at the top of the page, as shown in Figure 7-1.

View Service Provider Recommendations

On the right side of the page is a list of the most recent service provider recommendations in all categories—the ones that were added since the last time you signed in. The most recent recommendation appears at the top of the list.

To the left of each block of recommendation information is a yellow box with a number, which represents the total number of recommendations the member has received. Each recommendation block contains the following, from top to bottom:

- The name of the recommended LinkedIn member.
- How long ago they were recommended by another member.

Figure 7-1. **The Service Providers page**

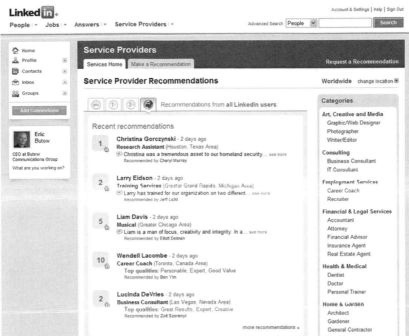

- The recommended member's position and where the member is located.
- A brief quote from the recommending member.
- Finally, the name of the recommending member.

Get More Recommendation Information

Within each recommendation block are three links to get more information about the recommended and recommending members. Click the name of the recommended member to view the Recommendation page, as shown in Figure 7-2. On this page, you can view the quote from the recommending member, the qualities of the recommended member, and the name of the recommending member.

From this page:

- If you want to send the recommended member a private message, click the Send InMail link. (You'll learn more about sending InMail in Chapter 10.)

Figure 7-2. **The Recommendation page**

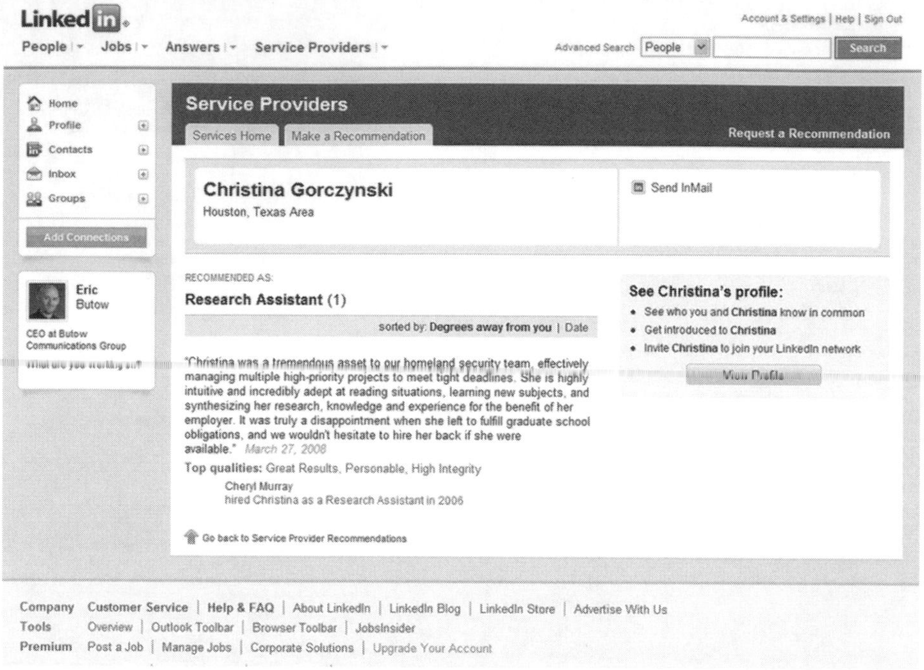

- If you want to view the recommended member's profile, click the View Profile button. Under the View Profile button, you also can view other top people in the same profession in the same geographic area, such as the top business consultants.

- If you want to view the profile of the recommending member, click the recommending member's name underneath the quote.

Get More Recommendations

Scroll down the list to view several more recommendations. If you want to view even more recent recommendations, click the More Recommendations link, as shown in Figure 7-3.

◠ *Figure 7-3.* **The More Recommendations link**

View More Top People

Below the Recent Recommendations list and the More Recommendations link are two lists of the top five recommended people in their industries or specialties. LinkedIn shows different lists so that, each time you visit (or refresh) the Service Providers page, the lists change. For example, you may see a list of top insurance agents and top doctors one time and a list of top graphic/Web designers and top career coaches the next time.

The person with the most recommendations appears at the top of each list. If you want to view more recommended people in each category, click the More link at the bottom of the list, such as the More Top Career Coaches link. The list of recommended service providers appears in the Service Providers page. Figure 7-4 shows lists of top photographers and top writers/editors, with the member having the most recommendations listed first.

 *Figure 7-4.* **The lists of top photographers and top writers/editors**

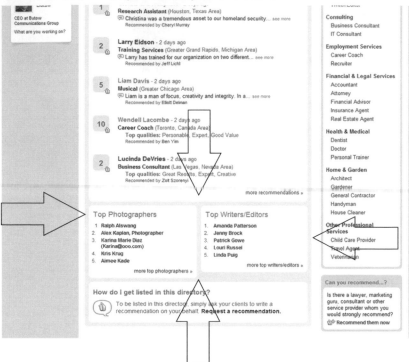

Searching for Service Providers

LinkedIn gives you five options when you want to search for a service provider:

1. Category,
2. Top results,
3. Date,
4. Degrees away from you,
5. Location.

View Recommendations by Category

In the Categories table on the right side of the page, you can select service providers in one of the following seven categories:

1. Art, Creative and Media, which includes the subsections Graphic/Web Designer, Photographer, and Writer/Editor.

2. Consulting, which includes the subsections Business Consultant and IT Consultant.

3. Employment Services, which includes the subsections Career Coach and Recruiter.

4. Financial and Legal Services, which includes the subsections Accountant, Attorney, Financial Advisor, Insurance Agent, and Real Estate Agent.

5. Health and Medical, which includes the subsections Doctor, Dentist, and Personal Trainer.

6. Home and Garden, which includes the subsections Architect, Gardener, General Contractor, Handyman, and House Cleaner.

7. Other Professional Services, which includes the subsections Child Care Provider, Travel Agent, and Veterinarian.

When you click on one of the subsections in a category section, the Service Providers page for the subsection appears. Figure 7-5 shows the Service Providers page for the Writer/Editor subsection in the Art, Creative, and Media category. The list of providers shows recommendations from all LinkedIn users, and the most recently recommended provider appears at the top of the list.

LinkedIn sorts the results by date automatically.

View Recommendations by Top Results

If you would rather see the service providers with the most recommendations at the top of the list, click the Top Results link above the first recommended name in the list. The list changes to show the service provider with the highest number of recommendations first, as shown in Figure 7-6.

If you want to sort by date again, click the Date link above the first name in the list.

Figure 7-5. **The Service Providers page for the Writer/Editor subsection**

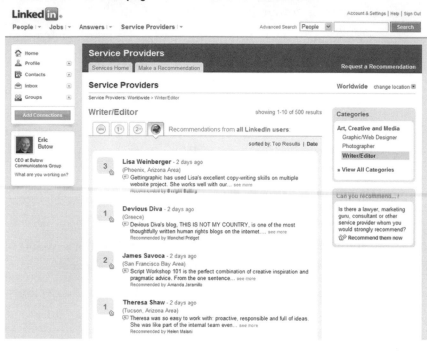

Figure 7-6. **The list sorted by top results**

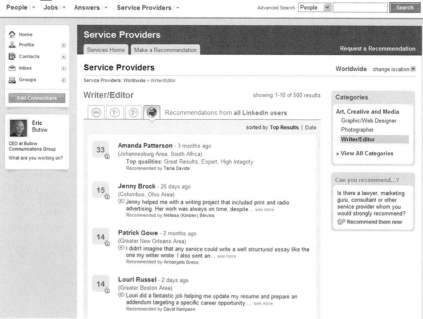

View Recommendations by Degrees Away from You

By default, LinkedIn displays recommendations from all LinkedIn users (including you) in the Service Providers page for the category you select. You can sort the list to show service providers that:

- Are in your second-degree network.
- Are in your first-degree network.
- You have recommended.

From the list that you sorted by top results (as shown in Figure 7-6), click the 2nd button tab above the first name in the list. The list changes, as shown in Figure 7-7, and displays the recommended writers and editors in your second-degree network.

Figure 7-7. **The recommended writers and editors in your second-degree network**

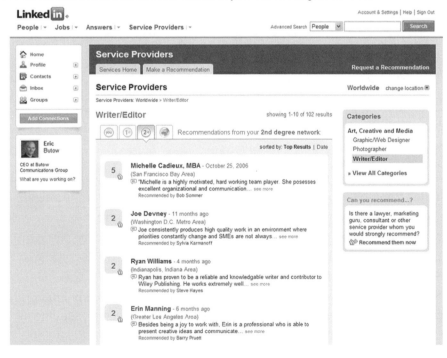

If you want to view recommendations only from those in your first-degree network, click the 1st button tab to the left of the 2nd button tab. Figure 7-8 shows the updated list with recommended writers and editors in your first-degree network.

Figure 7-8. **The recommended writers and editors in your first-degree network**

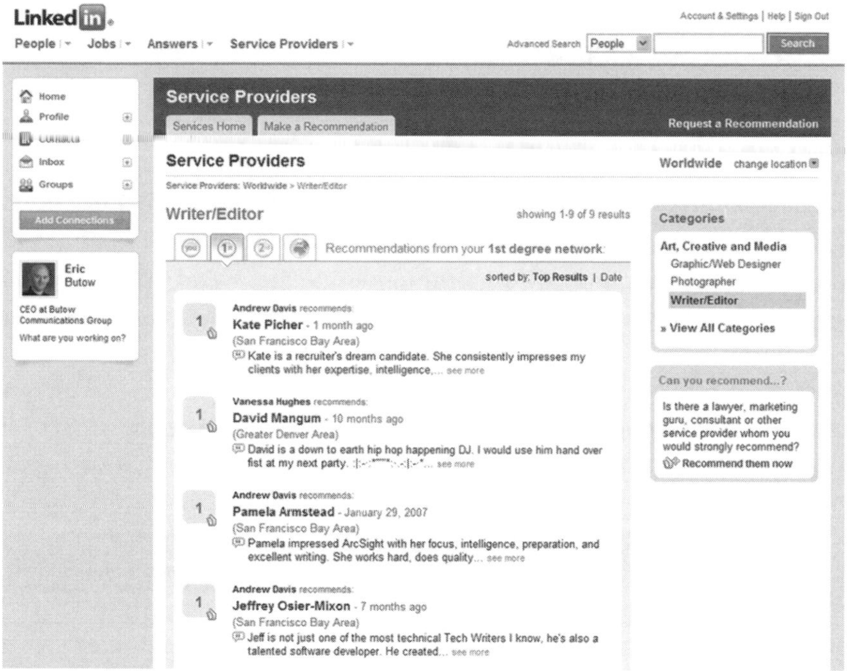

If you want to view only the writers and editors you recommend, click the You button tab to the left of the 1st button tab. If you have recommended any writers or editors, they appear in the list. If you haven't recommended any writers or editors (or any other service provider depending on the category you're in), LinkedIn invites you to recommend writers/editors by clicking the Recommend them now link, as shown in Figure 7-9.

You can also click the Has Recommended Some Already link to open the default Recommendations from All LinkedIn Users tab, or you can click on the globe icon button tab to the right of the second button tab.

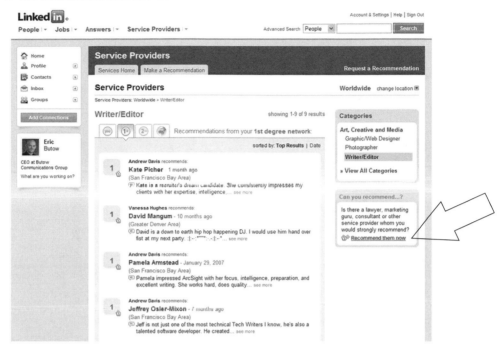

Figure 7-9. **The Recommend them now link**

View Results by Location

By default, LinkedIn displays all recommendations from around the world. If you want to narrow the geographic search area, click the Change Location link at the upper right area of the page. The Location box appears, as shown in Figure 7-10.

In this example, the default search country is the United States, but you can select a new country in the Country list. If you're in a country with a postal code, type the code in the Postal Code box. If the search area is in the United States, you can look up the ZIP code for the search area city and state by clicking the ZIP lookup link to the right of the Postal Code box. When you click the link, a new browser window opens and shows the United States Postal Service Web site's ZIP Code Lookup page. Once you find the ZIP code, close the browser window and type (or copy and paste) the ZIP code in the Postal Code box. After you finish selecting the country and typing the postal code, click the Change Lo-

Figure 7-10. **The Location box**

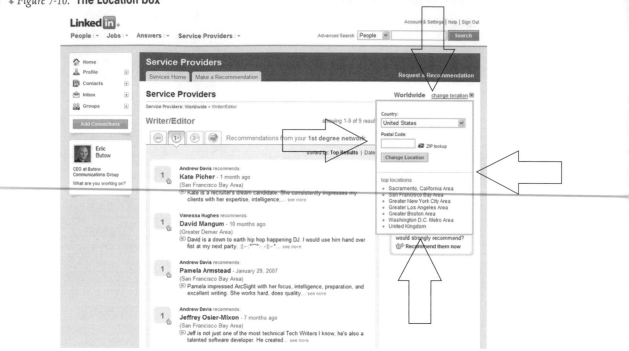

cation button to update the list with recommendations that are close to the search area.

If you prefer to search in another city, click on one of the links in the Top Locations list. Your metropolitan area is listed first, followed by other top locations you may be interested in. The last link is Worldwide, which is the default location.

You can close the location box by clicking anywhere outside the box.

View More Pages

However you sort the list of recommendations, it displays only 10 service providers per page. If you want to go to the next page, scroll down to the bottom of the page and click either the next link or the page number (from 2 to 50), as you learned to do in previous chapters.

Recommending a Service Provider

Suppose you want to recommend a connection who is also a service provider, or you want to recommend someone who currently isn't a LinkedIn member and you want to invite her to join LinkedIn and your network at the same time. Either way, recommending a service provider is easy. In the Service Providers page, start the step-by-step recommendation process by clicking the Make a Recommendation tab as shown in Figure 7-11. When you click the link, the Recommend a Service Provider page appears, as shown in Figure 7-12.

Figure 7-11. **The Make a Recommendation tab**

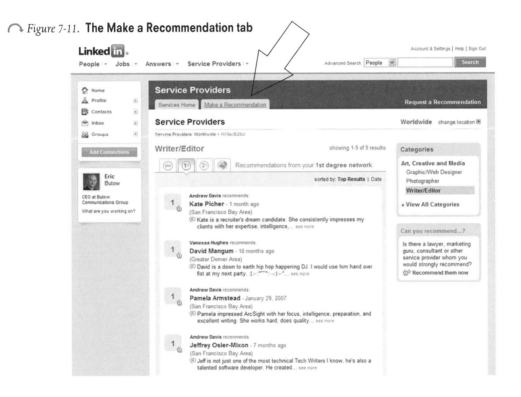

In Step 1, type the first name, last name, and e-mail address in the appropriate boxes. If you prefer to select an existing connection, click the Select from Your Connections List link. Figure 7-13 shows the Select Connection window that appears after you click the link. Select the connection you want to recommend by clicking the

Figure 7-12. **The Recommend a Service Provider page**

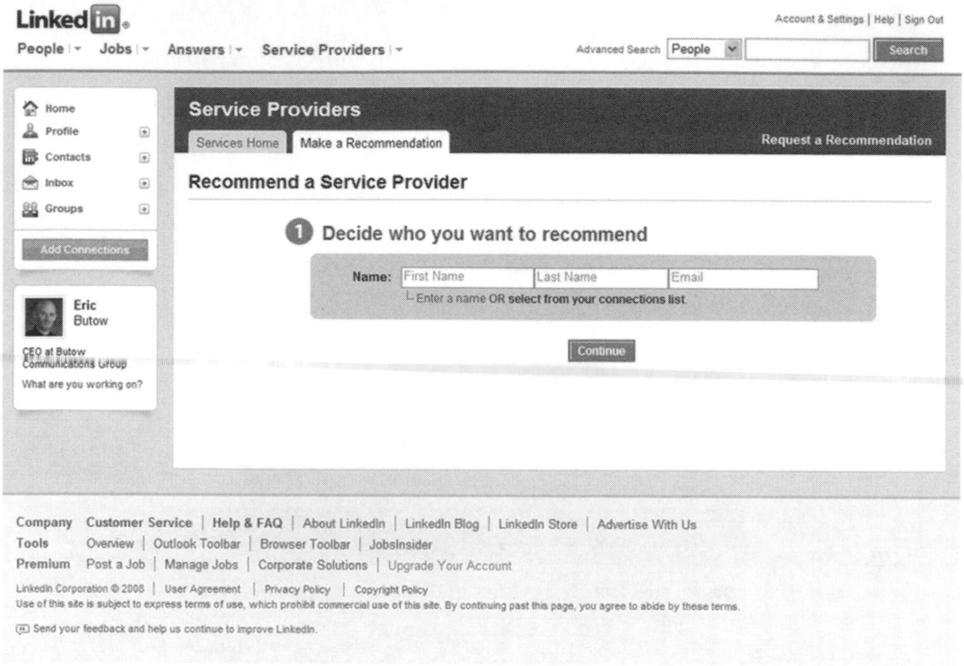

Figure 7-13. **The Select Connection window**

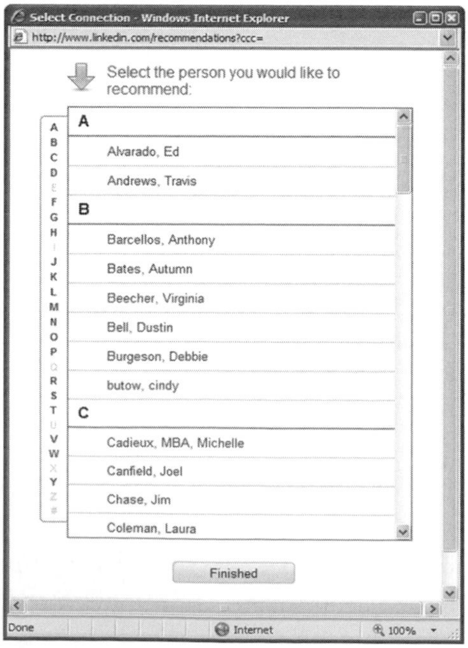

connection name in the list, then clicking the Finished button. The list window closes and the connection's first name, last name, and e-mail address appear automatically in the boxes. Click the Continue button to create your recommendation in the Recommendations People/Create page, as shown in Figure 7-14.

Figure 7-14. **The Recommendations People/Create page**

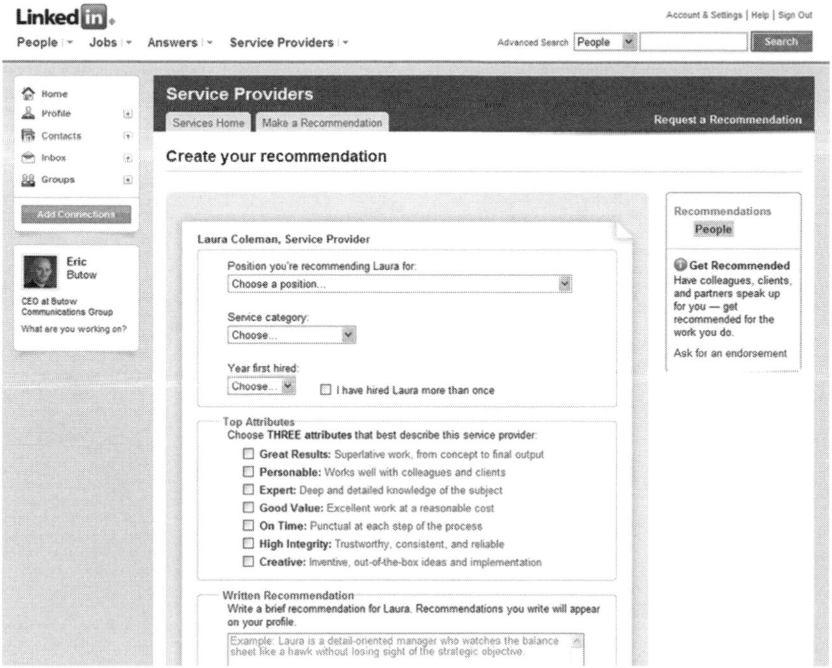

The recommendation form has three sections:

1. In the top section, choose the position you're recommending your contact for, the service category, and the year first hired from the appropriate lists. If you've hired the contact more than once, select the checkbox to the right of the Year First Hired list.

2. In the middle Top Attributes section, select three checkboxes that best describe the service provider.

3. In the bottom Written Recommendation section, write a brief recommendation for your connection or contact. The box has an example if you need help getting started.

LinkedIn automatically sends a message to the connection or contact you want to recommend. However, you can personalize the message by clicking the view/edit link below the Written Recommendation section. After you click the link, the Personalize this Message section appears, as shown in Figure 7-15.

Figure 7-15. **The Personalize this Message section**

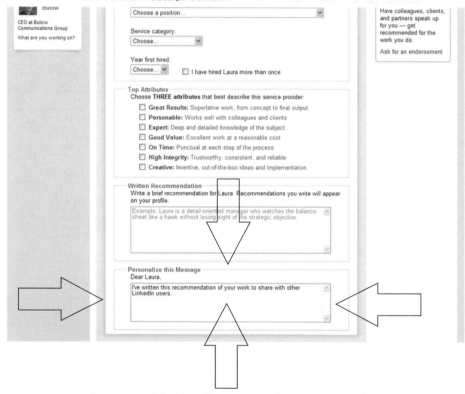

You can change the default text in the box by deleting it and substituting your own. When you're finished, click the Send button to send the recommendation. When you click the Send button, the LinkedIn home page appears with the message that your service provider recommendation has been created.

You will learn more about viewing recommendations for service providers, as well as managing your recommendations, in Chapter 8.

Becoming a Recommended Service Provider

While you are on the Service Providers page, take advantage of becoming a Service Provider yourself. This is a great way to get noticed on LinkedIn, because people can find you through your expertise and see what others have said about you. LinkedIn offers a quick tutorial on how to become a recognized service provider yourself at the top of the Service Providers page in the Tutorial Section. Under the How do I get listed in this directory? heading, click the Request a recommendation link, as shown in Figure 7-16.

Figure 7-16. **The Request a recommendation link**

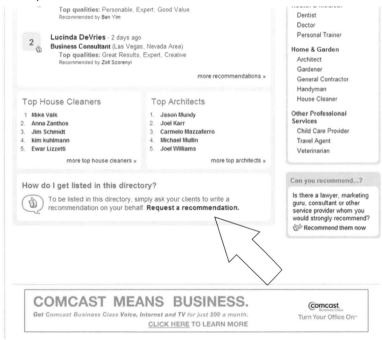

LinkedIn provides a very easy three-step process to become a Recommended Service Provider in the Request Recommendations page, as shown in Figure 7-17:

1. Choose a position.

2. Decide whom you'll ask.

3. Create your message.

Figure 7-17. **The Request Recommendations page**

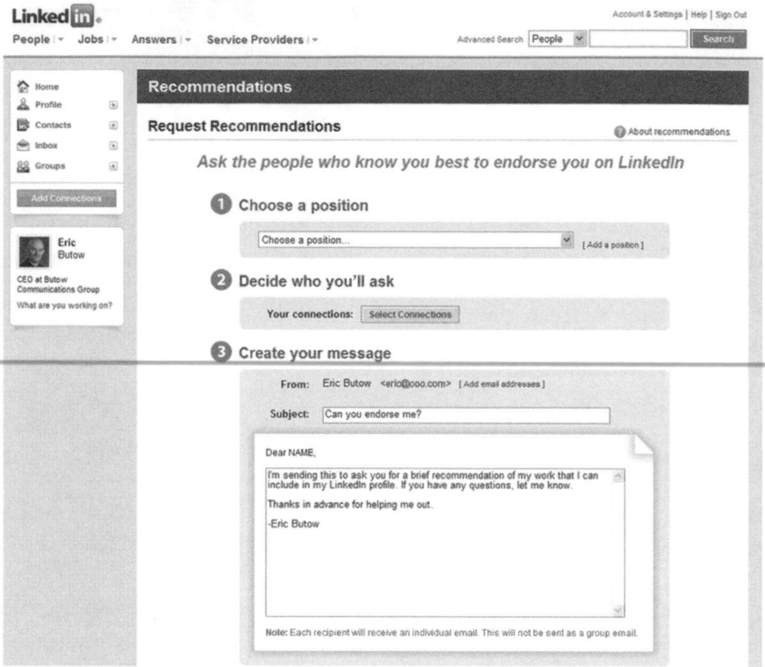

In Step 1, select the position for which you want your connections to recommend you. For example, if you own your own business and you want your connection to tell people what great service you provide, select the business from the position list. If you want to add a position instead, click the Add a Position link.

In Step 2, select the connections by clicking the Select Connections button. The Narrow Your Connections window appears, as shown in Figure 7-18. Select the connections you want to add to the list by selecting the check box to the left of the contact name. You'll learn about narrowing your connections further in Chapter 8. When you're finished, click the Finished button.

In Step 3, the message asking for a recommendation is already written for you, but you can change the text in the message box. When you're finished, click the Send button. LinkedIn sends each request for a recommendation as an individual e-mail message to each connection you selected in Step 2.

Figure 7-18. **The Narrow Your Connections window**

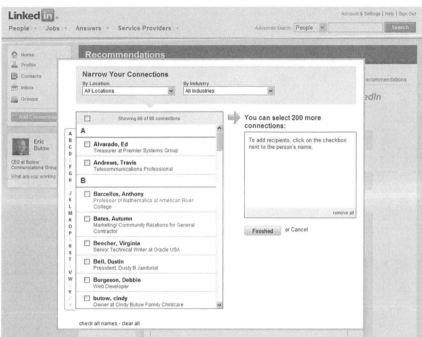

Hiding a Recommendation in the Service Provider Directory

When you make a recommendation for a service provider, it appears in the LinkedIn service provider directory, which everyone can see. If you don't want your recommendation to appear in the directory, you can hide it. This option is useful when your service provider doesn't want to be overwhelmed with a lot of business and/or you want to let only your trusted connections know about your great service provider.

Start on the LinkedIn home page by clicking the Profile link in the Navigation box, then clicking the Recommendations tab, as shown in Figure 7-19. In the Make & Manage Recommendations page that appears, look for the recommendation you want to change in the Manage recommendations you've made list, as shown in Figure 7-20. In the Display on my profile to: column, select No one from the list, as shown in Figure 7-21, Click the Save Changes button. At the top of the Recommendations page, a message states that the recommendation display settings have been updated, as shown in Figure 7-22.

(text continues on page 136)

Figure 7-19. **The Recommendations link**

Figure 7-20. **The Manage recommendations you've made list**

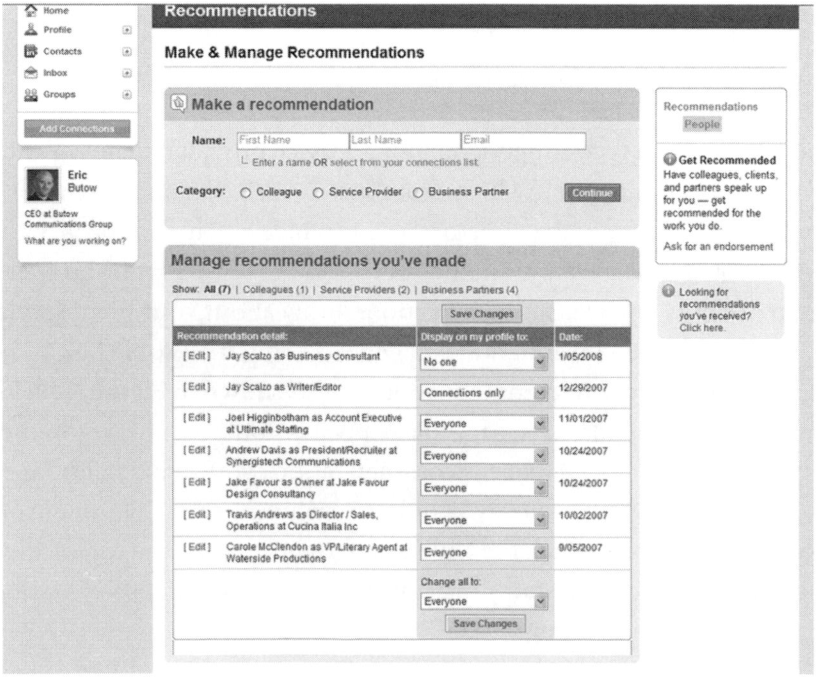

↷ *Figure 7-21.* **Select No one from the list**

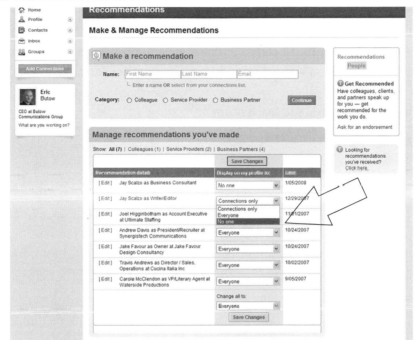

↷ *Figure 7-22.* **The recommendation display settings have been updated**

You can click the Show link to the right of the message to show the recommendation in the service provider directory. This is just one example of how to edit a recommendation, and you'll learn more about how to do that in the next chapter. You also can recommend others as colleagues or business partners, manage recommendations that you've made, and manage recommendations on your profile.

Continue to Chapter 8 to learn more.

Recommendations on Your LinkedIn Profile

One of the best ways to make your profile stand out on LinkedIn is to have recommendations from others. This is a great way to present your abilities with the help of others. Furthermore, recommendations save potential clients or employers a tremendous amount of time tracking down your references by phone or e-mail. You can add as many recommendations as you want to help build and promote your story for people who visit your profile.

How to Build Your Recommendations

You should approach building your recommendations with a couple of things in mind:

- Who will be reading the recommendations?
- What information in the recommendations is the most useful to them?

When considering asking for recommendations, keep in mind the value of your network and what it represents to your business.

Your best recommendations will be from those people who have had the most recent experience with you—their memories will be fresh. When you finish a project for someone, especially if it is extremely successful, it is the perfect time to ask the client to add a recommendation to your profile. A great way to get your client to write a recommendation about you is to ask whether he would like you to write a recommendation about him. By writing a recommendation about your experiences working with your clients, you're helping them build their reputation, and you're giving your client a strong incentive to write a recommendation for you. A reference from a CEO of a company you have just worked for has very high value on your profile page. The best recommendation to put on your profile page is one from the most senior person in the organization with whom you have worked.

Also, to show your diversity in working with many different kinds of clients, obtain references from a variety of companies. Five recommendations from one company might have two very different effects. They might prevent you from getting new clients, or they could show your particular expertise with that type of organization. So it is a good idea to have your recommendations tell the story from a couple of different perspectives. For example, as a recruiter, I find it helpful for my clients to see recommendations not only from other companies that have used me, but also from candidates I have recruited or placed at a company. The two perspectives present a more well-rounded story about my services and abilities.

Features of a Recommendation

A recommendation should be brief, and it should relate in a specific way to the work you did so that it tells a little story about you. For example:

> My Company engaged Kathy and her team to find talent that our HR team and other search firms had been unable to find throughout the U.S. Within two weeks of engaging Kathy, she was presenting us with qualified candidates for all our needs throughout the U.S.—many of whom we hired. I would hire her again without hesitation. She is extremely professional and serves her clients effectively.
>
> May 22, 2006

Duane Bell, executive vice president and chief financial officer of Tectura Corporation, was Kathy's client. In just a quick glance at such a recommendation, the reader can see:

- The client you did work for.
- What you did for the client.
- The results you delivered for the client.

When you write a recommendation, keep it brief, but certainly write things that are complimentary to the person's personality, capabilities, and talent, either in doing work for you or as your superior. Also remember to make your recommendations actual and truthful. If you don't, you not only harm your own integrity and that of the person you recommend, but you also diminish the integrity of the entire LinkedIn community.

Making a Recommendation

You can make a recommendation in LinkedIn in two ways. You can create a recommendation for anyone from the home page, or you can create a recommendation for a connection from within the connection's profile page. (If you read Chapter 7, the recommendation process should be familiar to you.)

From the Home Page

To make a recommendation from the LinkedIn home page, click the down arrow to the right of the Service Providers link at the top of the page. In the drop-down menu that appears, as shown in Figure 8-1, click the Make a Recommendation link. When you click the link, the Recommend a Service Provider page appears, as shown in Figure 8-2. In addition to recommending a service provider, you can use this page to recommend someone as a colleague or business partner.

The first step is to decide whom you want to recommend. You can type the person's first name, last name, and e-mail address in the First Name, Last Name, and Email boxes, respectively. If you would rather recommend someone in your connections list, click the Select from Your Connections List link. A new browser window opens, displaying the Select Connection window, as shown in Figure 8-3. Scroll up and down the list until you find the connection you want to add, then click the name in the list. The contact name and e-mail information appear in the Recommend a Service Provider page boxes. Close the Select Connection window by clicking the Finished button. You can change the connection by clicking the Select from Your Connections List link again. When you select the person you want to recommend, click the Continue button. The Recommendations: People/Create page appears, as shown in Figure 8-4 so that you can create your recommendation. The name of the person you want to recommend appears at the top of the Create your recommendation form.

(text continues on page 142)

Figure 8-1. **The Make a Recommendation link**

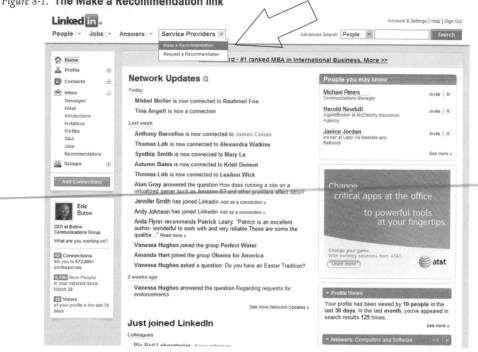

Figure 8-2. **The Recommend a Service Provider page**

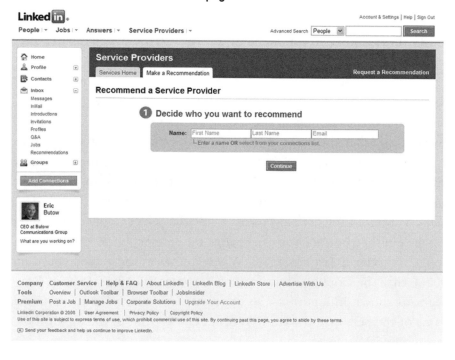

Figure 8-3. **The Select Connection window**

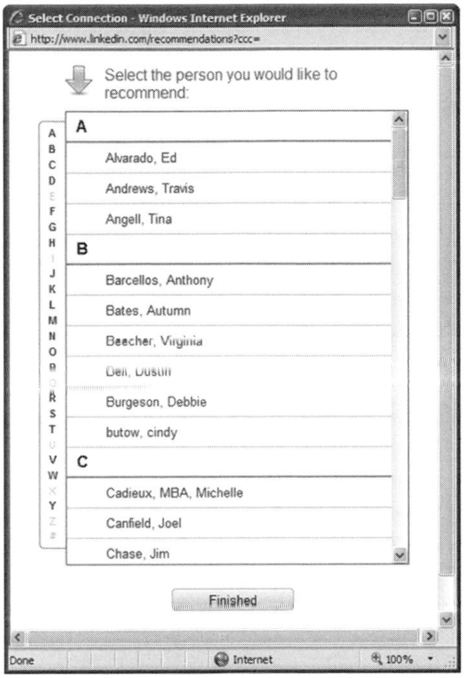

Figure 8-4. **The Recommendations: People/Create page**

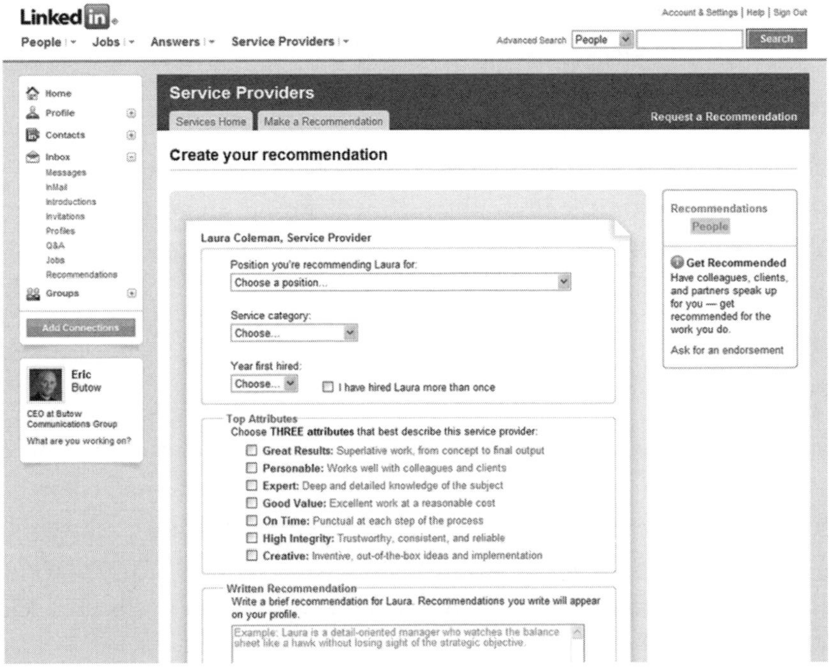

Position Information

Underneath the name is a box that lists the positions the person has held, the service category, and the year first hired. Here are some notes and options to consider when selecting options in these lists:

- If you're recommending the person for a position not yet listed in the person's profile, select the Position Not Yet Listed option in the list. If the person doesn't have a position listed yet, you won't be able to select a position.

- If the service category isn't in the list, select the Other option. When you select this option, a box appears for you to type the service in the box.

- If you never hired the person, select the year you started working with the person in the Year First Hired list. If you have hired the person more than once, then select the check box to the right of the list.

Top Attributes

In the Top Attributes area, as shown in Figure 8-5, select three of the seven check boxes that best describe the person you're recommending.

Written Recommendation

In the Written Recommendation box, as shown in Figure 8-6, you can write a brief recommendation for the person, which will appear on your profile as the person's profile. Remember that what you write reflects on both you and the person you recommend.

Edit Your Personal Message

LinkedIn sends a default message to the person informing her of your recommendation. If you want to make this message more personal, click the View/Edit link below the Written Recommendation box. When you click the link, the Personalize this Message box appears, as shown in Figure 8-7. You can change the default message in the box to suit your desires. When you're finished, click the Send button.

↷ *Figure 8-5.* **The Top Attributes area**

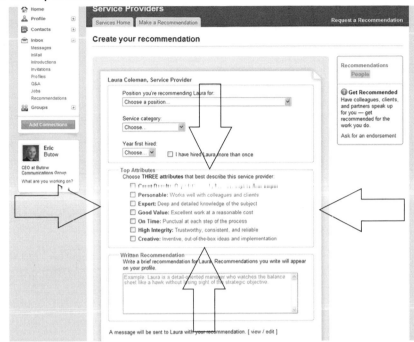

↷ *Figure 8-6.* **The Written Recommendation box**

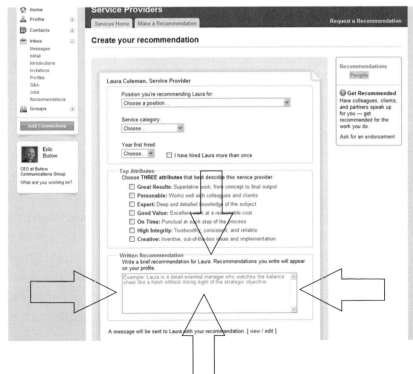

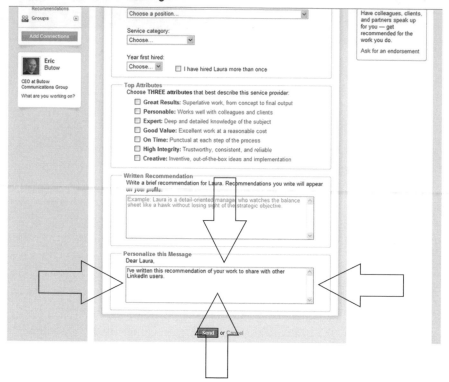

○ *Figure 8-7.* **The Personalize this Message box**

If you don't select from all the options on the page and don't select exactly three attributes for the person, the page reappears with a red bar at the top that prompts you to correct the marked fields.

After you successfully send the recommendation, the LinkedIn home page appears and a green bar at the top of the page informs you that your service provider recommendation has been created.

From a Connection's Profile Page

Add a recommendation from a connection's profile page by clicking the Contacts link in the Navigation box, as shown in Figure 8-8. In the My Connections page that appears, click the name of the connection in the list, and the profile page for the connection appears. To the right of the connection name, click the Recommend this person link, as shown in Figure 8-9. The Recommendation box appears, as shown in Figure 8-10, and lets you recommend the person as a colleague with whom you've worked, as a service provider, or as a business partner. Click the appropriate button

↷ *Figure 8-8.* **The Contacts link**

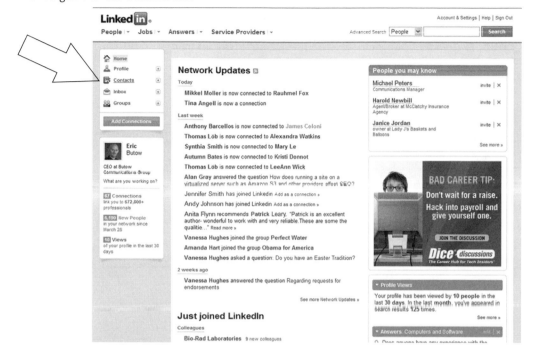

↷ *Figure 8-9.* **The Recommend this person link**

Figure 8-10. **The Recommendation box**

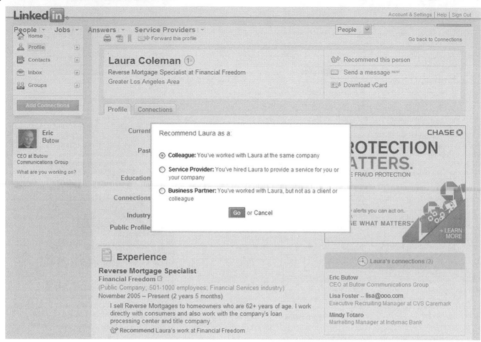

and then the Go button. The Recommendations People/Create page appears. The page options that appear differ depending on the type of recommendation you're creating. You already know about how to create a recommendation for a service provider from earlier in this chapter and Chapter 7.

Recommend as a Colleague

If you are recommending a person as a colleague, the Create your recommendation form for a colleague appears, as shown in Figure 8-11. In the Relationship area, tell others how you worked with the person in the Basis of recommendation list, then select your title and the person's title at the time. If you had a different position than the one listed in the Your title at the time list, click the Add a position link to add a new position to your profile. You can then write a recommendation, change the message to send to the person with your recommendation if you want, and click the Send button.

⌒ *Figure 8-11.* **The Create your recommendation form for a colleague**

Recommend as a Business Partner

If you are recommending a person as a business partner, the Create your recommendation form for a business partner appears, as shown in Figure 8-12.

In the Relationship area, tell others whether you worked with the person when she was at a different company or was a client in the Basis of recommendation list, then select your title and the person's title at the time. If you had a different position than the one listed in the Your title at the time list, click the Add a position link to add a new position to your profile.

You can then write a recommendation, change the message to send to the person with your recommendation if you want, and click the Send button. The person receives an e-mail message with the details of the recommendation and a link to display the recommendation on his profile.

Figure 8-12. **The Create your recommendation form for a business partner**

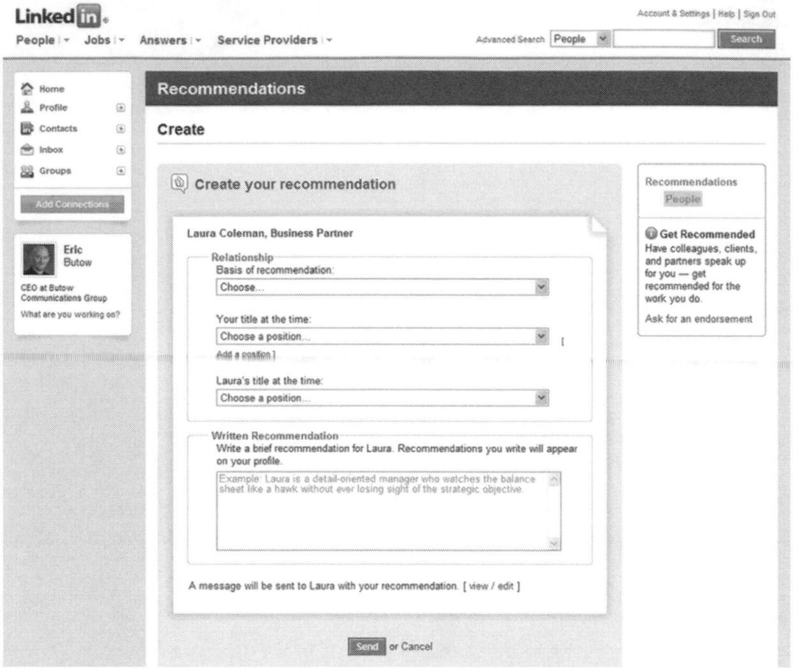

Request a Recommendation

LinkedIn makes it easy for you to ask as many as 200 of your connections at one time to send you their recommendations. Start on the LinkedIn home page by clicking the down arrow to the right of the Service Providers link at the top of the page. In the drop-down menu that appears, as shown in Figure 8-13, click the Request a Recommendation link. After you click the link, the Request Recommendations page appears, as shown in Figure 8-14. You can get more information about recommendations by clicking the About Recommendations link in the upper right corner of the page. Start the process by choosing a position that you entered in your profile from the Choose a Position list in Step 1 on the page. If you want to add a different position, click the Add a Position link to the right of the list. Select the connections you want to contact by clicking the Select Connections button in Step 2 on the page. The Narrow Your Connections box appears, as shown in Figure 8-15.

↷ *Figure 8-13.* **The Request a Recommendation link**

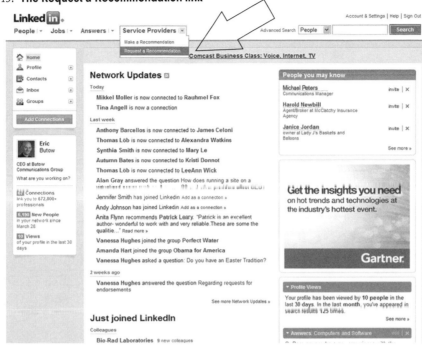

↷ *Figure 8-14.* **The Request Recommendations page**

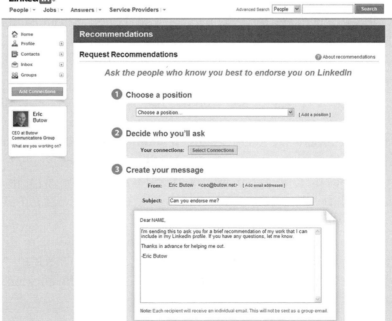

Figure 8-15. **The Narrow Your Connections box**

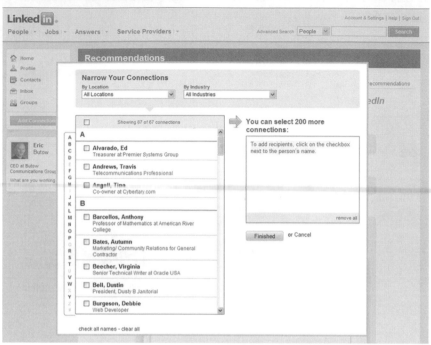

In Chapter 7, you learned how to select a connection and add it to the list of people you want to contact. To the left of this list is an alphabetical index. You can click on the letter in blue to go to names in the list starting with that letter, such as the letter "W" to jump to last names in the list that start with "W."

You can narrow your list further by filtering the list by location and/or by industry. The By Location list contains the locations for all your connections, and the By Industry list contains the industries for all your connections. When you select a location and/or industry in one or both lists, LinkedIn automatically updates the list with the names that meet your criteria. If you want to view all locations and/or all industries, select All Locations and All Industries in the By Location and By Industry lists, respectively.

As you add names, they appear in the connections box to the right of the connections list. If you want to add all names, click the Check All Names link at the bottom of the box. You also can clear all selections by clicking the Clear All link at the bottom of the box or the Remove All link at the bottom of the connections box.

When you're finished selecting your connections, click the Finished button. The connections you selected appear in the Request Recommendations page, as shown in Figure 8-16.

Figure 8-16. **The connections you selected**

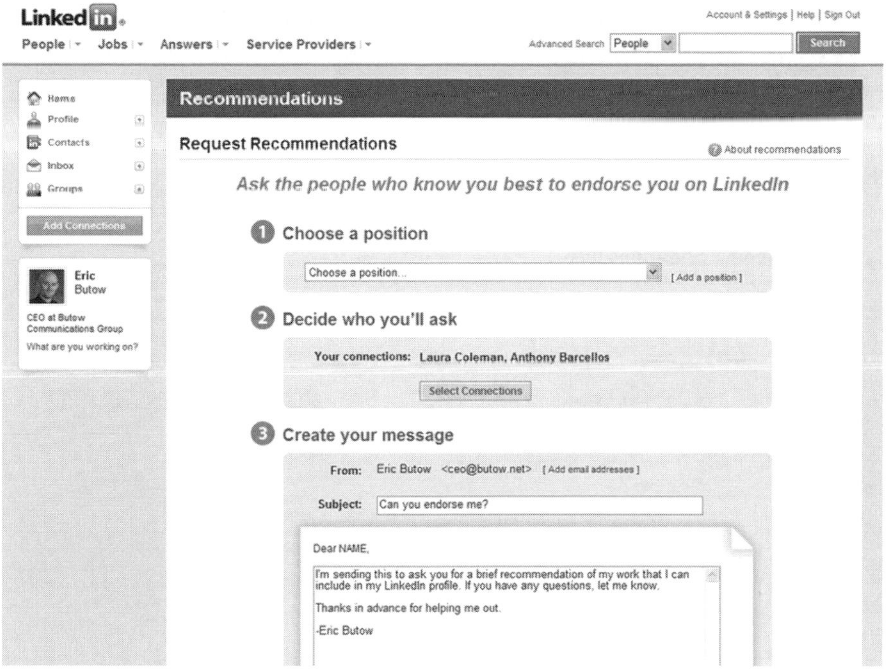

In Step 3 on the page, you can change the default subject and default text in the Subject and Message boxes, respectively. When you're finished, click the Send button. After LinkedIn sends the recommendation request, the LinkedIn home page appears with a green bar at the top of the page informing you that the request for a recommendation has been sent.

Each person on your list receives an e-mail message with the text of your message requesting a recommendation and a link to endorse you. It's up to the recipient to decide whether to recommend you. Be sure to thank those folks who do so, either with a sincere note or with a recommendation for them.

Manage Recommendations

Now that you know how to send and request recommendations, LinkedIn makes it easy for you to manage those recommendations so that you can see what you've written, make changes, and even remove recommendations if necessary.

Manage your recommendations from the home page by clicking the plus sign to the right of the Inbox link in the Navigation box. In the drop-down menu, as shown in Figure 8-17, click the Recommendations link. The Recommendations page appears and displays the recommendations you've received, as shown in Figure 8-18. The page lists all recommendations you've received for all positions in your profile. If you have no recommendations for a particular job, you can request a recommendation for the position by clicking the Ask to Be Endorsed link.

Figure 8-17. **The Recommendations link**

If you have recommendations from others for one of your positions that you want to manage, click the subject of the recommendation in the Subject column, as shown in Figure 8-19. When you click the link, the recommendation page appears, as shown in Figure 8-20.

Figure 8-18. **The Recommendations: Received page**

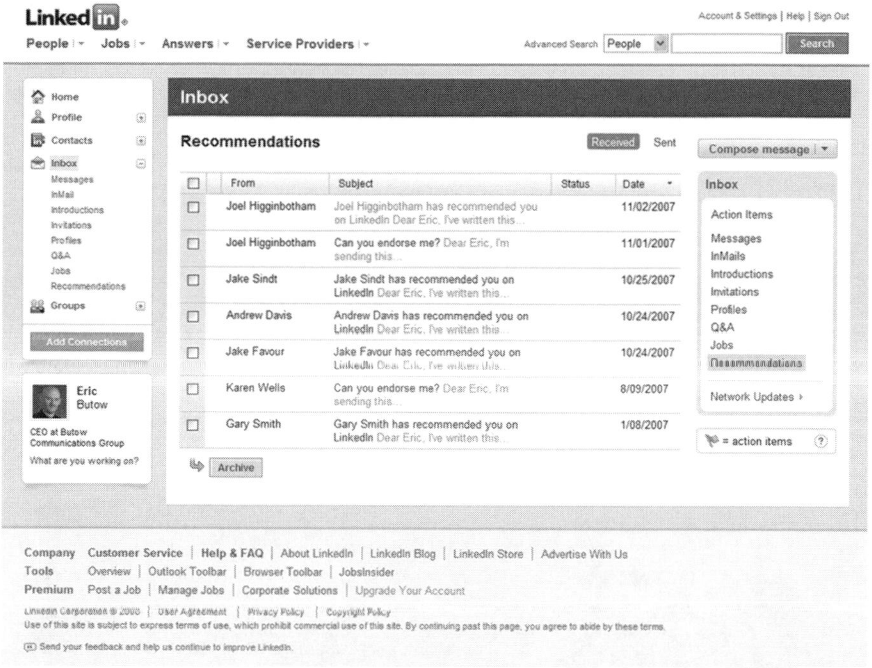

Figure 8-19. **The recommendation subject**

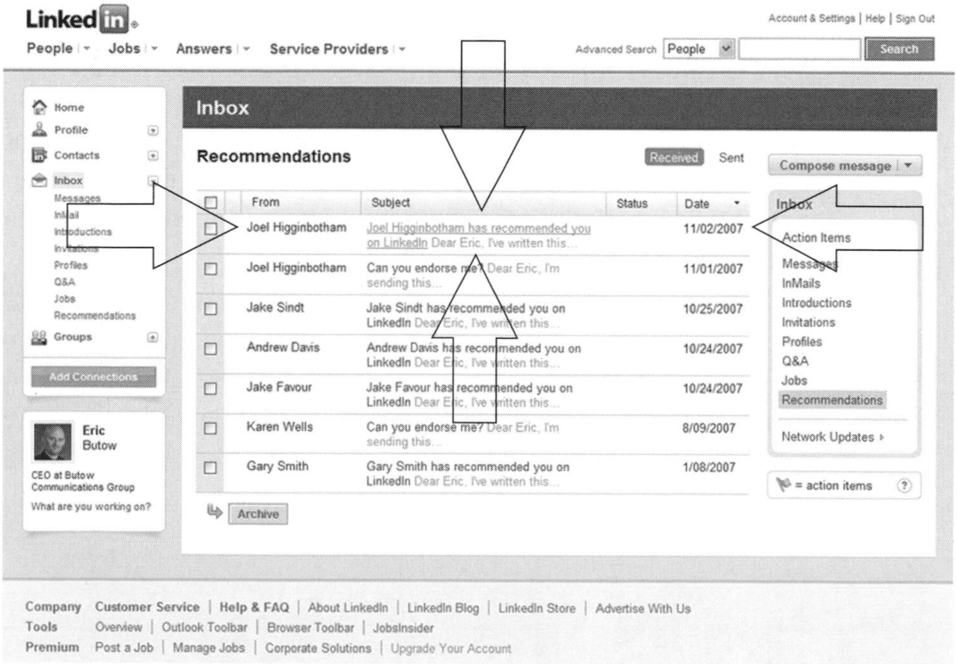

Figure 8-20. **The recommendation page**

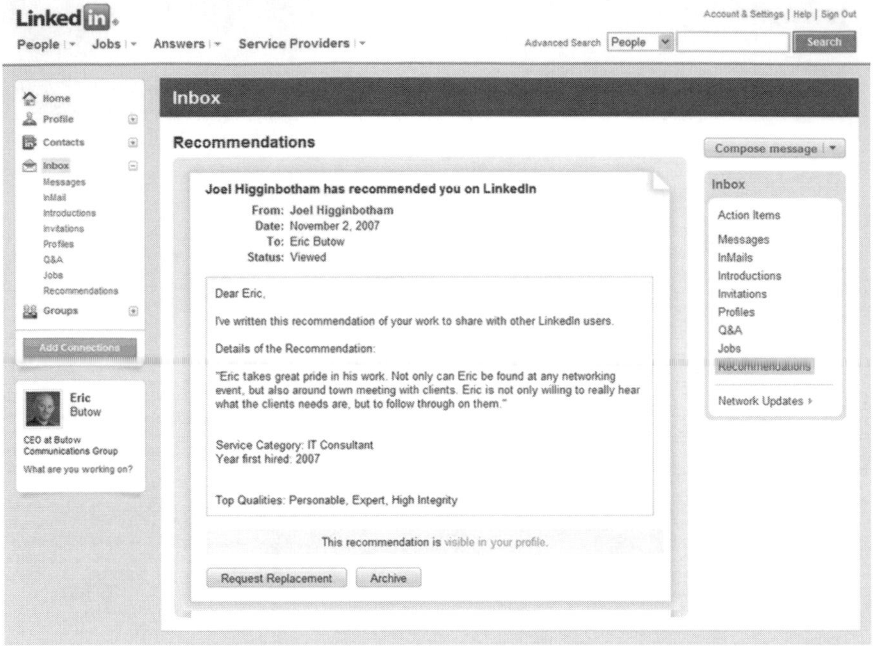

At the bottom of the recommendation text, a box indicates that the recommendation is visible in your profile. If you want to make changes to the recommendation, click the visible in your profile link. The Received Recommendations page appears, as shown in Figure 8-21. This page lists the number of recommendations you have received for different jobs. You can manage recommendations for each job by clicking the Manage link. The Manage Received Recommendations page appears, as shown in Figure 8-22.

The first recommendation you received appears at the top of the list. To the left of each recommendation is a check box that, if selected, indicates that the recommendation is currently being shown in your profile. By default, all the show check boxes are checked. If you want to hide any recommendations, select the corresponding check boxes to clear them. Apply the changes by clicking the Save Changes button below the last recommendation in the list.

↷ *Figure 8-21.* **The Received Recommendations page**

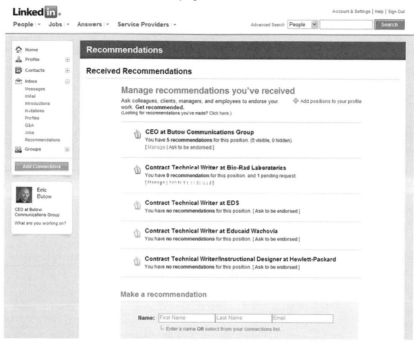

↷ *Figure 8-22.* **The Managed Received Recommendations page**

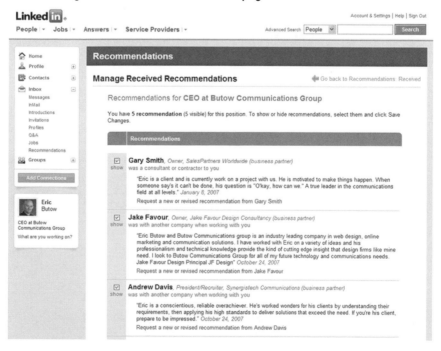

Get a Revised Recommendation

If you read the recommendation and decide that you want to have the recommendation revised for some reason—for instance, if you want the recommendation to include information about a recent job you did for the client—click the Request Replacement button under the recommendation text, as shown in Figure 8-23. When you click the link, the Request Recommendations page appears, as shown in Figure 8-24. In the Create Your Message box, you'll see the default text for asking the person who recommended you to update his recommendation, including the original recommendation. You can change this text in the box to fit your requirements, and you can change the text in the Subject box too, if you want. When you finish creating the update message, click the Send button.

Figure 8-23. **The Request Replacement button**

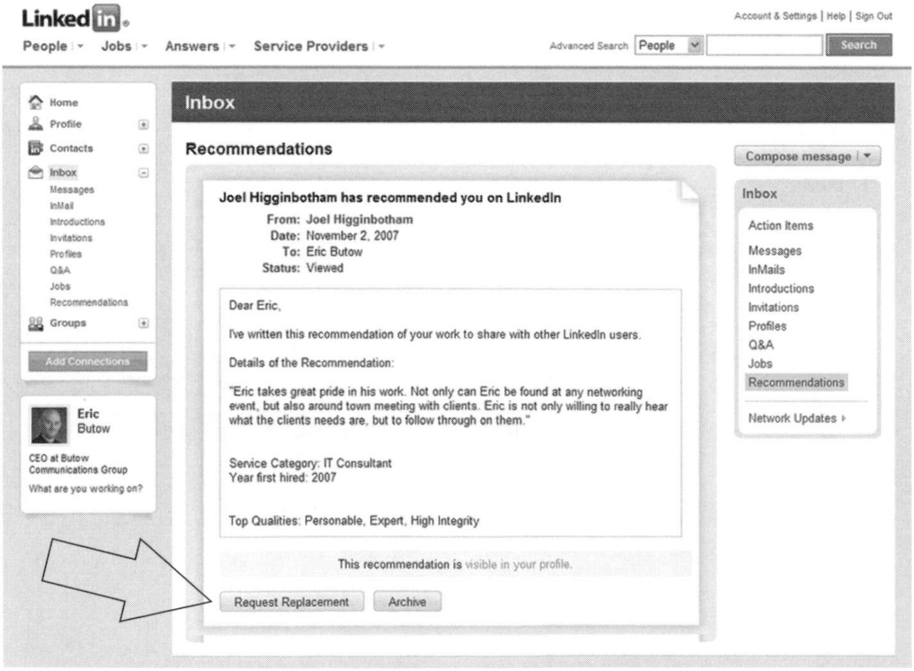

Figure 8-24. **The Request Recommendations page**

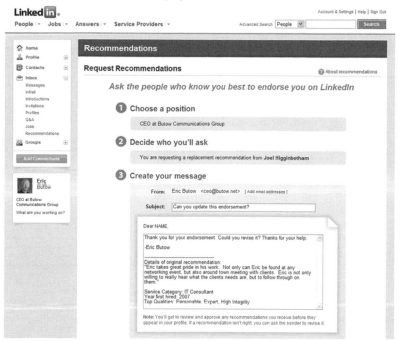

View Recommendation Requests

To view all the recommendation requests that you have sent to others, click the Sent link at the top of the Recommendation list, as shown in Figure 8-25. The recommendations you sent appear in the Sent list, as shown in Figure 8-26.

You can resend the messages to these contacts (you'll learn more about how to do that in Chapter 11).

Manage Recommendations You've Made

If you want to manage recommendations you've made for another LinkedIn member, click the invitation subject in the Subject column. At the bottom of the recommendation, click the Manage your recommendations link, as shown in Figure 8-27. When you click the link, the Make & Manage Recommendations page appears, as shown in Figure 8-28, which gives you the opportunity to add more recommenda-

(text continues on page 160)

Figure 8-25. **The Sent link**

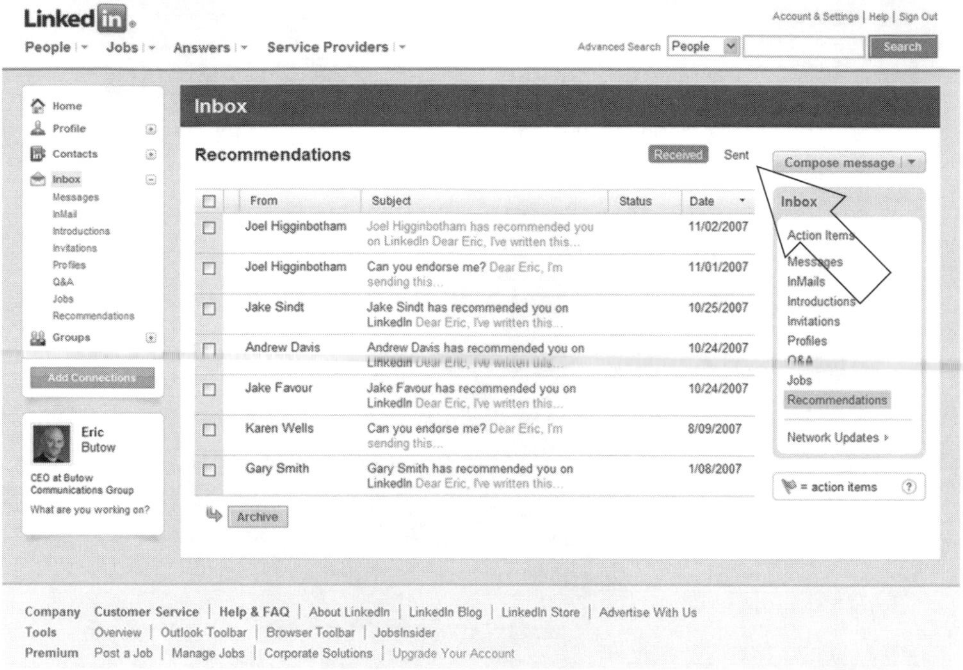

Figure 8-26. **The Sent list**

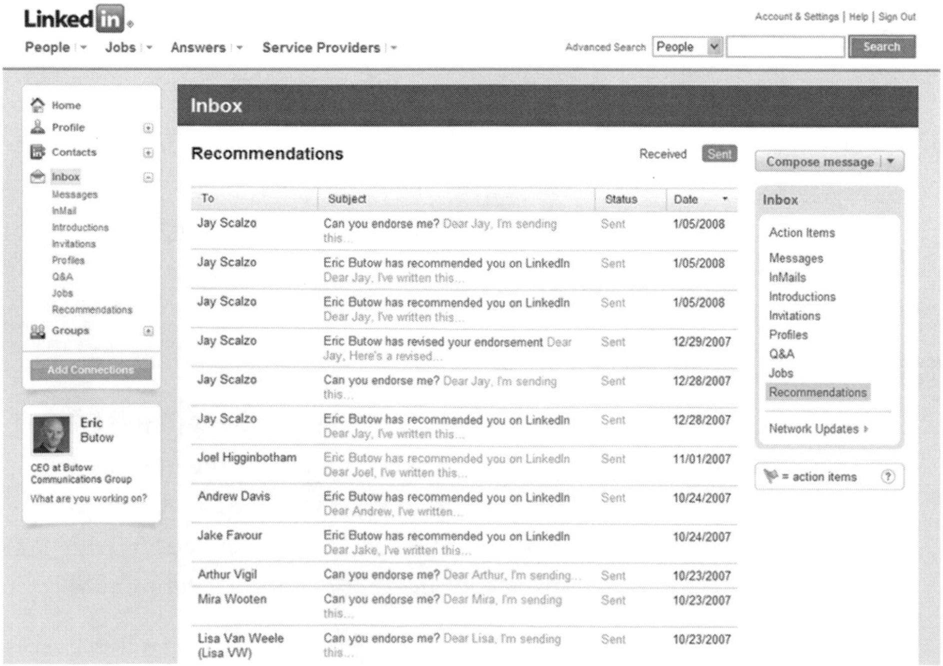

Figure 8-27. **The Manage your recommendations link**

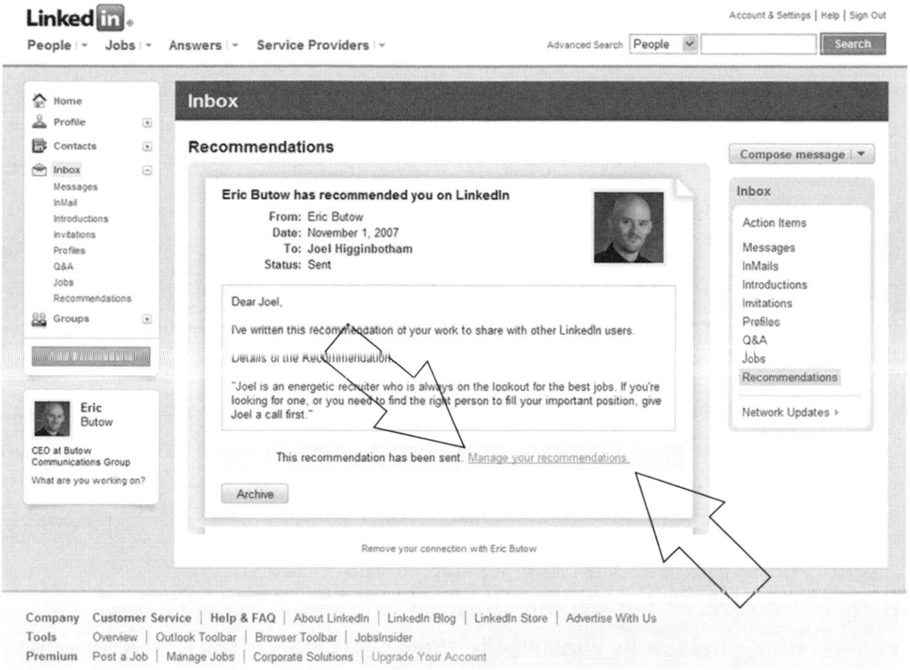

Figure 8-28. **The Make & Manage Recommendations page**

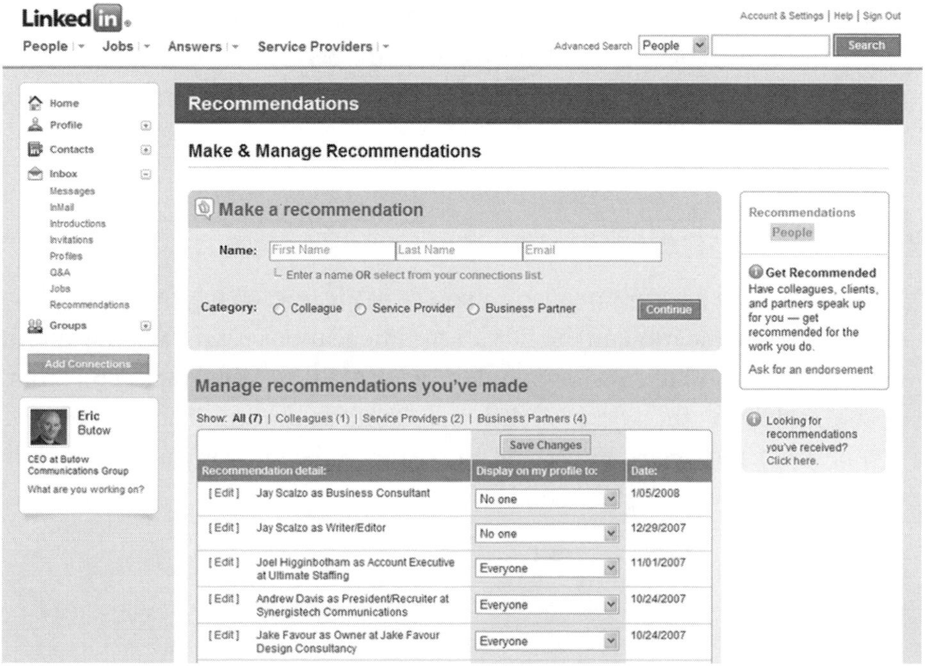

tions at the top of the page and also lists all the recommendations you made in the Manage Recommendations You've Made list.

The list displays all your recommendations by default. You also can filter your list by showing only colleagues, service providers, or business partners. For each person on the list, you can display your recommendation on your profile either to everyone (which is the default), or only to your connections, or to no one by selecting the appropriate option in the list in the Display on my profile to column. You also can change the display option for all recommendations in the list by selecting the appropriate option in the Change all to list at the bottom of the Manage recommendations you've made list. When you've finished updating the display information, click the Save Changes button at the top or bottom of the list.

If you want to edit a recommendation, click the Edit link to the left of the recommended person's name in the list. When you click the link, the Recommendations / Edit your recommendations page appears, as shown in Figure 8-29. This page displays the recommendation as it currently appears. You can make changes to the recommendation, including the service category and the year first hired, the attributes, and the text of the recommendation. You also can change the personal message to send to the person by clicking the View / Edit link below the Written Recommendation box. When you're finished, click the Send button.

LinkedIn sends an e-mail message to the person, informing her of the updated recommendation and inviting her to click a link to display your revised recommendation on her profile. After you click the Send button, the Recommendations: People page appears with a green bar at the top informing you that the recommendation has been updated.

Remove a Recommendation

You can remove a recommendation you've made by clicking the Edit link to the left of the recommendation. In the Edit Recommendations page, click the Withdraw this recommendation link, as shown in Figure 8-30. In the small dialog box that appears in the middle of the window, click the Confirm button. The person you recommended will not receive any notification from LinkedIn that you have withdrawn the recommendation.

Figure 8-29. **The Edit Recommendation page**

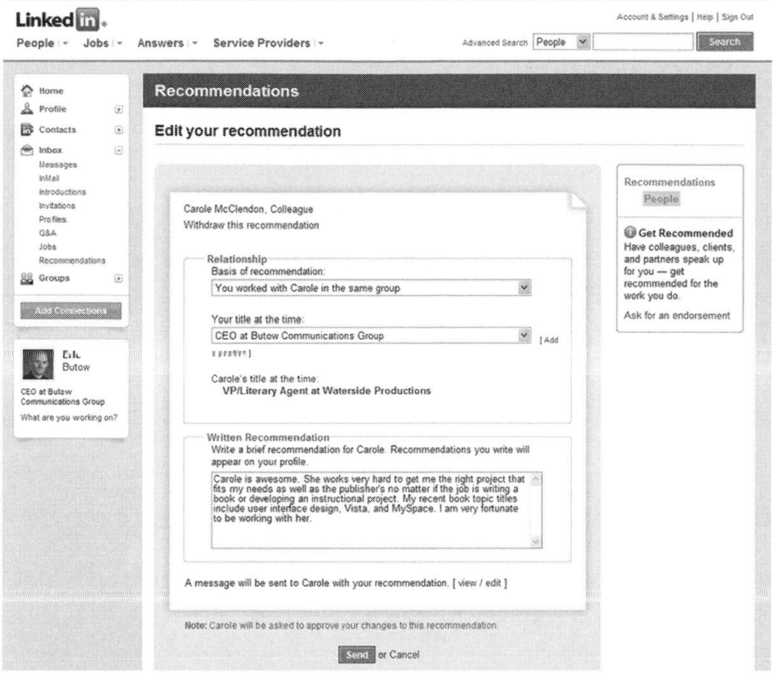

Figure 8-30. **The Withdraw this recommendation link**

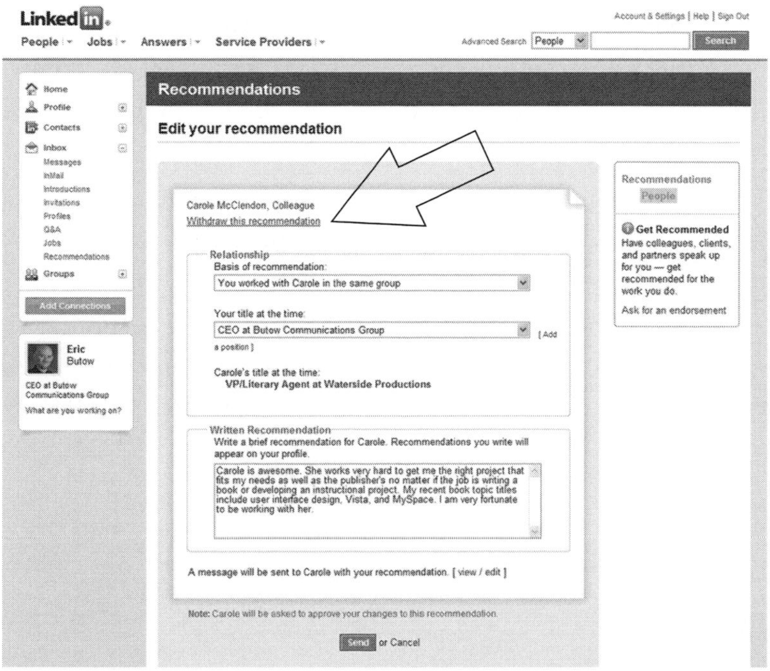

Tips for Building and Finding Recommendations

Building Recommendations

Now that you know how to create and manage your recommendations, how do you find them and how many do you need?

Though you don't want to seek a recommendation from everyone in your network, it makes sense to have more than three. Your goal should be 9 to 12 recommendations from a variety of people: people who have hired you, people you have worked closely with, and perhaps people you have hired. When you receive recommendations, you have the option to accept or refuse them. Remember to pick the recommendations that carry the most weight with visitors who view your profile.

Finding Recommendations

If you can't find any recommended service providers with the talent you're looking for, it's probably for a couple of different reasons:

- Your connections have not written many recommendations. You may want to contact your connections to find out whom they recommend and whether they know someone on LinkedIn, to encourage them to write recommendations about providers, and to let you know when the recommendations are written. Then you can go on your connections' profiles and read the recommendations.

- You might need to add connections to your list. Refer to Chapter 5 to learn more about how to add connections to your profile.

Even if you can't find talent this way, don't worry. There is another way to find what you are seeking. It takes a few more steps, but the talent will emerge that you are seeking. You'll learn more about finding these answers in Chapter 9.

9

Searching for Answers

LinkedIn is a place for you not just to network with other people, but also to ask questions and get answers from other LinkedIn members in your network in the LinkedIn Answers section. For information gathering to help your business, project, or personal life, LinkedIn Answers is a fantastic tool.

For example, try asking, "What is your best success story using LinkedIn?" In response, LinkedIn lets you know that a similar question was asked and that there are more than 23 answers to the question. As more people ask more questions and offer more answers, LinkedIn creates a large repository of information that you can use to get answers to questions from a trusted network, as opposed to searching Google or some other search engine and getting information from people you don't know. This answer repository certainly encourages you to think "outside the box" about how to use LinkedIn to find jobs, get ideas to run your business, and much more.

You also can look for information by looking through other people's questions. Let's say that you are an IT consultant. While scrolling through people's questions, you come across a question such as, "I am a CIO at NPQ company and I am looking for a top-notch IT consultant who has an understanding of CRM solutions. Is there anyone you can recommend?" You can reach that person in a couple of ways. You may ask one of your connections who is networked to this person to recommend you as a consultant, or you can reach out to the person yourself. Perhaps you have done work that he might be interested in; that's a great way to open up the conversation in e-mail. Such an e-mail response might say:

> I saw your question on LinkedIn, and thought I would make you aware of some consulting I just completed for Acme and their CRM solution. I can certainly share with you the kind of work I did there. Does your calendar permit a quick introductory phone call?

Another great way to use LinkedIn Answers is to help promote your clients' work. Nothing gets your clients' attention faster than sending business their way. When it comes time to calling consultants for a job, your name rises to the top of their list because you have helped them and demonstrated concern and caring about their business that perhaps other consultants have not. A constant thought to keep in mind when using LinkedIn is the give-and-take of the service and how you can help others so that it comes back to you.

LinkedIn Answers is also a great way to become a subject matter expert. Answering as many questions as possible in a question category, such as staffing and recruiting, gets you noticed as having a high number of responses. And your answers have an opportunity to be picked as the best answer, giving you top billing when that question comes up again. As your knowledge base grows from participating not only in answering questions but in asking them as well, you become more valuable in the marketplace and raise your profile within your network.

Viewing and Browsing Questions

Before you ask a question, you should view questions to see if anyone has already provided answers to it. If you don't find the exact answer you're looking for from the questioner's network, you still can ask the question to your network. In other words, you have many more people from whom you can seek answers. The main Answers page contains a list of new questions from people in your network, and you can also browse questions in a number of different categories and subcategories to get the exact answers you want.

Start on the home page by clicking the Answers link at the top of the page, as shown in Figure 9-1. When you click the Answers link, the Answers Home page appears, as shown in Figure 9-2, displaying two columns of information. Three boxes appear in the left column:

1. Featured Category.

2. My Q&A.

3. Browse.

At the top of the Answers Home page is the featured category, which LinkedIn selects automatically. LinkedIn selects and displays five questions from your

◠ *Figure 9-1.* **The Answers link**

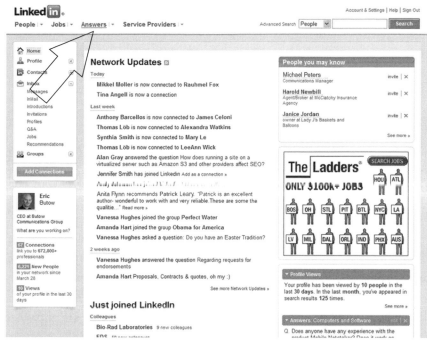

◠ *Figure 9-2.* **The Answer Home page**

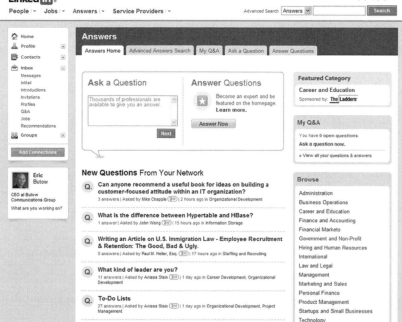

network in this category. When you open the Answers Home page, LinkedIn reads your profile and immediately opens a category with questions and answers that may interest you. Recruiters, for example, may see questions in one of the following areas:

- Hiring and Human Resources.
- Management.
- Technology.

The My Q&A section appears underneath and shows any questions you may have asked, and it contains links for you to ask a question and view your questions and answers. The Browse section contains links to 16 different categories of questions.

The Ask a Question and Answer Questions box appears at the top of the right column. You can ask a question by typing the question in the Ask a Question box or learn how to answer questions by clicking the Learn More link or Answer Now button.

The New Questions from Your Network section appears underneath the box. This section lists the five most recent questions asked by members of your network. You can view more questions by clicking the More Open Questions link at the bottom of the list.

Below the new questions is a section detailing This Week's Top Experts. The past week's top experts are the people in your network who have provided the most answers. LinkedIn lists the top five experts with the person who has the most answers in the past week. If you want to view more experts in the list, click the More Top Experts link at the bottom of the list. Scroll down the page to view the This Week's Top Experts list, as shown in Figure 9-3.

Reading a Question

In the New Questions from Your Network list, each question contains:

- The title of the question.
- How many answers have been submitted in response to the question.
- The person who asked it.
- How many degrees the person is away from your network.

Figure 9-3. **The This Week's Top Experts list**

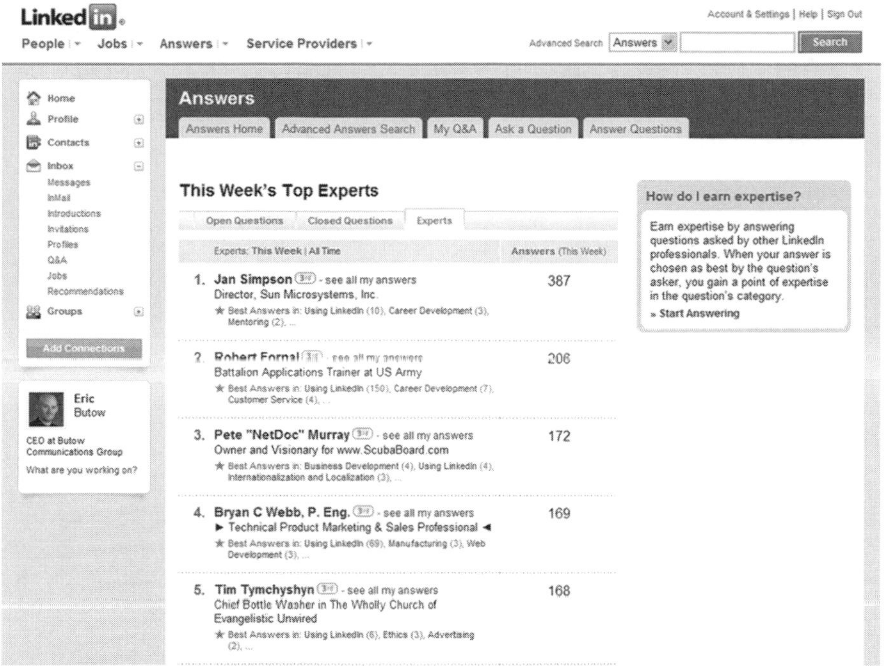

- How long ago the question was asked.
- The category in which it was submitted.

You can read the question and the associated answers by clicking the question title. When you click the title, the Question page appears, as shown in Figure 9-4. The question appears in the yellow box at the top of the page. The box is shaped like a comic strip talk bubble. In this case the bubble points to the name of the person who is asking the question, and the name appears to the left of the yellow question box.

Browsing for a Question

If you want to see questions in a particular category, the Browse area in the Answers Home page gives you 16 categories to choose from:

1. Administration
2. Business Operations

Figure 9-4. **The Question page**

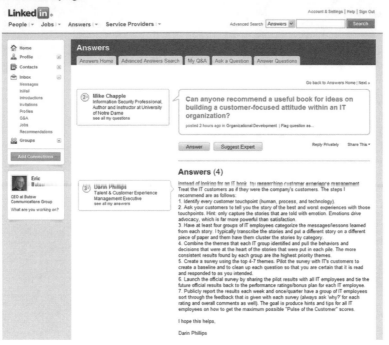

3. Career and Education

4. Finance and Accounting

5. Financial Markets

6. Government and Non-Profit

7. Hiring and Human Resources

8. International

9. Law and Legal

10. Management

11. Marketing and Sales

12. Personal Finance

13. Product Management

14. Startups and Small Businesses

15. Technology

16. Using LinkedIn

Click on the section link that most closely matches the topic you're looking for. For example, click the Marketing and Sales link to open the Answers: Marketing and Sales page, as shown in Figure 9-5. The Answers: Marketing and Sales page, like all Questions pages in any category, lists the five most recently asked open questions. You can view a list of more open questions by clicking the More Open Questions link at the bottom of the list.

Figure 9-5. **The Answers: Marketing and Sales page**

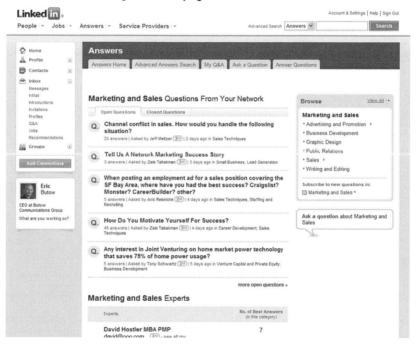

If you want to view closed questions—that is, questions that a person has asked and is no longer accepting answers for from others—click the Closed Questions tab above the first question in the list. The list of closed questions appears, as shown in Figure 9-6. The closed questions list contains the 10 most recently asked closed questions. Click the question title to open the question and to view all the answers that were asked in that category. If you want to see the next 10 pages, scroll down to the bottom of the page and click the Next link.

Figure 9-6. **The list of closed questions**

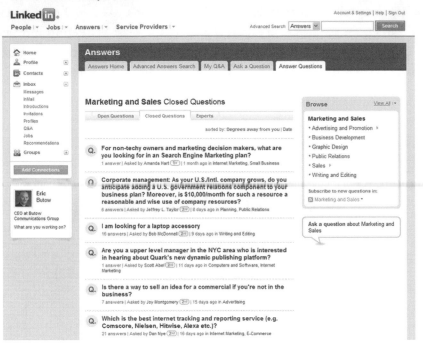

View the Experts List

An expert is someone who has been recognized by other LinkedIn users as the best person who has answered their questions. LinkedIn measures its members' expertise with a point system. When you answer a question in a public LinkedIn forum in a particular category and the questioner picks your answer as the best one, LinkedIn gives you a point. As you accumulate points, LinkedIn lists you as an expert in that category, thus increasing your visibility to other LinkedIn members looking for answers. (Unfortunately, only answers in public forums, not private answers, count for points.) Therefore, if you see someone who is classified as an expert, you can be reasonably assured that she provides answers that you can use, and you should check her answers first if you have a similar question. Or you may want to ask the expert a question of your own.

You can view all the experts in this area by scrolling down the page and viewing the list of experts in the category, as shown in Figure 9-7. You can view

Figure 9-7. **The Marketing and Sales Experts list**

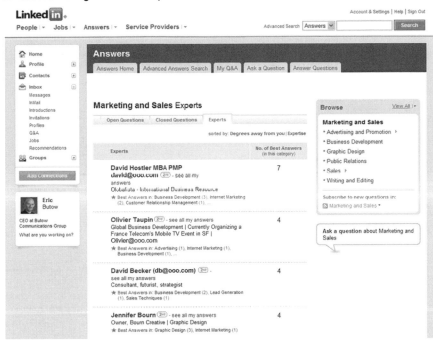

more experts for the category by clicking the More Experts link at the bottom of the list.

View Question Subcategories

The Answers page offers a number of subcategories under the primary category. For example, in Figure 9-8 the Marketing and Sales category contains six subcategories, from Advertising and Promotion to Writing and Editing. Click a subcategory to view questions and experts in that subcategory. For example, when you click the Writing and Editing subcategory, the Answers: Writing and Editing page appears, as shown in Figure 9-9.

If one of the subcategory names has a right arrow to the right of it, there are even more sub-subcategories underneath that subcategories. For example, if you click the Sales subcategory, Figure 9-10 shows the three sub-subcategories in that category.

⌒ *Figure 9-8.* **The Browse list for the Marketing and Sales category**

⌒ *Figure 9-9.* **The Answers: Writing and Editing page**

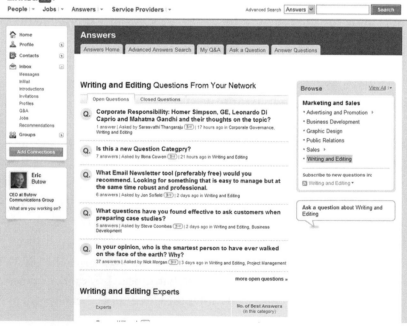

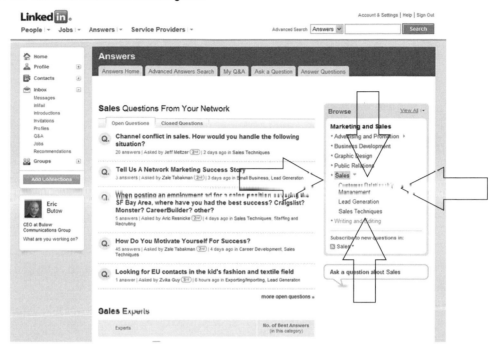

Figure 9-10. **The three Sales sub-subcategories**

Click on one of the sub-subcategories to narrow the list of questions and experts even further and find exactly what you need.

Identify Someone as an Expert

If another LinkedIn member has asked a question and picked an answer as the best one, that may satisfy you. If you still put the question out there in your network and receive an answer that you think is the best one, you may mark the answer as the best, and others in your network see that, thereby helping to make someone a subject matter expert. For example, Kathy Taylor asked the question, "I am looking for creativity software to use with kids to develop a new toy, any recommendations?" She received 10 answers and was given the option of rating the best as well as good answers, as shown in Figure 9-11.

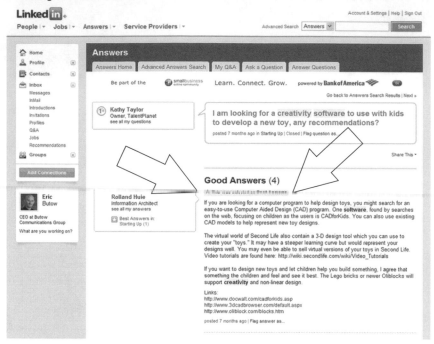

Figure 9-11. **Rating the best answer**

Ask a Question

You can ask a question of your network members in LinkedIn in several ways:

- In the LinkedIn home page, click the down arrow to the right of the Answers link at the top of the page. In the drop-down menu that appears, as shown in Figure 9-12, click the Ask a Question link.

- In the Answers Home page, type a question in the Ask a Question box, as shown in Figure 9-13, then click the Next button.

- In the Answers Home page, click the Ask a Question Now link in the My Q&A box on the left side of the page.

- Click the Ask a Question tab at the top of the Answers page.

All these methods get you to the Ask a Question page. The only difference among these four methods is that, when you type a question in the Ask a Question box and click Next, the question appears in the question box at the top of the Ask

⌒ *Figure 9-12.* **The Ask a Question link**

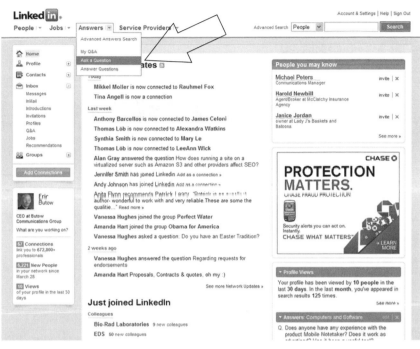

⌒ *Figure 9-13.* **The Ask a Question box**

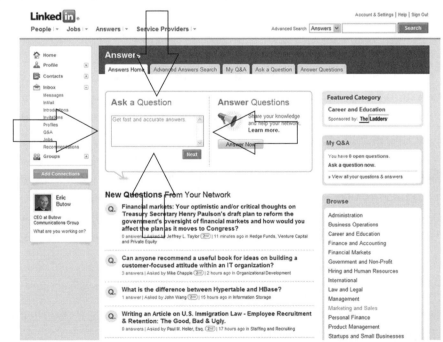

a Question page. With the other two options, the question box, as shown in Figure 9-14, is empty.

Figure 9-14. **The Ask a Question page**

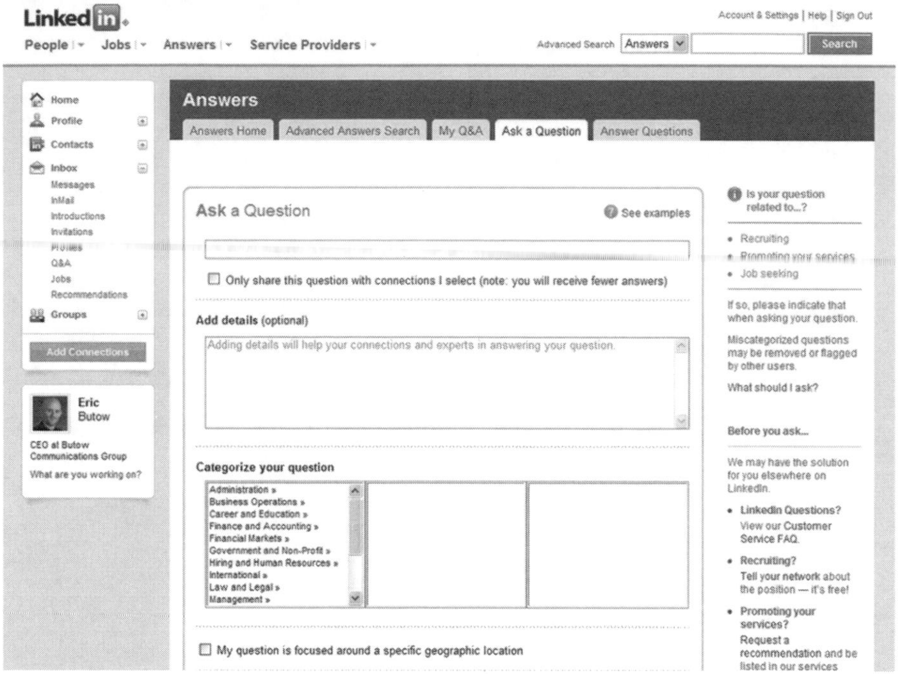

Now, type a question in the question box. If you type the question in the Ask a Question box in the Answers Home page, you can edit your question in the box. If you want to share the question only with specific connections, select the check box below the question box.

In the Add Details box, you can add more details about your question to help others in your network answer it. For example, if you're a recruiter looking for someone to fill a particular position, you can add information about the background and experience you want the candidate to have. Though entering information in this box is optional, it's a good idea to add as much detail about your question as possible.

How to Ask a Question

If you're not sure of the type of question to ask, view examples by clicking the See Examples link above the question box.

Although LinkedIn suggests, as a matter of etiquette, not to ask a question to promote your business, many people do just that. By asking a question and putting it out to your network of people, it reminds them that you are in the business of providing your services and that you're available to help them should they need your services. For example, recently someone who was an executive recruiter asked the question, "What are your biggest challenges in doing search?" Of course, many recruiters responded, but his profile was also raised significantly.

Categorize Your Question

After you ask the question and provide additional details, select the category for your question by clicking the category in the left box. When you do that, the subcategory appears in the middle box. If there is a sub-subcategory, a right arrow appears to the right of the subcategory name. When you click a subcategory name that contains sub-subcategories, the sub-subcategories appear in the right box, as shown in Figure 9-15 for the Sales subcategory.

Figure 9-15. **The sub-subcategories for Sales**

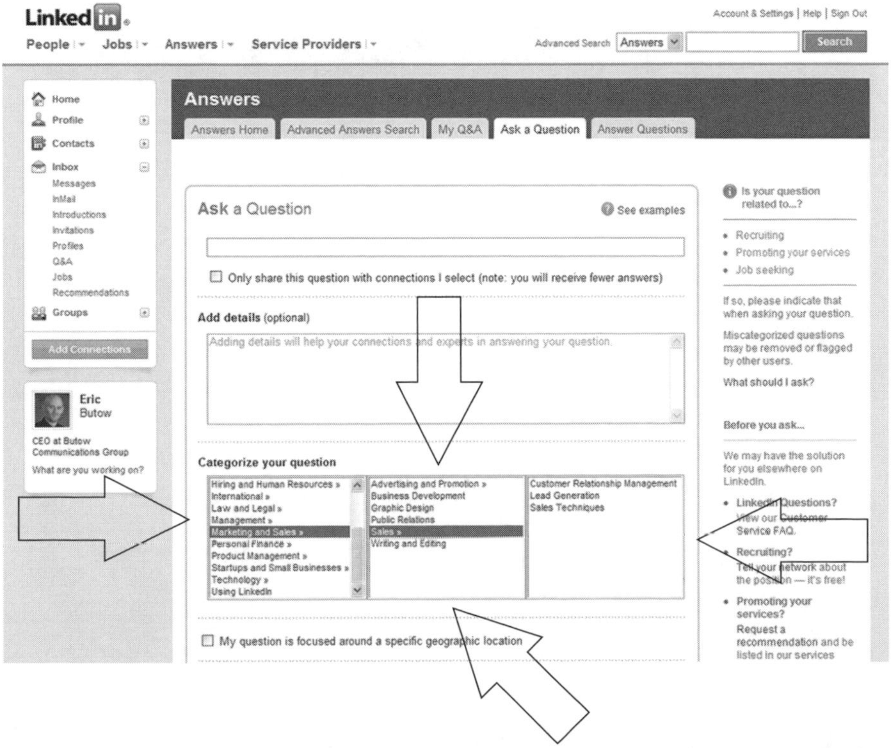

If your question is focused on a specific location, such as the metropolitan area in which you live, select the My Question Is Focused Around a Specific Geographic Location check box.

Finally, you need to tell LinkedIn whether your question is related to recruiting, promoting your services, and/or job seeking by typing the question in the Add Details box.

Flagging Questions

If you ask a question that others believe is miscategorized or inappropriate, they may flag it to alert the LinkedIn customer service staff about their concern. If a question is flagged by enough users, the LinkedIn staff automatically hides the question but also reviews it to decide whether to put it back on the system.

To flag a question, click the Flag question as . . . link at the bottom of a question. The Flag question as box appears below the question (as shown in Figure 9-16)

Figure 9-16. **The Flag question as box**

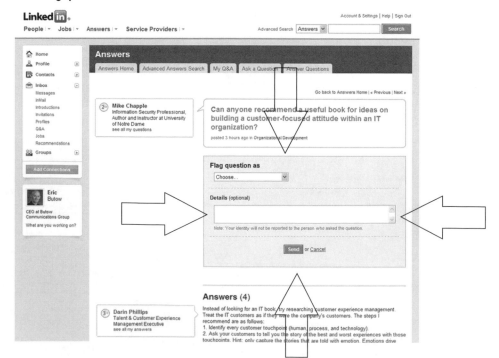

so that you can choose the type of concern you have with the message from the list, such as if you believe the question has inappropriate content. You also can type optional details in the details box. When you're finished flagging the question, click the Send button. (If you make a complaint about a question, the complaint is also sent to the questioner but not your identity.)

You also can flag an answer if you believe the answer is inappropriate by clicking the Flag answer as link at the bottom of the answer. The Flag answer as box appears underneath the link, as shown in Figure 9-17.

Figure 9-17. **The Flag answer as box**

You can choose the type of concern you have with the answer from the list, such as your belief that the answer constitutes an advertisement, and you can type optional details about your complaint in the Details box. When you're finished, click the Send button. Just as when you send a complaint about a question, the complaint about the answer goes to the answerer without identifying who wrote the complaint.

Answer a Question

Answering a question is easy, and you can either share your answers with others publicly or reply privately to the questioner.

Answer Publicly

When you view a question, you can answer it right away by clicking the Answer button below the question, as shown in Figure 9-18. The Your Answer box appears below the question, as shown in Figure 9-19.

Figure 9-18. **The Answer button**

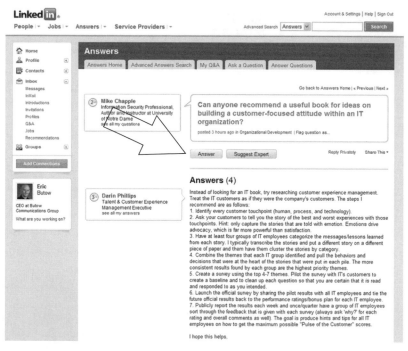

Type the answer in the Your Answer box. You should be thorough but brief so that the person asking the question—and anyone else who may be interested in the answer—can get your information quickly and easily.

If you want to reference Web sites, type the URL (Web site address) in the Web Resources box. As you click the box with the instructions for typing the Web

Figure 9-19. **The Your Answer box**

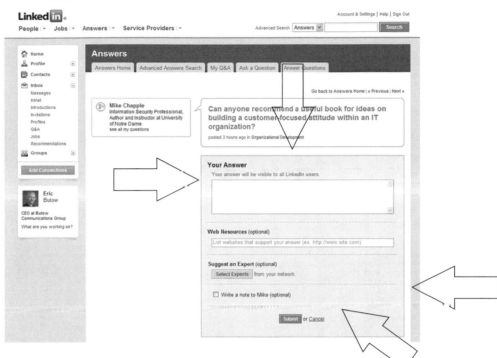

site, another box appears above it so that you can add a new Web site. If you click on the box with the instructions a third time, the box goes blank because you can add only up to three Web sites.

You can add the contact information for an expert from your network by clicking the Select Experts button so that the person asking the question (as well as anyone else reading the answers) can contact your expert for more information. After you click the button, the Narrow Your Connections window appears, as shown in Figure 9-20.

You can add as many as three connections by scrolling up and down the contact list, then selecting the check box to the left of the contact name. LinkedIn automatically adds the name you selected to the connections list at the right side of the box. You can add as many as three connections as experts for the questioner. When you're finished adding connections as experts, click the Finished button.

If you want to write a personal note to the person answering the question, select the Write a Note check box. A message box appears below the check box for you to type your personal note. This is a good opportunity to introduce yourself

Figure 9-20. **The Narrow Your Connections window**

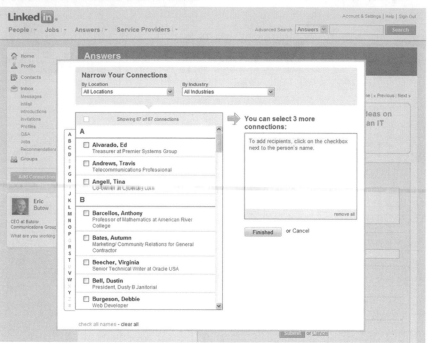

professionally, and your message will be sent only to the person who wrote the question.

When you're finished posting the answer, click the Submit button. LinkedIn adds your answer to the bottom of the question page as the most recent answer posted in response to the question.

Reply Privately

Reply privately to the person asking the question by clicking the Reply Privately link, as shown in Figure 9-21. After you click the link, the Q&A page appears, as shown in Figure 9-22, so that you can compose your private message to the questioner. In this page, you can change the default subject in the Subject box and then type your message in the Message box that appears below the question. If you want to add more Web resources, type as many as three site addresses into the Web Resources area boxes.

Below the Web Resources area, you also can select up to three experts to refer to the questioner from your network, just as when you answer publicly by clicking the

Figure 9-21. **The Reply Privately link**

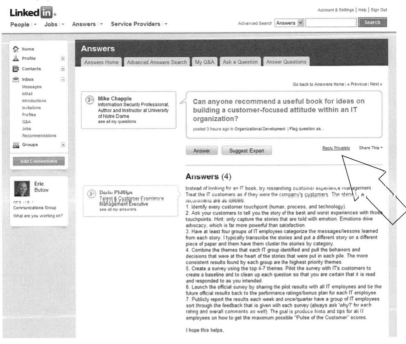

Figure 9-22. **The Q&A page**

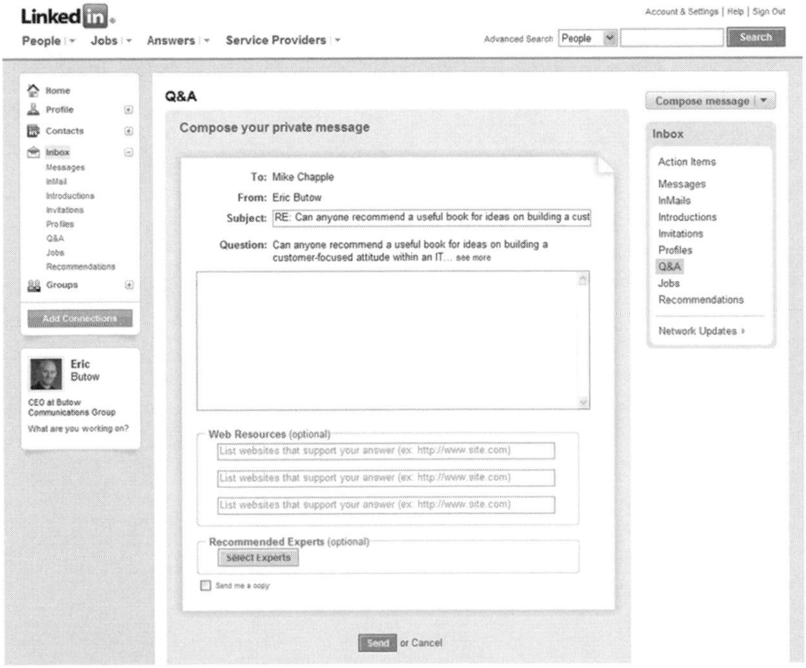

Select Experts button. Finally, select the Send Me a Copy check box at the bottom of the page if you want to receive a copy of your message sent in your e-mail box. When you're finished preparing the message, click the Send button.

Share a Question

You can share a question in two ways: You can suggest an expert on LinkedIn to the person asking the question, which not only helps the questioner get the right answer but also makes you look helpful (and you are). You can also share the information with other people by including the link to the question on another online medium such as an e-mail message, a blog, or a Web site.

Suggesting an Expert

You can select experts from your network by clicking the Suggest Expert button underneath the question, as shown in Figure 9-23. The Suggest an Expert area appears

Figure 9-23. **The Suggest Expert button**

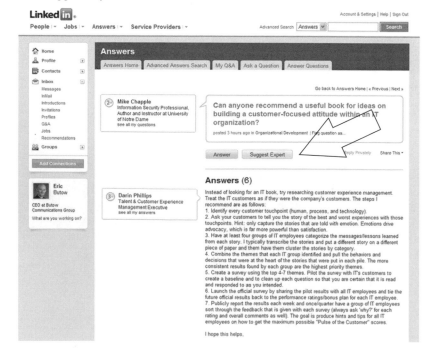

Figure 9-24. **The Suggest an Expert area**

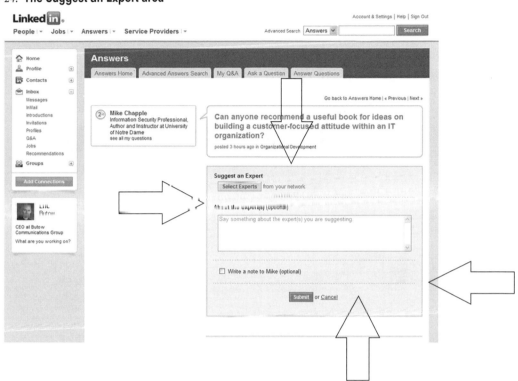

underneath the question, as shown in Figure 9-24, so that you can select experts from your network and write information about them. You can select up to three experts by clicking the Select Experts button, then selecting the experts as you did when answering publicly, as explained earlier in this chapter. When you're finished, you may want to say something about the experts and why the person asking the question should contact them by typing that information in the About the Expert(s) box. (Doing so is optional.)

If you want to write a personal note to the questioner to introduce yourself, select the Write a note check box, then type the note in the box that appears underneath the check box. The note is sent only to the person who posted the question. When you're finished suggesting your experts, click the Submit button.

Sharing with Others and with Online Media

You can share the question with others in your network, put it on related Web sites (including del.icio.us and Digg), and link the question Web site to other online media, such as a Web site, blog, or an e-mail message. Share the question by clicking the Share This Link under the question. The Share This box appears underneath the link, as shown in Figure 9-25.

Figure 9-25. **The Share This box**

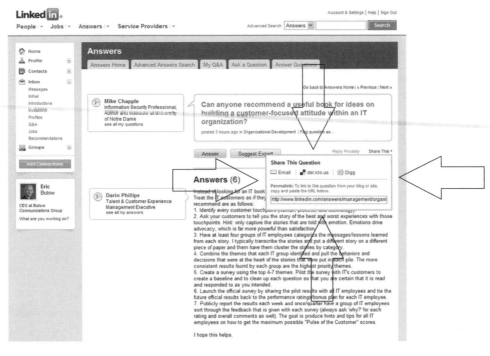

E-mail the question to connections in your network by clicking the Email link. The Q&A page appears so that you can forward the question to other connections in your network, as shown in Figure 9-26.

You can select your connections by clicking the Select Connections button and then selecting your connections in the Narrowing Your Connections box, as explained in Chapter 8. To edit the subject and/or message, type in the Subject and/or Message box, respectively. You also can send a copy of the forwarded message to your own e-mail address by selecting the Send me a copy check box. When you're finished, click the Send button.

Figure 9-26. **The Q&A page to forward a question**

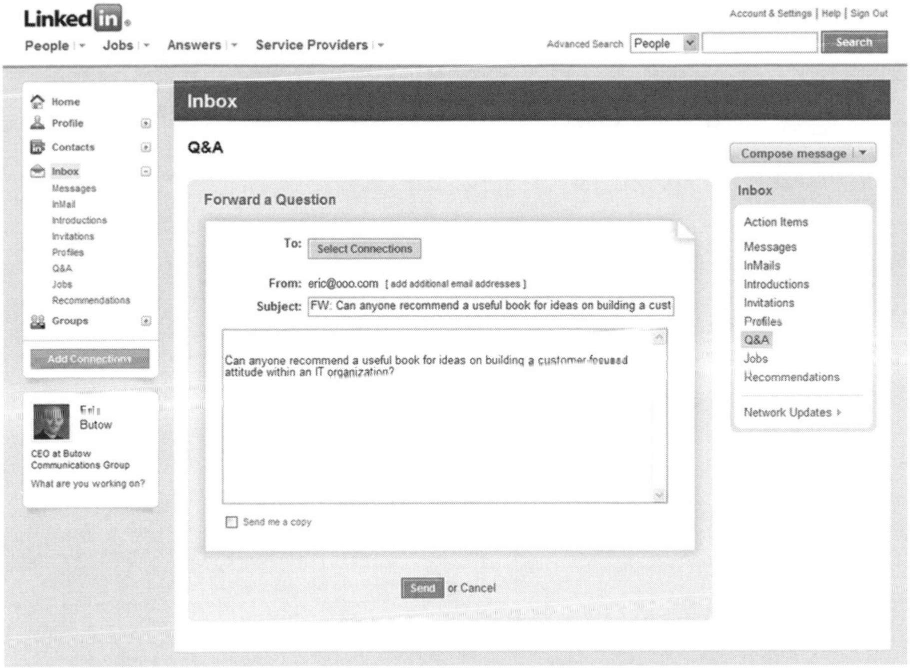

If you have an account with the del.icio.us social bookmarking Web site and/or the Digg content-sharing Web site, you can log into your account and share the question information with others on those two sites.

In the Share This Question box, LinkedIn includes a box with the URL, or Web site address, for the question so that you can copy and paste that address into another location, such as a Web site or blog. You also can paste the URL into an e-mail message to someone else.

Search for an Answer

If you still can't find the answer you're looking for, you can search for it by clicking the Advanced Answers Search tab at the top of the page, as shown in Figure 9-27. Type the search criteria in the Keywords box and then click the Search button. The

Figure 9-27. **The Advanced Answers Search tab**

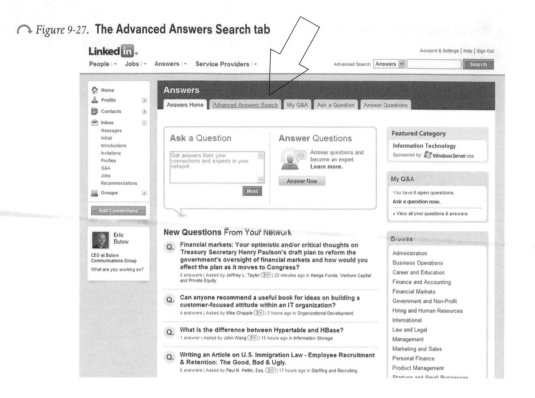

Search Results page appears with the results of your search in the Search Results page. For example, when you type "hiring salesperson" in the Keywords box, the Search Results page shows the first 10 questions that meet that criteria, as shown in Figure 9-28.

You'll notice that, in some question descriptions, your search terms are highlighted. If no search terms are highlighted, one or more answers to the questions contain the search terms, and you can view the search terms when you view the questions and their answers.

If you want to view the next 10 questions, scroll down to the bottom of the page and then click the next link. You can refine your search in the Refine Search box by changing your search criteria, searching for your keyword match in both questions and answers or only questions, searching within a specific category, and showing only unanswered questions. You also can sort the questions by viewing open questions, sorting by the relevance to your criteria, and sorting by the dates the questions were posted.

Figure 9-28. **The Search Results page**

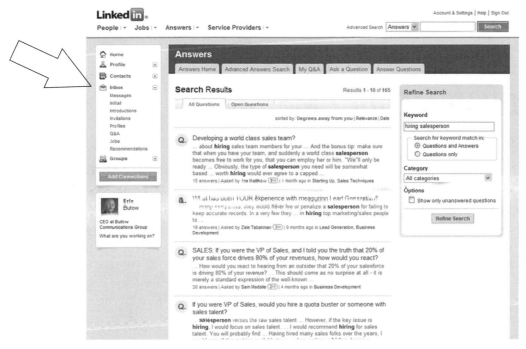

As part of learning about questions and answers, you learned how to contact the person asking the question directly. LinkedIn contains many more tools for contacting other LinkedIn members directly, and you'll learn more about them in Chapter 10.

10.

Contacting Other Members

LinkedIn provides a number of methods for contacting other members, whether they are connections in your network or people you would never have a chance to meet otherwise but want to get to know through LinkedIn. You can contact your members directly using LinkedIn's Inbox, and you can also create groups of users with the new LinkedIn Groups feature.

The Inbox

Access the Inbox in the home page by clicking the Inbox link in the Navigation box, as shown in Figure 10-1. When you click the link, the Inbox: Action Items page appears, as shown in Figure 10-2. The Action Items page shows flagged items that you need to attend to, such as InMails from other LinkedIn members that you need to read, invitations from others in your network, and information about jobs from your network.

If you have no flagged items, the page tells you that you have no items in your Inbox, as you see in Figure 10-2. On the left side of the page is a button to compose a message and the Inbox menu box that contains options for viewing information from other members of your network, such as invitations or questions and answers. You also can get the latest updates from your network by clicking the Network Updates link. After you click the link, you see the latest updates for the current week, as shown in Figure 10-3, but you can also view network updates as far back as four weeks.

⌒ *Figure 10-1.* **The Inbox link**

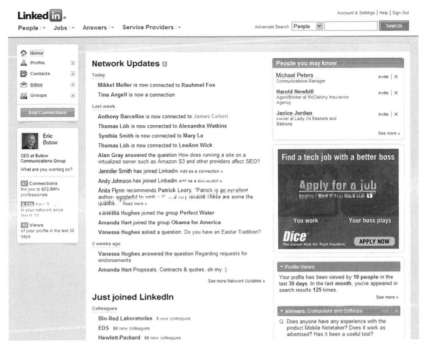

⌒ *Figure 10-2.* **The Inbox: Action Items page**

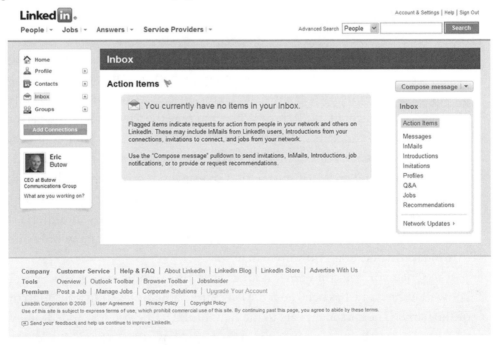

Figure 10-3. **The Network Updates page for the current week**

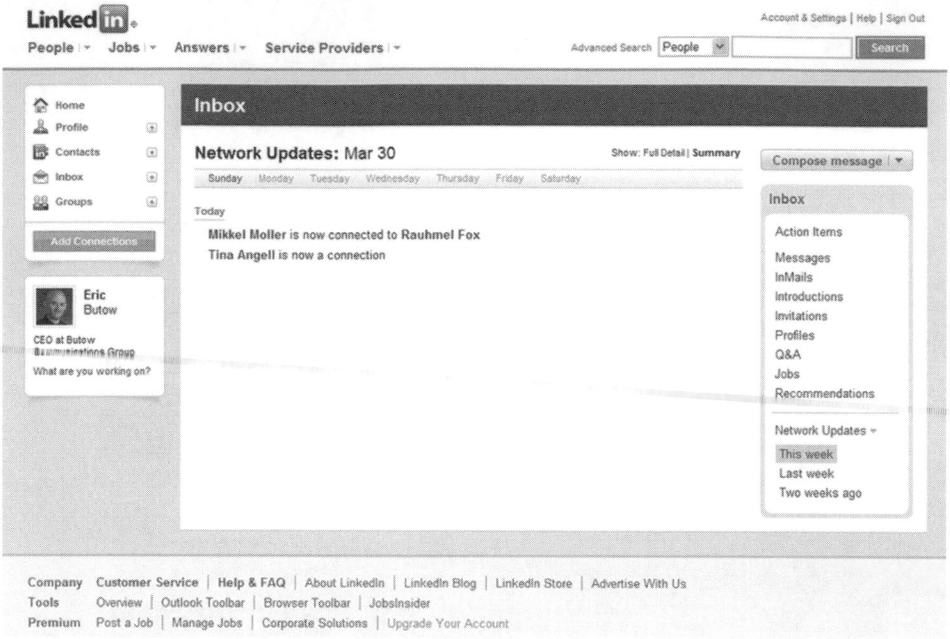

Compose a Message

You can quickly compose a message to one or as many as 10 other connections in your network by clicking the Compose message button. After you click the button, the Messages page appears, as shown in Figure 10-4. Start your message by typing the name of the recipient in the To box. When you type the first letter in the person's first or last name, a list appears below the To box with names from your connections list that match the name. For example, in Figure 10-5, when I type the letter "B," the list of all first and last names that start with B appears underneath the To box. If you find a name in the list you want to add, click it. You also can keep trying the name of the person, and the list shrinks as the number of names that meet your criteria shrinks. For example, if I type "Barc" in the To box, the list shrinks to show only one name that meets that criteria: Anthony Barcellos.

Once you select a name, it appears in the To box, in a gray box to let you know that the name has been added. Delete the name by clicking the "X" to the right of the name. The cursor appears to the right of the name you just added, and you can add more names by typing new ones in the box. Above the To box, LinkedIn tells you

↷ *Figure 10-4.* **The Messages page**

↷ *Figure 10-5.* **The list of all first and last names that start with "B"**

how many more connections you can add. You can send a message to as many as 10 connections at one time.

If you'd rather add your connections from the Narrow Your Connections box, click the little address book to the right of the To box. The Narrow Your Connections box appears for you to select the names from your connections list. (Refer to Chapter 8 to learn how to use the Narrow Your Connections box.)

Add an E-Mail Address

The e-mail address you're sending the message from appears below the To box. If you want to send your message from more than one address, click the Add email address link to the right of the e-mail address. A new browser window appears, and the Email Addresses page appears, as shown in Figure 10-6. You can add a new e-mail address (such as your work e-mail address) by typing the address in the box and then clicking the Add email address button. When you're finished adding the e-mail address, close the browser window that contains the Email Addresses page.

After you type the subject in the Subject box and the message in the Message

Figure 10-6. **The Email Addresses page in a new browser window**

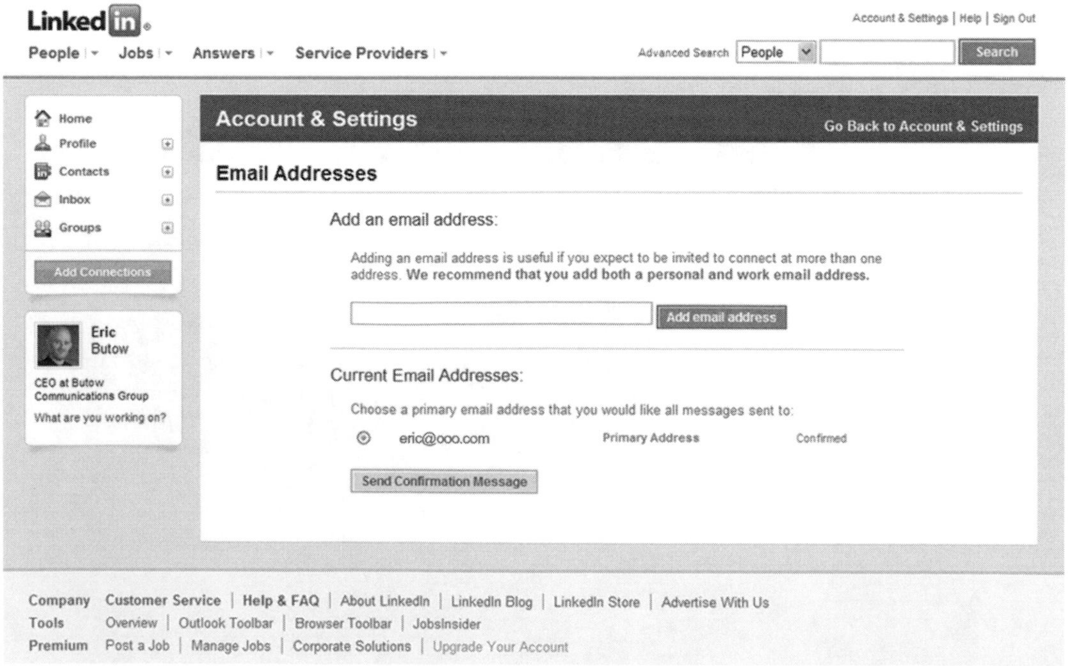

box, you can clear the Allow recipients to see each other's names and e-mail addresses if you have multiple recipients for the same message and you don't want each recipient to know who else received the message. You also can select the Send Me a Copy check box if you want to receive a copy of the message in your e-mailbox. When you're finished preparing your message, click the Send button.

Other Composing Options

Note that you also can compose a message by moving the mouse pointer over the Compose message button, then clicking the Send message to a connection link that appears in the Compose message menu, as shown in Figure 10-7.

Send InMail or Introduction

LinkedIn offers two methods of introducing yourself to a contact. One of the services available from the LinkedIn OpenLink Network is InMail, which is available to

Figure 10-7. **The Send message to a connection link in the Compose message menu**

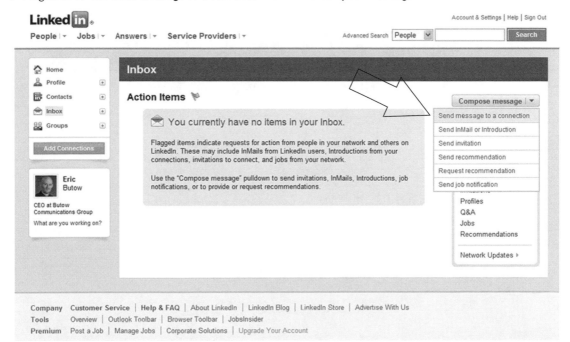

premium account holders and which lets you communicate to a LinkedIn member's e-mail address. InMail displays your message on the member's LinkedIn home page so that the member recognizes that you are a fellow LinkedIn member and that your message is important. An introduction lets a connection recommend you to another member whom your connection knows to get the ball rolling toward your having a relationship with that member. You can have five introductions open at one time with a free personal account. If you want more introductions open at one time, you must purchase one of the premium accounts. (See Chapter 2 to review the different types of accounts.)

The first step is to search for the person you're looking for by clicking the Send InMail or Introduction link in the Compose message menu. When you click the link, the InMail and Introductions page appears, as shown in Figure 10-8. To send In-Mail and/or an introduction, click the Search now button. The People page appears, as shown in Figure 10-9.

Refer back to Chapter 4 for more information about how to search for people. Because I'm signed in as Eric Butow, for the purposes of this example I'll type "Kathy Taylor" in the Name Search box and then click the Search button. As the

Figure 10-8. **The InMail and Introductions page**

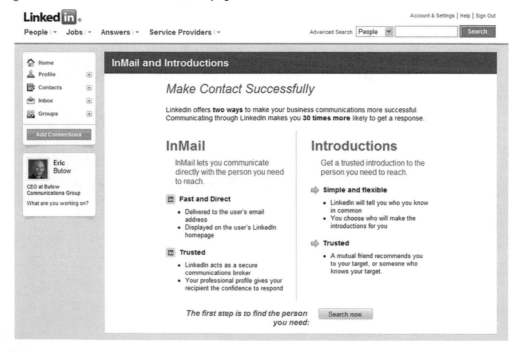

Figure 10-9. **The People page**

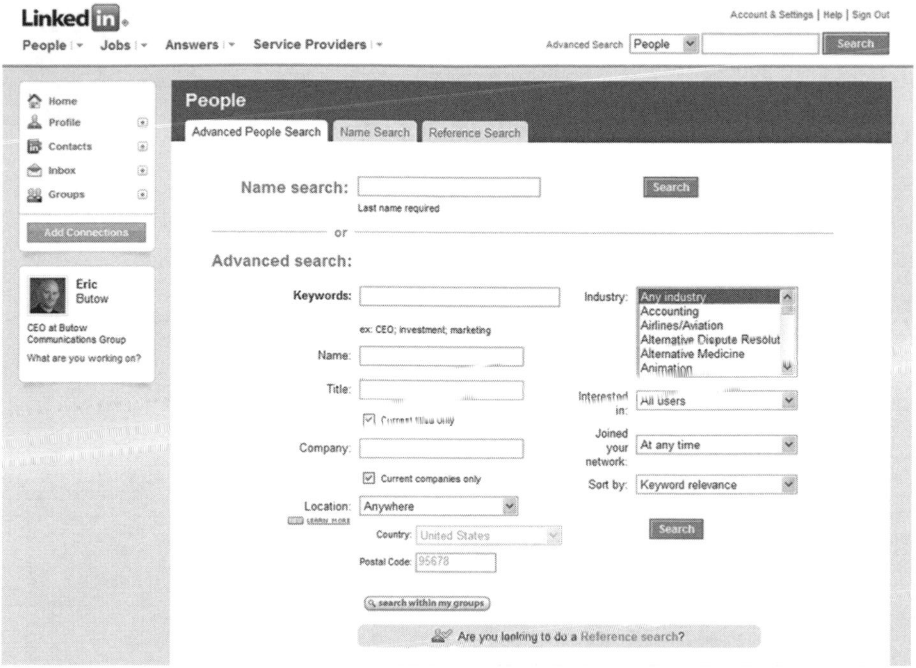

Name Search Results page shows in Figure 10-10, Kathy is a first-degree connection in my network. However, there is another Kathy Taylor in the list who is a third-degree connection in my network, and I want to connect with her. When I click on Kathy's name to open her profile, to the right of her e-mail are links to send an In-Mail message and also to get introduced through a connection, as shown in Figure 10-11.

Send InMail

Click the Send InMail link to open the InMail page, as shown in Figure 10-12. By default, your contact information is included when you send an InMail message. If you would rather not send your contact information to the recipient, clear the Include my contact information check box. The default contact information you share is your e-mail address, but, if you want to include your phone number so that the recipient can contact you directly, type your phone number (and don't forget your area code) in the Phone box.

⌒ *Figure 10-10.* **Two Kathy Taylors in the Name Search Results list**

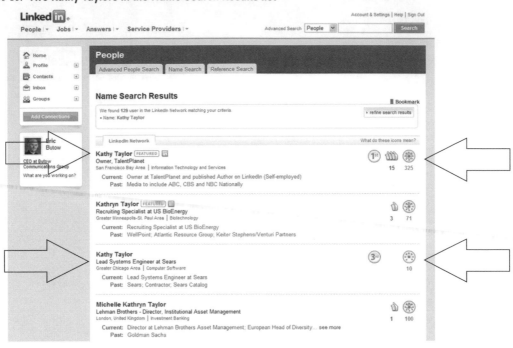

⌒ *Figure 10-11.* **Links to send an InMail message and get introduced through a connection**

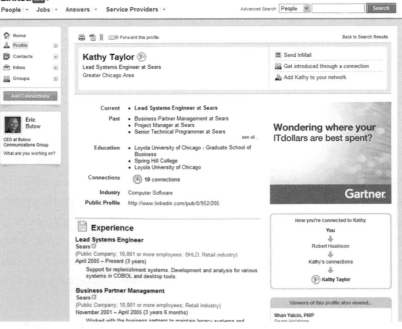

Figure 10-12. **The Compose your message page**

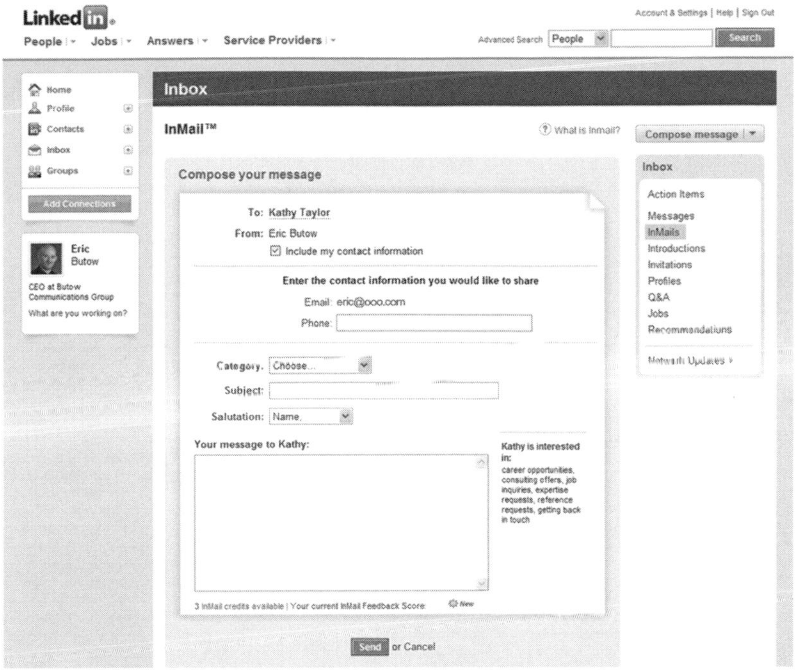

Below the Phone box, you can choose the type of message you want to send in the Category list. To the right of the message box is a list of what your recipient is interested in, so you may want to tailor your message to meet the recipient's interests.

After you type the subject in the Subject box and your message in the Message box, click the Send button. LinkedIn sends the message to the member and alerts the member about the message on his home page.

Get Introduced

If you want to get introduced to a member through one of your mutual connections, click the Get introduced through a connection link on the member's profile page. When you click the link, the Request an Introduction page appears, as shown in Figure 10-13. If LinkedIn finds that more than one connection can introduce you, select the connection you want to introduce you by clicking the appropriate button and then clicking the Continue button. The Compose Introduction page appears, as shown in Figure 10-14.

You request an introduction as you compose an InMail message, but with one

Figure 10-13. **The Request an Introduction page**

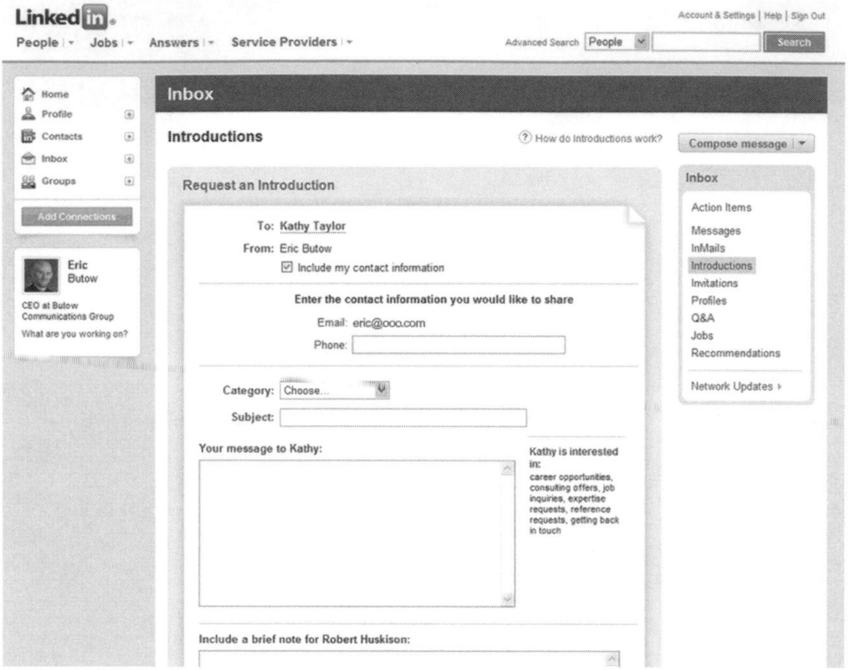

difference: You also need to write a brief note to the connection. After you click the Send button, the connection receives your request for an introduction and decides whether to forward it to the member or to reject your request.

Send Invitation

You can send an invitation to one or more people in your personal address book to join LinkedIn and join your network. To send an invitation from the Inbox page, click the Send invitation link in the Compose Message menu, as shown in Figure 10-14. When you click the link, the Add Connections page appears, as shown in Figure 10-15, so that you can add friends or colleagues to your network.

You can send up to six invitations at one time by typing each user's first name, last name, and e-mail address. If you want to check to see who in your address book uses LinkedIn, click the Check Webmail contacts button on the right side of the page if you use Gmail, Yahoo!, or AOL. If you use Outlook to check your e-mail, click the Check Outlook contacts button to check your Outlook address book. If you

Figure 10-14. **The Send invitation link**

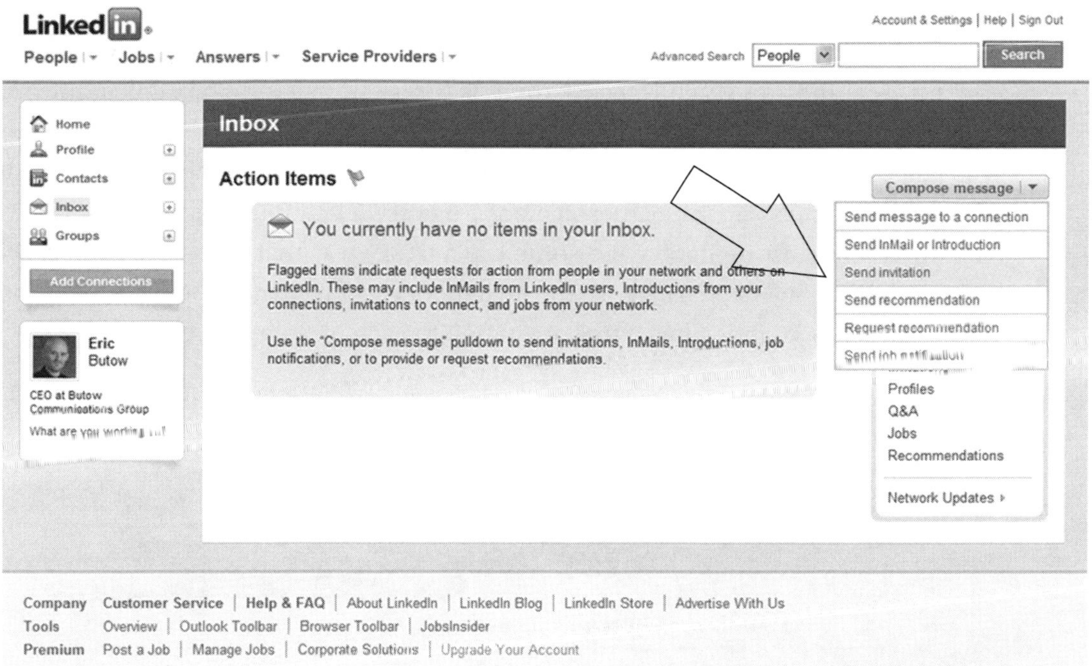

Figure 10-15. **The Create Invitations page**

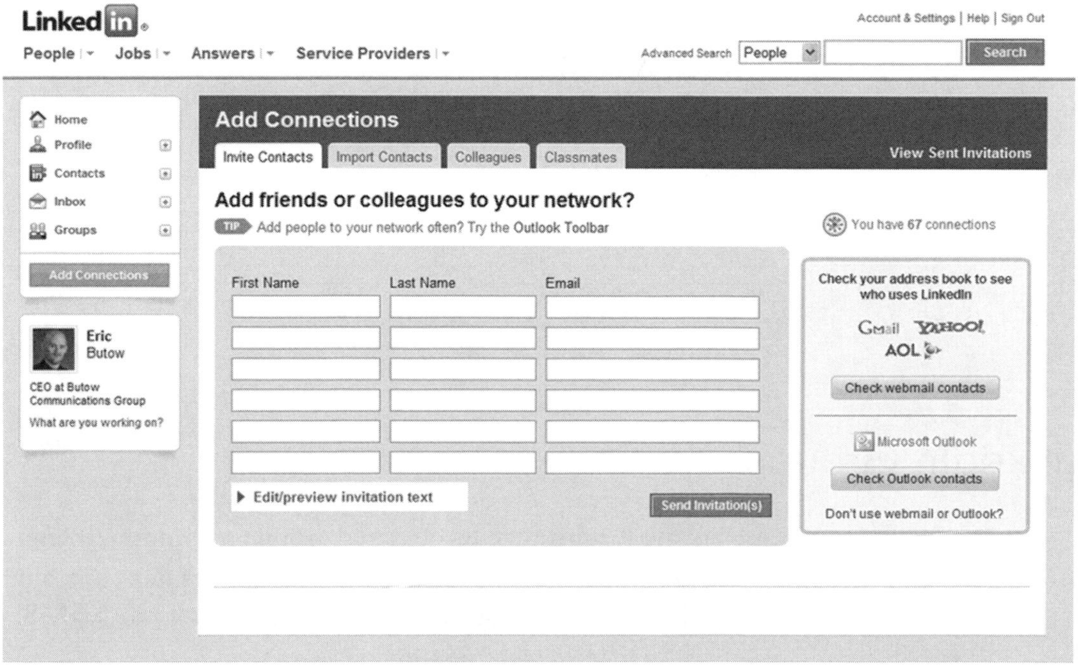

use none of these programs, click the Don't use Webmail or Outlook? link for more options.

LinkedIn sends standard invitation text to each of your invitees, which you can preview and edit when you click the Edit/preview invitation text link at the bottom of the page. The message appears below the link, as shown in Figure 10-16. You can edit the subject in the Subject box, change the salutation in the Name list, and edit the invitation message in the message box. In every invitation, LinkedIn also adds a link to accept your invitation and some explanatory text that you can't edit. When you're finished making changes to the invitation, click the Send Invitation(s) button. LinkedIn sends an individual e-mail invitation to each of your invitees.

Figure 10-16. **The invitation message**

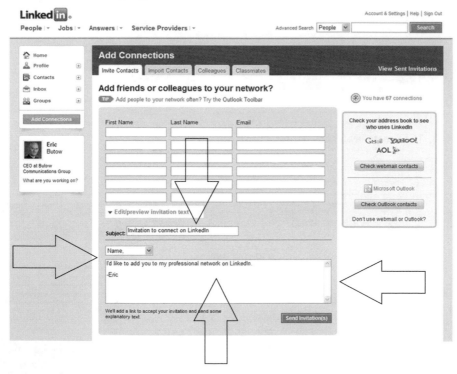

LinkedIn Groups

LinkedIn Groups are private forums that are centered around a common theme or background, such as university alumni or people who used to work at a company. If you want to keep in touch with a certain group of people and collaborate with them without having to interact with the general LinkedIn membership, you can create your own group and invite members to join.

You can access LinkedIn Groups by clicking the Groups link in the Navigation box. as shown in Figure 10-17. When you click the link, the About LinkedIn Groups page appears, as shown in Figure 10-18, and lists the groups to which you belong. You can view a directory of groups, including featured groups for alumni of several business schools, Hewlett-Packard alumni, and technical groups, by clicking the Groups Directory tab at the top of the page.

Figure 10-17. **The Groups link**

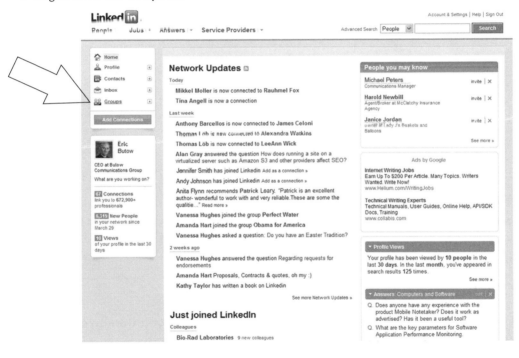

Viewing Existing Groups

If you want to see existing groups in other categories, click a category name in the category list. For example, if you click the Professional Groups link, the Professional Groups page appears and lists all the current professional groups. When you click on a group name, a new browser window opens so that you can view more information

Figure 10-18. **The About LinkedIn Groups page**

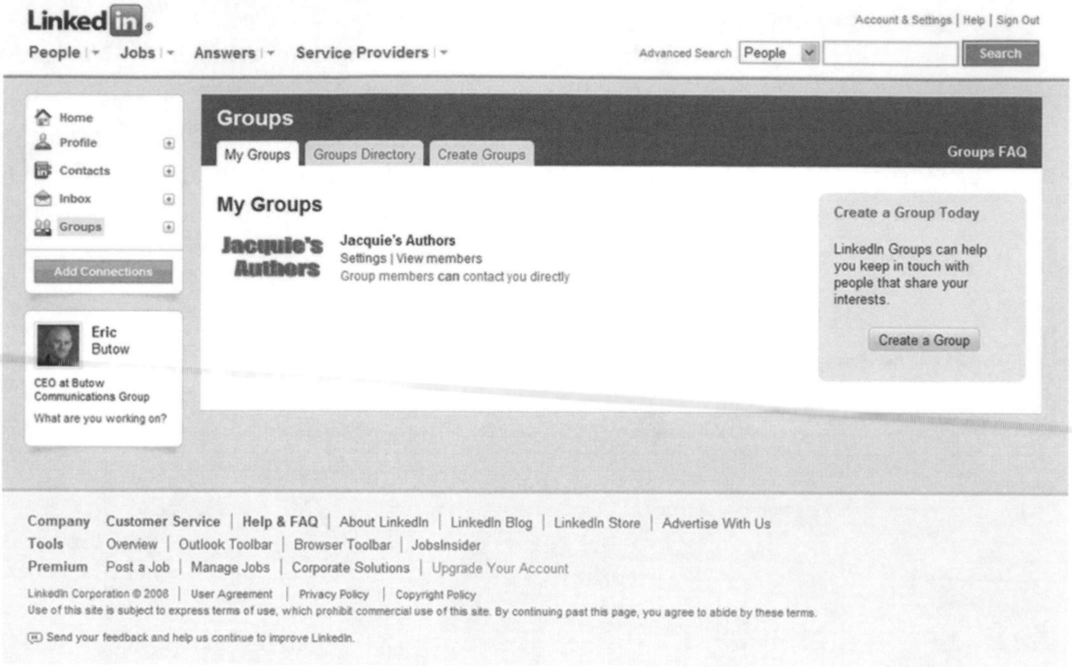

about the organization. You cannot join a group itself; you must be invited by the managers of the group, and in many cases you must join the organization before you are invited to join the LinkedIn group.

Starting Your Own Group

If you have an organization or a group of professionals that you want to collaborate with through LinkedIn, you can start your own group. Start the process by clicking the Create a Group button, as shown in Figure 10-19. In the Create a Group page that appears, as shown in Figure 10-20, you can upload your group logos as well as enter information about your group.

In the Upload Group Logos section, you need to upload a large 100-by-50-pixel logo and a small 60-by-30-pixel logo. LinkedIn uses both logos to identify your group in its listings. After you finish creating your logos, you can browse for each logo by clicking the Browse button to the right of each in the Group logo box example. Click the Browse button at the top to browse for the large logo, and click the Browse button on the bottom to browse for the small logo.

Figure 10-19. **The Create a Group button**

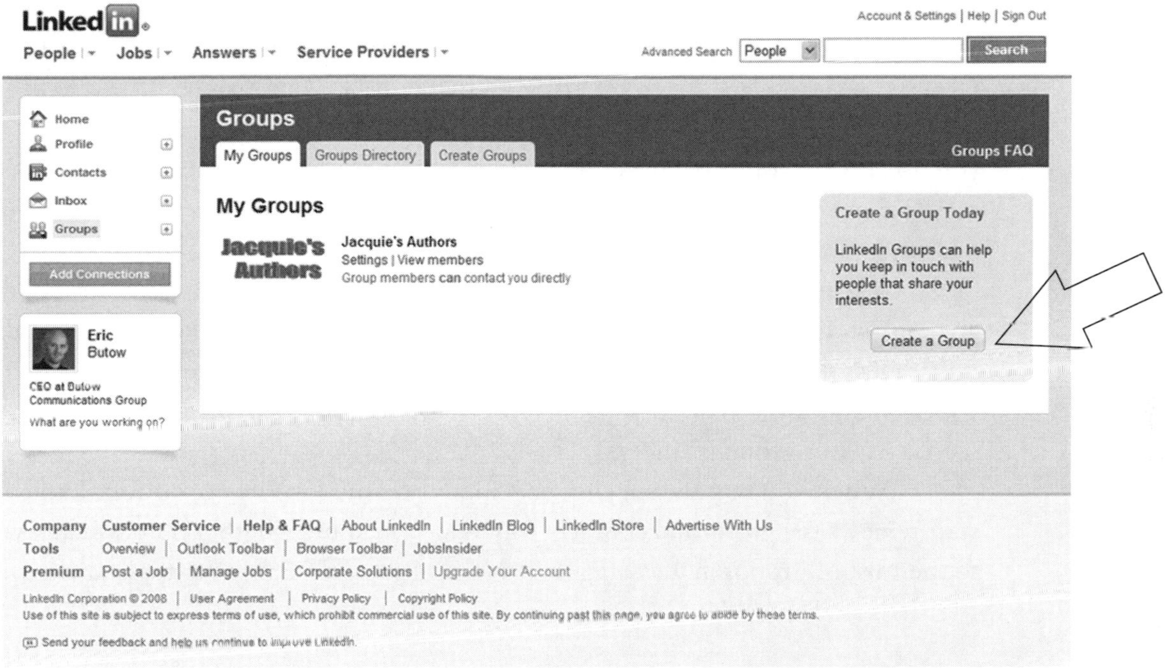

Figure 10-20. **The Create a Group page**

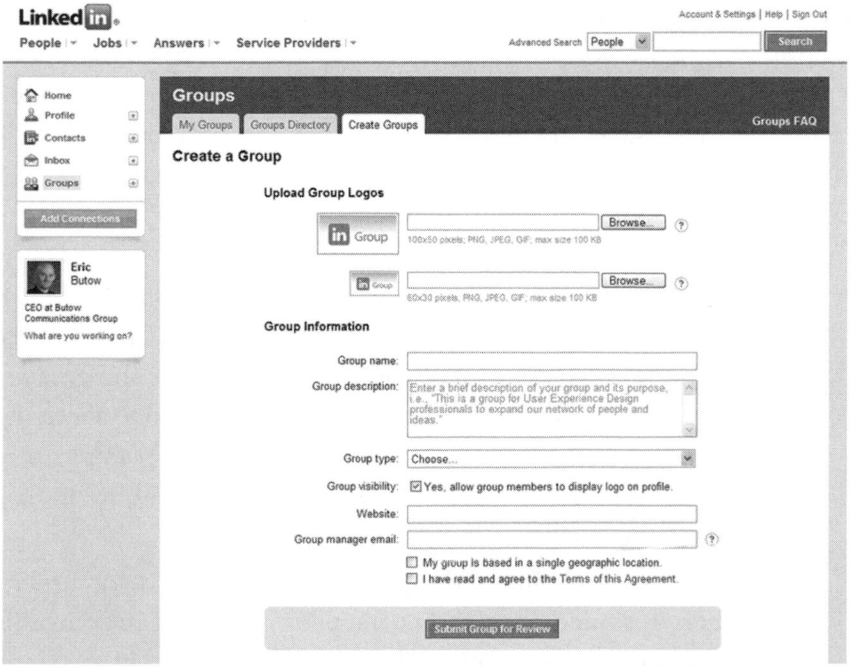

In the Group Information area, type the group name in the Group Name box and the group description in the Group description box. For those who are not sure about what to type in the Group description box, the box contains an example. In the Group type list, select the group category that best fits your group.

Group members can display your group logo on their profile by default. If you don't want your members to do this, clear the Yes, allow group members to display logo on profile check box. In the Group Manager Email box, type your e-mail address.

If your group is in a single geographic location, such as a city or metropolitan area, select the My group is based in a single geographic location check box. You also must select the check box indicating that you have read the terms of the agreement, which includes the requirement that you must supply LinkedIn with a list of the names of your group members.

When you're finished, click the Submit Group for Review button. LinkedIn staff reviews the group and contacts you to let you know whether they will add you to their list of groups in the category you specified or decline your application.

Tips for Contacting Other Members

When you find you need to contact others in your network, consider why you are doing so.

If you are in a fast-paced business like recruiting, you are usually conducting a search with a sense of urgency. If so, the best way to go about a search is to contact people directly. In such cases, in doing a search when you don't know the person but you do share the same contacts, you should take a couple of steps.

- When filling in the subject line, choose a compelling message to grab attention, such as "SVP Marketing of Oracle and Larry Ellison." Pick a name from your list of shared contacts that has the greatest impact in reaching out to the intended person. Again, thinking about the level of title of your shared contact is a good idea. For example, a reference to someone with vice president as title gets more attention than, say, your cousin in Omaha.

- Insert a compelling message that conveys a sense of urgency. Perhaps there is someone you want the person to meet or a meeting that you would like her to attend. Then the message should say something like,

"I would like to get connected with you before August 3 as my hiring manager is in town on August 7 and, if it made sense, we could get the two of you together, especially if you are interested." This should encourage a sense of urgency with the reader and motivate her to act quickly.

- Your message also should reflect that you have spent some time looking at the person's profile on LinkedIn and that there is genuine interest in speaking to him because of his life successes. As a recruiter, I always like to point out a thing or two on the profile. For example, "I see you worked in the e-commerce space with Xuma and our client is very interested in that kind of background."

Figure 10-21. shows an example of a compelling message.

Figure 10-21. **An example of a compelling message**

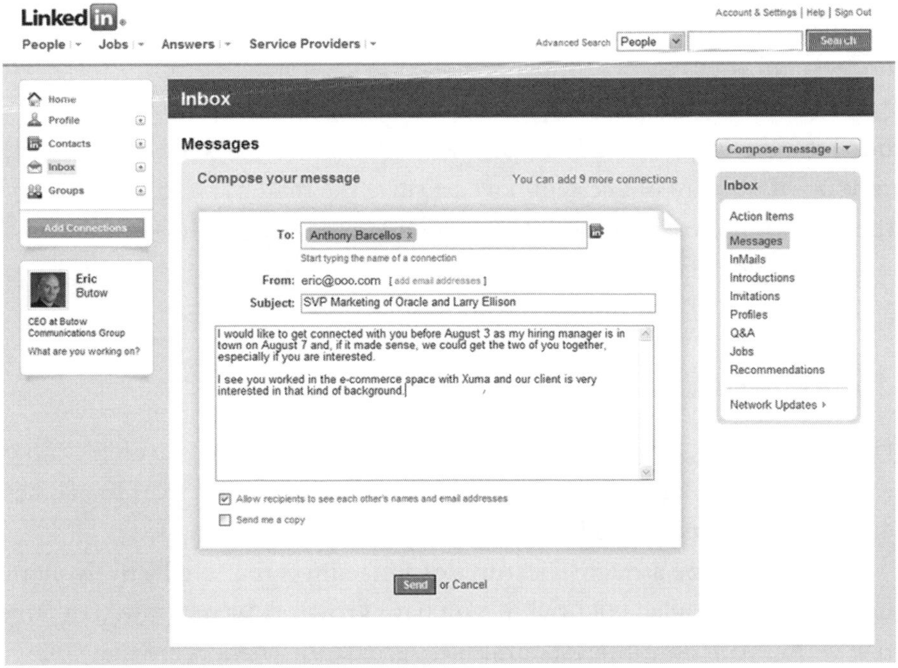

Whatever the reason you are contacting someone, give the impression that you are truly interested in him, not just looking to network with him only to connect with someone else.

Be Discreet

Another time to use direct contact is when the subject matter is of a highly sensitive or personal nature—something the contactees wouldn't want anyone in their network to know about, such as:

- They are job hunting.
- You are contacting them about a job.
- You might be looking to replace someone at your company, and you would not want that disseminated for public knowledge.
- You are asking them for a reference on someone.
- The conversation you need to have is highly confidential, and you and/or they would not want others to know about it.

These are entirely appropriate reasons for contacting someone directly as opposed to going through your network. Those on the receiving end most certainly will understand your reasons for being direct.

Think of these messages as a telephone conversation. Would you want anyone listening in on the call? If not, use discretion. When in doubt, err on the side of caution. If you are not certain how sensitive the material is in your e-mail message, then do not write that information in an InMail message. Those on the receiving end will appreciate your discretion.

Asking for Referrals or Introductions

Have you ever wanted to do business with someone whom you didn't know? In these cases, you really have no way to make a connection other than to call her office at 7:30 A.M. and hope to catch her at the desk.

One of the attractive features of LinkedIn is that it effectively eliminates the need for the so-called cold call. If you have grown your network to a large enough size within your core interest or business group, the chances are that you will be connected to the person you want to speak with. This removes the you-don't-know-me-but phone call and allows you to make contact through your shared connections. It takes the sting out of a call or e-mail coming out of the blue.

By way of example, allow me to share a story about a CEO friend of mine.

He told me a story of wanting to work for a company in northern California that was in the wine supply manufacturing business. He believed his resume did not tell the story that would best portray him as a fit and knew that it wouldn't make the cut with a recruiter. He went into his LinkedIn network and put a message out to some of his contacts that he was seeking a conversation with a certain recruiter. Through his network, he found someone who was two degrees away from the recruiter. He contacted his contact, asking him to forward a message to his contact that the CEO wanted to speak with the recruiter about this position. The message was forwarded through LinkedIn and phone calls. Subsequently, the CEO was able to speak with the recruiter and was able to set up a lunch to explain his background in more detail. That put him in a stronger position in vying for the job.

What is the best way to go about asking for referrals or introductions? The strength and relevancy of the message are very much determined by the contact who is going to relay the message. In other words, pick the contact who has the greatest impact on the person you are trying to connect with.

If several of your contacts are connected to the person you are trying to contact, then you need to ask yourself some questions:

- What person would carry the most weight in terms of reaching my desired contact?

- What person would be the most likely to pass my message on in the timeliest fashion?

- How many messages have I asked these contacts to pass along recently?

- Does the person know enough about my services and me to send along the appropriate message introducing me?

So you may have a couple of CEOs on your list who would garner the attention desired, but will they take the time to pass on your message? Obviously, the choice of intermediary is a fine balancing act of picking the best person who will carry the highest value in your network and one who will take the time to pass it along.

Once you have an intermediary, the message is also important. Figure 10-22 shows an example of a strong message that addresses the preceding questions when you ask for a referral or introduction.

Whomever you pick should be appropriately thanked. Let her know you would be happy to return the favor by helping her in any way possible.

Figure 10-22. **An example of a strong message**

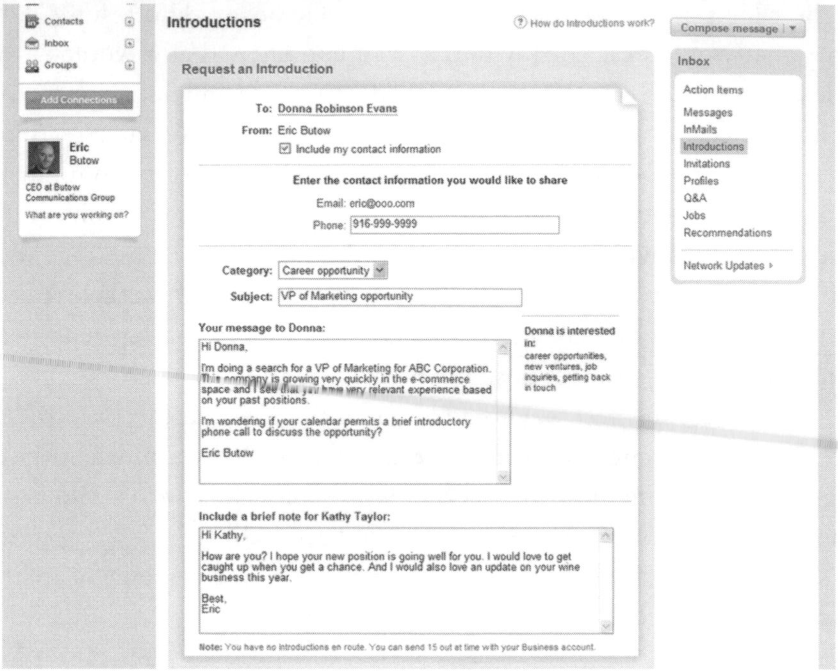

Along with reaching out to someone new through your trusted network, also remember that you have "reminded" one of your key contacts that you are in business and would be available to do work for her or for someone in her network. Every time you reach out to someone in your network, it has a halo effect that informs others of your work.

When Other Members Contact You

As a busy professional, you must make sure that your time is well spent, focusing on your current work demands as well as looking for new business. You may sometimes find that, when people ask you to do things to help them out with their businesses, you wouldn't get any of your own work done if you answered every single request. LinkedIn is a great way to vet requests to see whether the person making the request could help your business, is a good contact to have, or is doing something you are highly interested in either personally or professionally. How do you do that? You do it by checking the requestor's network.

You can discover, through their references, whether a request is something you should pursue. Check with your references who know the requestor or his business, and then decide whether the request is something you should honor.

You can reach this intermediary in a variety of different ways. One way is to send an InMail message directly to him, bypassing any intermediate connection. Instead, your message goes directly to the party you wish to contact. The drawback is that if the person doesn't know you, there may be hesitancy to respond to your InMail message. Or it may languish for days while he considers whether to answer your InMail message.

One idea is to include the person whom you and the contactee mutually know in the subject line of the InMail message, thereby making a connection. If you are e-mailing someone with a consulting opportunity and you both know John Smith, you might say in the subject line. "Consulting opportunity and John Smith." With this subject line, you grab attention with both the position and the name of a mutual friend. This generally is a successful strategy because the name in the subject line draws attention and, more often than not, a response. The implied message is that you have that person's permission to send the e-mail. This approach is tricky, but, if your e-mail message reflects only that you both know this individual, you should be on safe ground.

Another way is to send a request through the connection you and the contactee share. Choose the best common name, based on influence within your list of connections. For example, let's say you are approaching Mary Jones about a consulting opportunity, and you see you have seven connections to her. You must now choose which one is the best to go through. Think through a few things before you send this request and an InMail message:

- Don't go through anyone she currently works with in case she's working with the other person on a current project. You could put her in an awkward situation.

- Don't pick a name you have used numerous times. The person may begin to feel used.

- Pick the name that you think would wield some influence.

- Be mindful of the intermediary's title. If the connection is a busy CEO, the message may not get passed along for quite some time.

Once you have made your choice, send a friendly note, engaging the person you have asked to pass along your request. This might be along the lines of:

> Hi Joe,
>
> It's been awhile since we last spoke. Hope you are doing well. I would certainly like to catch up with you when you have a moment. In the meantime, do you mind passing this note along to Mary Jones?
>
> Thanks,
>
> Tom

If the message is urgent and you know the person you are asking to forward the e-mail, you send a separate e-mail to him to let him know you are asking for help in connecting you with your desired person. This is a matter of personal choice, of course. Very often, the decision can be made based on how quickly the response is desired.

Finding People Outside Your Network

You also can find people outside your network, reaching out to people whose names you do not know and who don't have a connection with you in your network. This feature of LinkedIn is particularly useful when you are looking outside your industry or region. For example, if you work in high tech and you are looking for a structural engineer, then your database probably does not contain many structural engineers because you previously have not worked that network of people.

In such an instance, keep the search field fairly broad at first to see what kind of talent comes up for you. Then narrow the search as you discover keywords within their bios that would help you focus more specifically. For example:

- Keyword: Engineer, Structural
- Title: Engineer

Keep geographic parameters the same as when you are searching inside the network. Your search may pull up one or two profiles with names on them, but the majority will not have names attached to their profile. It might look something like Figure 10-23. Depending on how large your search field is in terms of distance and keywords, you could have several profiles with no names on them because you are not connected to them through your network.

Figure 10-23. **An example of profiles without names attached to them**

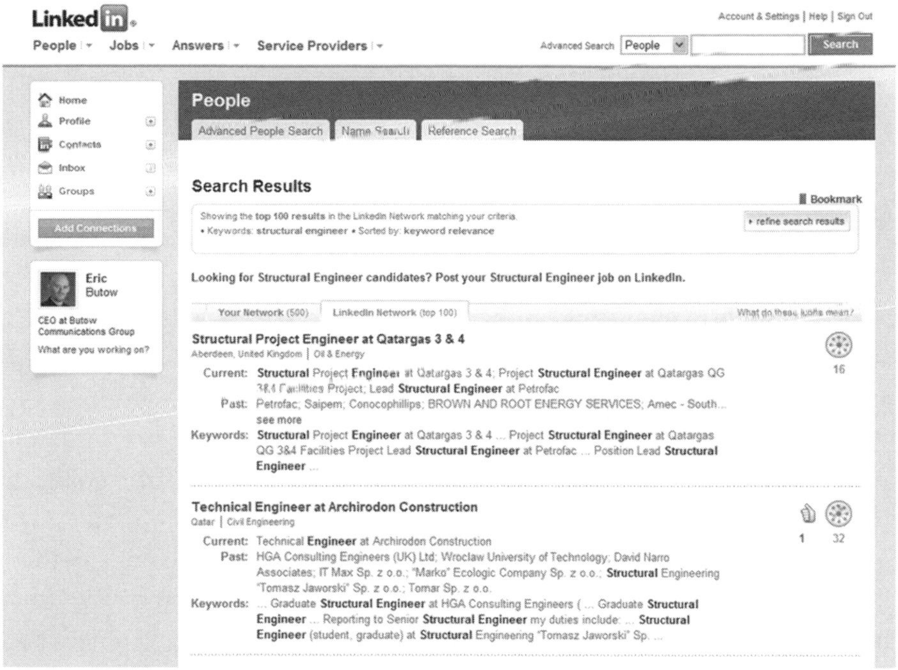

Upon reviewing the profiles, you may see a service provider who could be the answer to your needs. The only way to contact the provider is through an InMail message because you have no one in your network connecting the two of you. It then becomes very important to put together a message that garners a response. Perhaps you want to discuss the scope of the work or the particular challenges that would make it compelling for someone to get back to you. It really depends on the kind of project you are doing and what kind of service provider you are seeking. For example:

> Hi Don,
>
> I am doing a search for a Structural Engineer for Shaffer and Stevens in Omaha. They are a boutique firm that has done a variety of interesting projects, including the Henry Doorly Zoo and the new Paxton development in downtown Omaha. This is a great opportunity to join an exciting and growing firm. Your background looks very interesting. I would like to hear back from you to give you more details about the position.
>
> Kathy Taylor
>
> Principal
>
> TalentPlanet

Include all your contact information in your InMail message, including your name, your e-mail address, and your phone number. Also include as much information as possible in your e-mail message and mention that you have read his profile and see his background as a fit for your project. This helps to ensure that you will receive a return e-mail and/or phone call.

There are drawbacks to finding people outside your network. You have no way of checking them out through your connections; it is like going though the phone book and pulling names out of the *Yellow Pages*. However, one way to investigate prospects is to see whether their job history includes a company that someone in your network has either worked for or is connected to in some way. Otherwise you have to trust your judgment and then, of course, check the references they provide to you.

Now that you know more about contacting other members, what happens when you don't receive a response from a member you really want to talk to? Let's continue that discussion in Chapter 11.

11

Managing the Nonresponding LinkedIn Member

Occasionally, LinkedIn members just do not respond to a request. This can happen for a variety of reasons, including:

- They are too busy to respond.
- The message isn't compelling enough for them to respond.
- The LinkedIn message fell into their spam or junk folder, and they don't know it is there.
- The shared connection or connections have not passed your request along.
- They don't recognize the shared connection and therefore they may not recognize you.

Before you decide to find out what's happening, you should determine the status of these members and whether they have had an opportunity to review your request(s). LinkedIn provides several methods and tools for doing just that. You learned about a lot of them earlier in this book, and now it's time to bring them all together (with all figures included) to manage the nonresponding LinkedIn member.

Get Message Status Updates

You can find out which messages have received a response and determine whether you want to resend the messages or withdraw them. Start in the home page by clicking the Inbox link in the Navigation box, as shown in Figure 11-1. We'll use the sent invitations and Q&A messages in this figure as the example in this chapter. Therefore,

Figure 11-1. **The Inbox link**

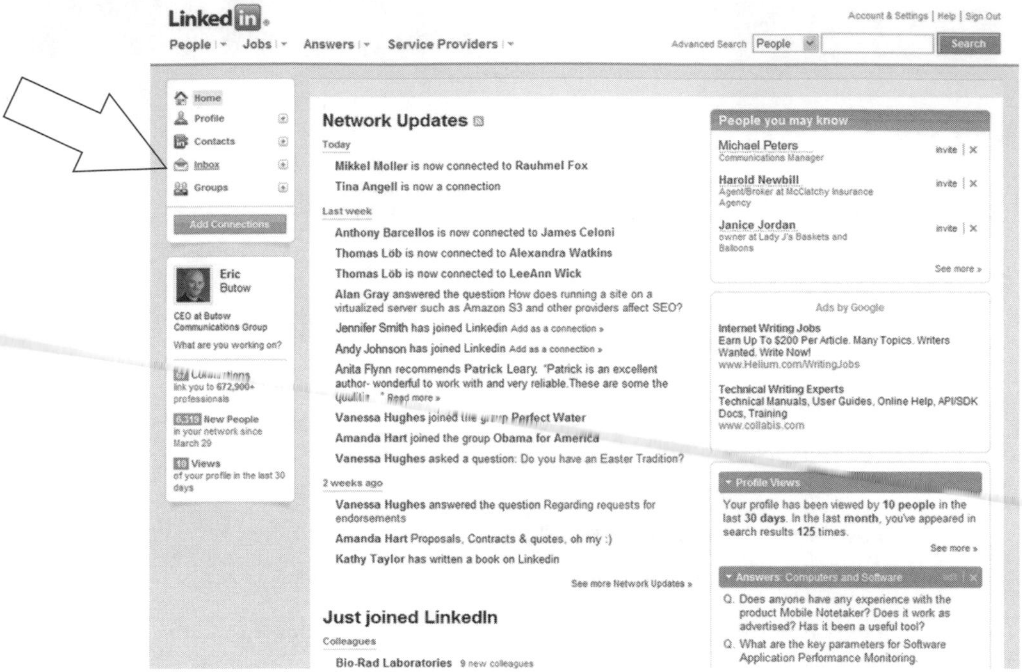

in the Inbox: Action Items page that appears, as shown in Figure 11-2, click the Invitations link. The Invitations page opens and shows the invitations you have received. You also can view all invitations you have sent by clicking the Sent link, as shown in Figure 11-3. The Status column for each invitation you have sent shows you the invitations that have been accepted, the invitations that have been sent but that have not received a response, and the invitations that have expired because they have not received a response after several weeks.

You can review the message you sent by clicking the subject title in the Subject column. The invitation page appears, as shown in Figure 11-4, with the text of the invitation you sent. You can resend the invitation by clicking the Resend button or withdraw it by clicking the Withdraw button. When you click the Resend button, the Compose your message page appears, as shown in Figure 11-5, so that you can recompose your message. You can either keep the text in the message box or retype the message to make sure that it's more compelling. (You also can get tips about making your messages more interesting later in this chapter.) When you're finished, click the Send button to resend the invitation. The Invitations: Sent page appears with the text of the invitation you just sent.

Figure 11-2. **The Invitations link**

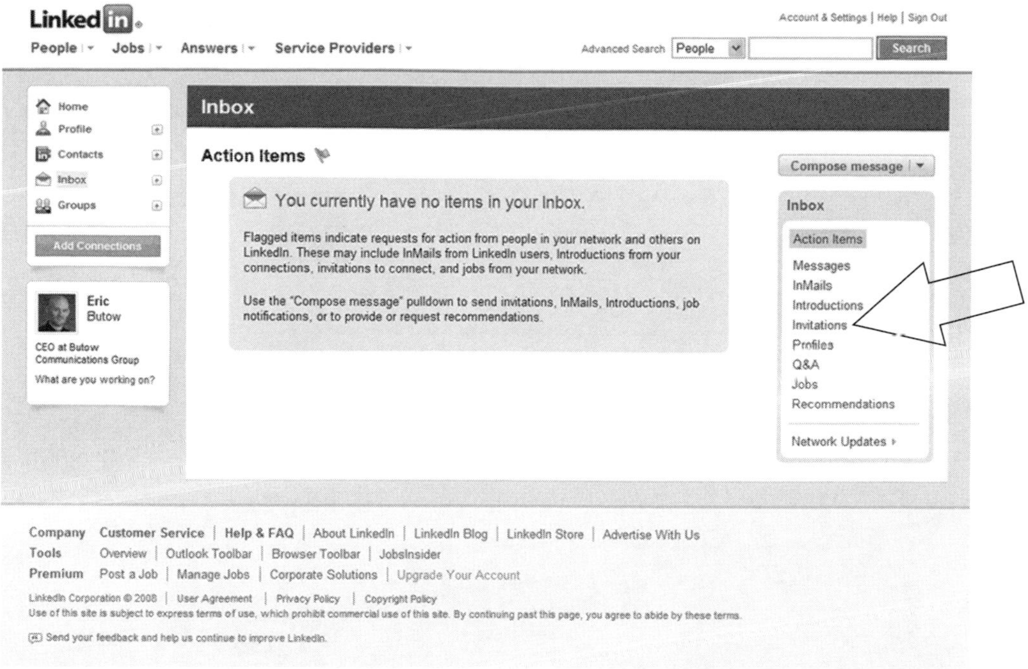

Figure 11-3. **The Sent link**

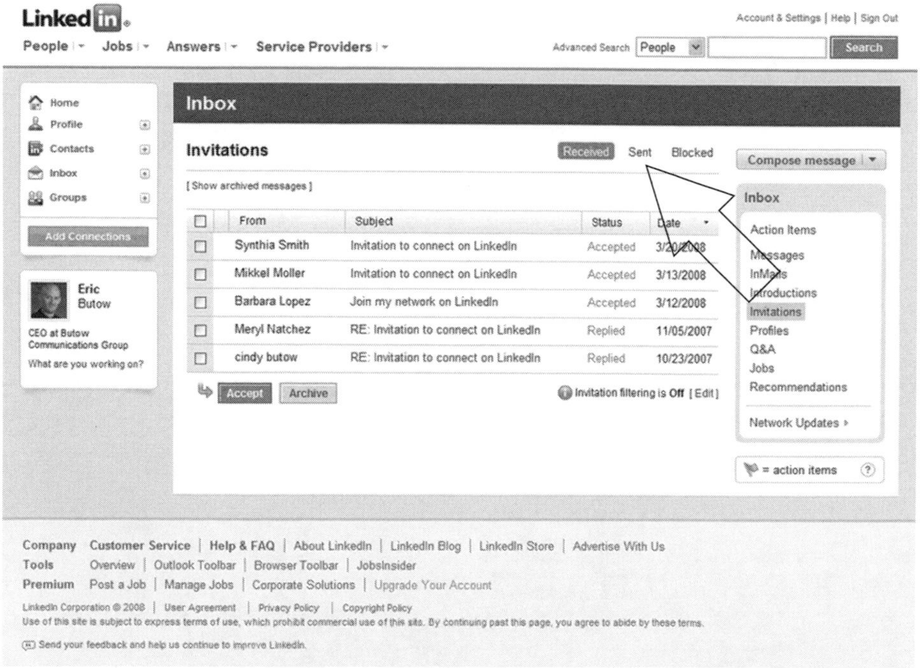

Figure 11-4. **The Invitations: Sent page**

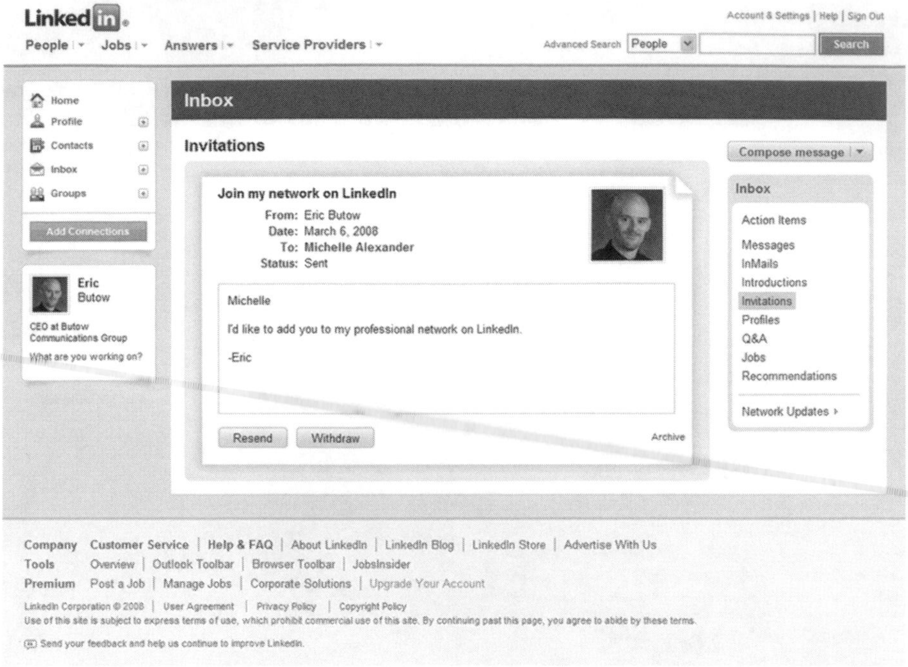

Figure 11-5. **The Compose your message page**

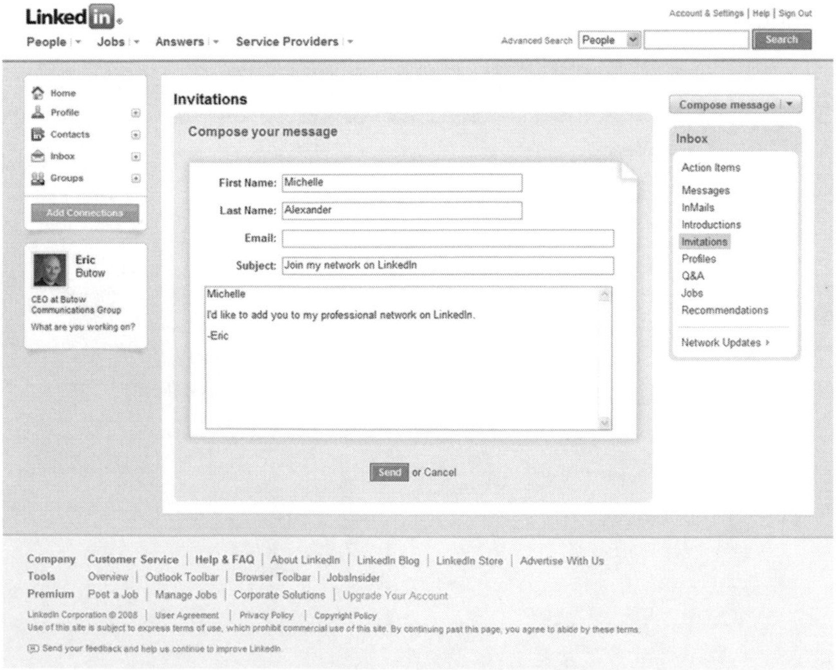

Now you can view the questions and answers you've sent to others by clicking the Q&A link on the page. The Q&A: Received page appears, and you can view all sent questions and answers by clicking the Sent link, as shown in Figure 11-6. You can view all the answers for a particular question by clicking the question title in the list. When you click the title, the question appears on the page, as shown in Figure 11-7. This page shows you the question, the network members you sent the question to, and the current message status.

Figure 11-6. **The Sent link**

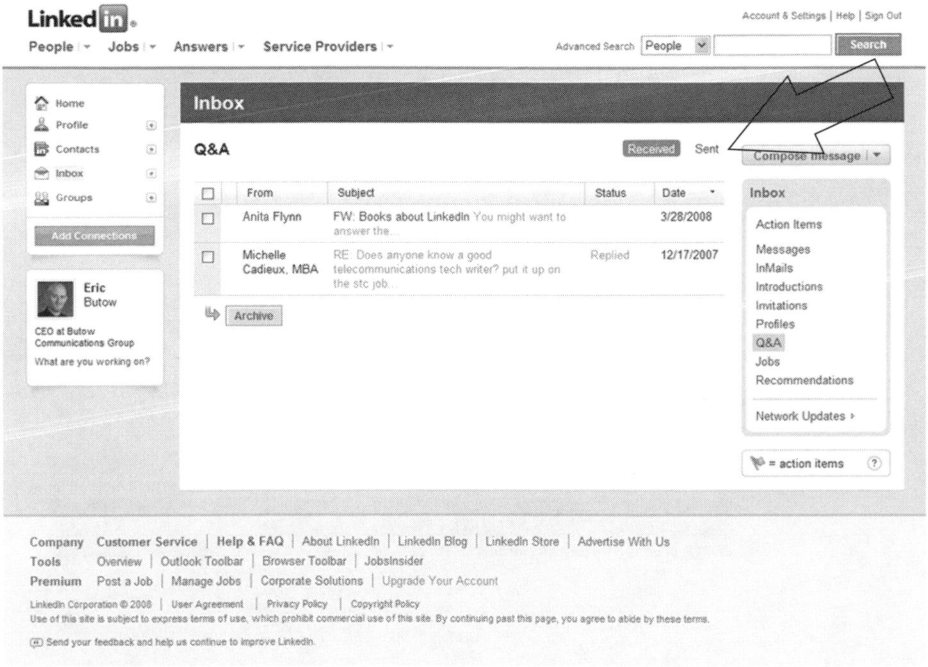

View all the answers associated with the question by clicking the View Question button. The Answers page appears, as shown in Figure 11-8. This page shows the question at the top and all the answers, both public and private, underneath your question. If your question is closed and you want to reopen it, click the Reopen This Question to Answers link. LinkedIn reopens the question, sends the question to the people you sent the question to previously, and invites you to send the question to other connections in your network. You also can share the question by e-mail with other connections in your network and with other users on del.icio.us or Digg, or you can copy and paste the URL into an e-mail message or Web site by clicking the Share This link below the question.

Figure 11-7. **The Question page**

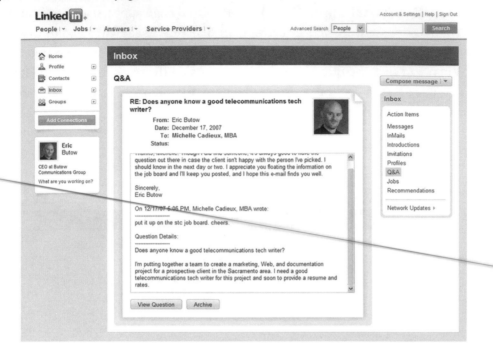

Figure 11-8. **The Answers page**

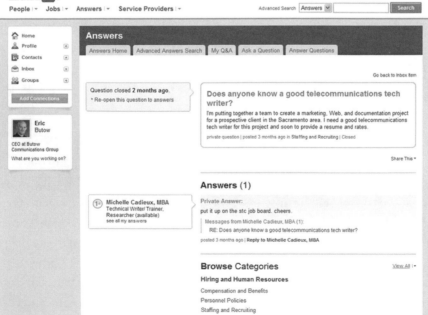

Pending Recommendation Requests

If you've sent recommendation requests to other members but have yet to receive a response, you can check the status of those requests in two ways. You can click the Recommendations link in your inbox, or you can manage the recommendations you have received.

View Recommendations in Your Inbox

Open Recommendations in Your Inbox by clicking the plus sign to the right of the Inbox link in the Navigation box and then clicking the Recommendations link, as shown in Figure 11-9. In the Recommendations page that appears, you see all recommendation requests you've received. You can also click the Sent link, as shown in Figure 11-10, to view all the recommendation requests you've sent. In the Recommendations: Sent page that appears, as shown in Figure 11-11, click the recommendation request that you sent in the list. The recommendation contains the text "[Your Name] has recommended you on LinkedIn," where "[Your Name]" is your own name. At the bottom of the recom-

Figure 11-9. **The Recommendations link in the Navigation box**

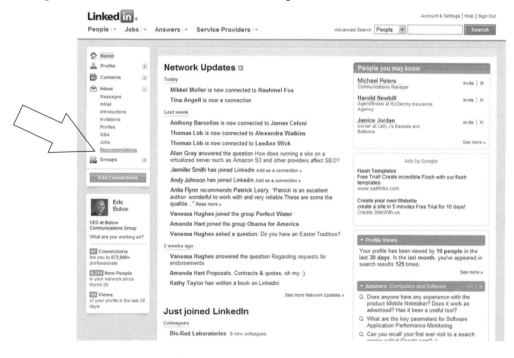

Figure 11-10. **The Sent link**

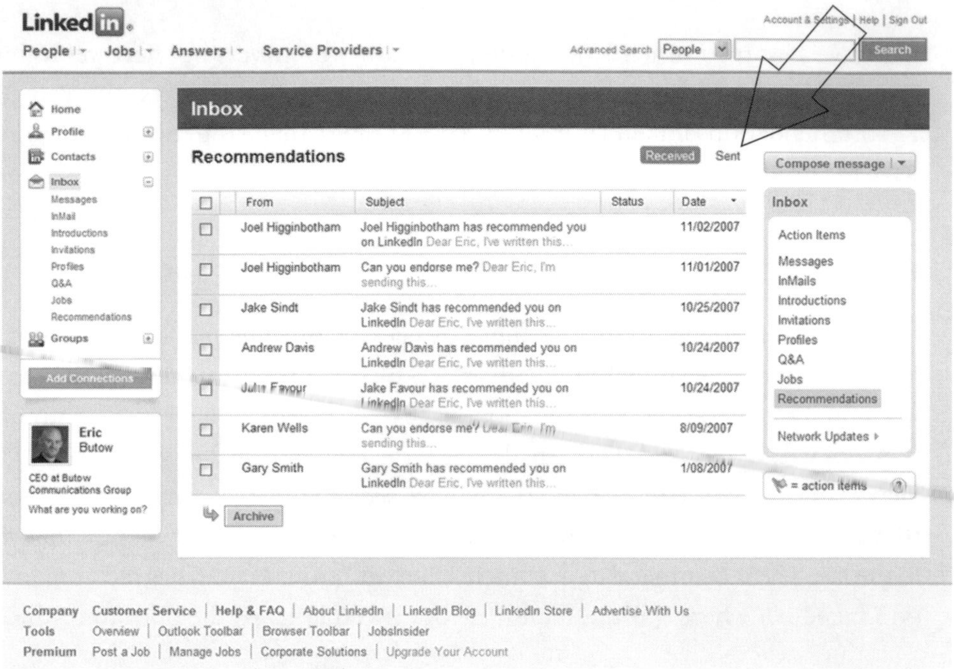

Figure 11-11. **The Recommendations: Sent page**

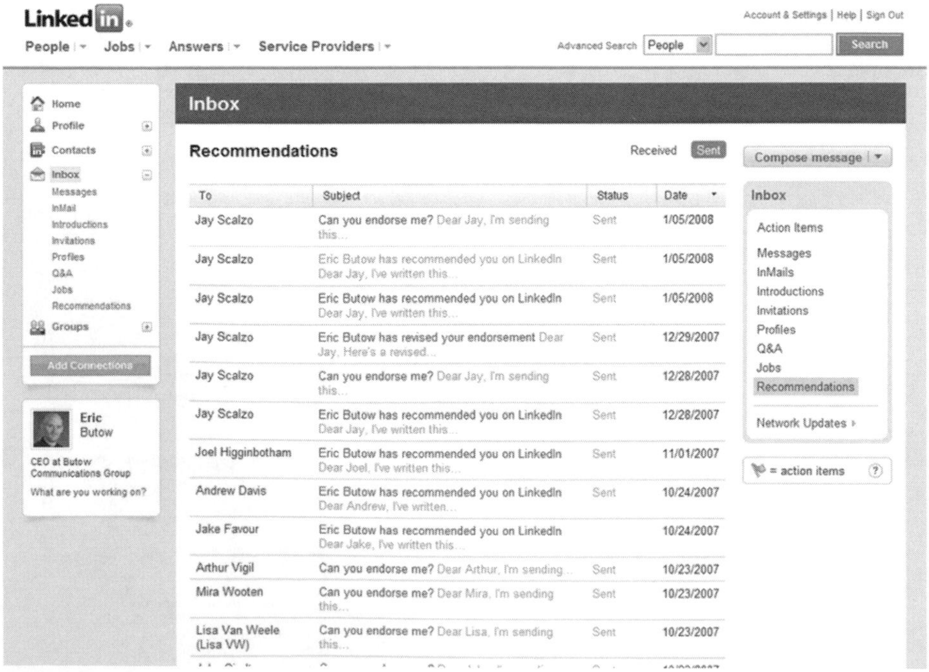

mendation text, LinkedIn informs you that the recommendation has been sent and that you can manage your recommendations by clicking the Manage Your Recommendations link at the bottom of the list. You can manage this recommendation and others by clicking the link to open the Recommendations: People page.

Manage Recommendations

You also can access the Recommendations page from the home page by clicking the Inbox link in the Navigation box. In the Inbox page, click the Recommendations link. The Recommendations page appears, as shown in Figure 11-12. If you have any pending recommendation requests for a particular position, click the Sent link, as shown in Figure 11-13.

In the Sent list, scroll down the page to view the list of sent recommendation requests, as shown in Figure 11-14. If you want to resend a recommendation to a recipient, move the mouse pointer over the Compose message button, then click Request Recommendation. The Request Recommendations page appears, as shown in Figure 11-15. You can rewrite your message in the Create Your Message box. If you're not sure how to change your message so that it becomes more effective, consider

Figure 11-12. **The Recommendations page**

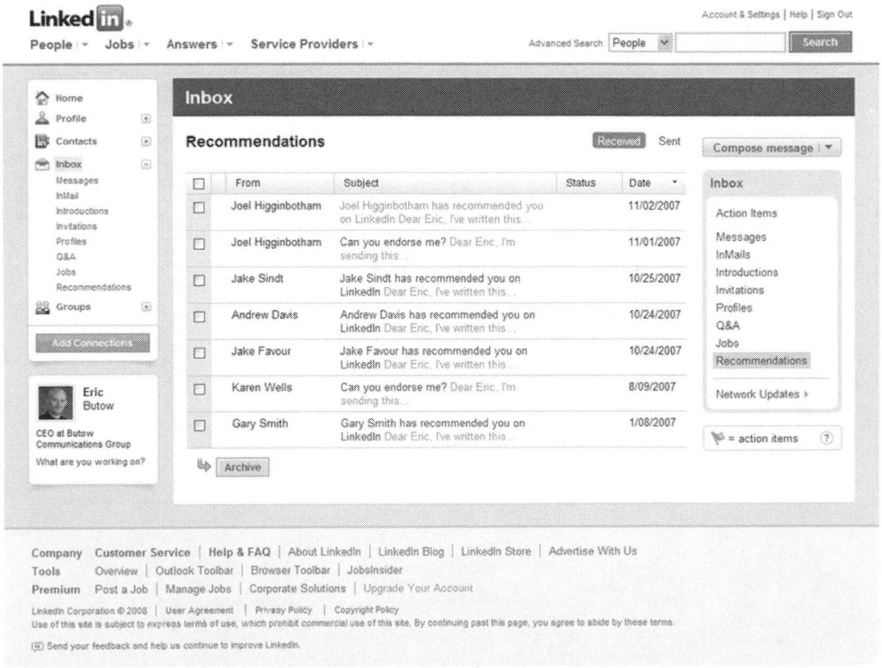

Figure 11-13. **The Sent link**

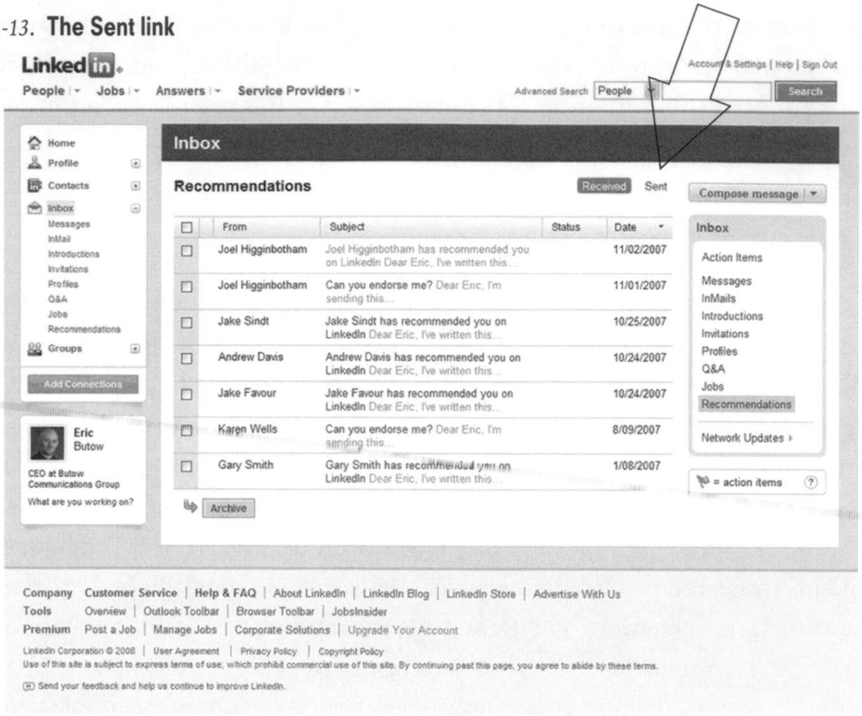

Figure 11-14. **The list of pending recommendation requests**

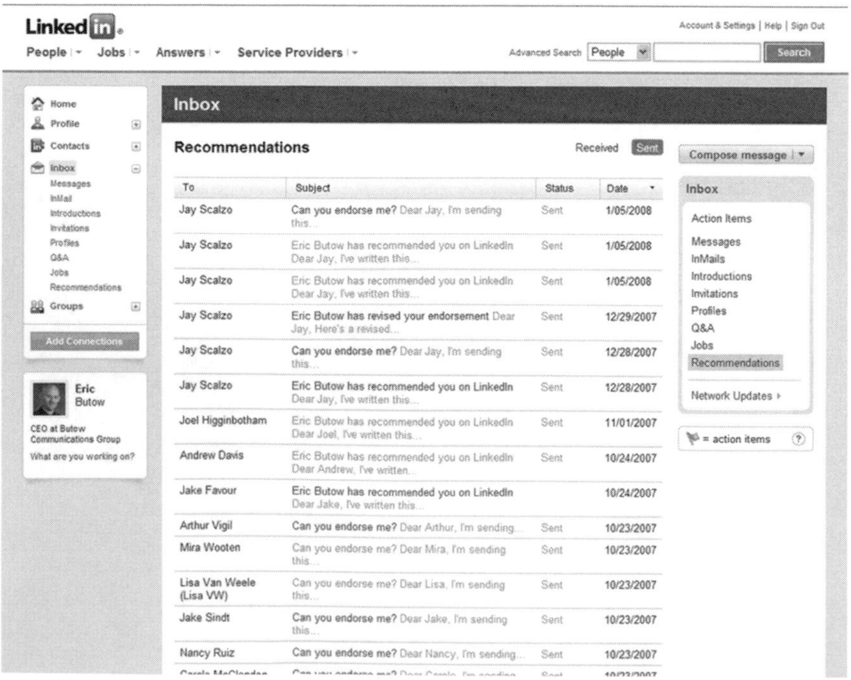

Figure 11-15. **The Request Recommendations page**

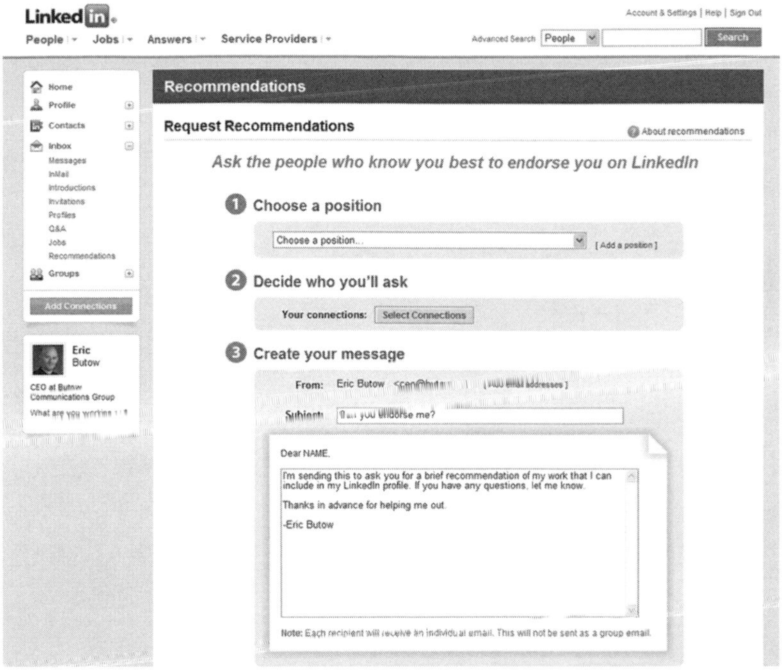

implementing the tips in Chapter 10 and those found later in this chapter. Or you can leave the message as it is. When you're finished updating the message, click the Send button.

Getting Attention

So what do you do to get a member's attention? If you are only mildly interested in getting to know the member or if your request does not have a specific timeline, then the best action is to do nothing for a while. Just assume they have been out of town or too busy to respond for the moment. Don't take any action for at least a week, and then send a message again, perhaps with a more compelling message, as shown in the example in Figure 11-16.

Notice how both parties you are sending e-mails to have more of a compelling message. To Jean, the person you are trying to reach, you have conveyed a sense of urgency to take action by offering a "fresh database of names" and by stating that you are "actively seeking a new challenge." If she hesitates in getting back

⤶ *Figure 11-16.* **An example of a more compelling message**

to you, she may lose the talent. To Tiffani, the person you are asking to pass the message along, you are offering her help on "refreshing your information on compensation comparables." You are giving her a reason to help you by offering her something in kind.

Some people have very high spam filters, and often LinkedIn messages can fall into a user's junk mailbox. In that case, there isn't much you can do except to send another message or two and see whether they eventually get through. If you know your shared connection really well, call her to see whether she has the e-mail address of that person and ask whether you can go directly to her without using LinkedIn.

You can check to see whether your shared connection has passed your message along by checking your Inbox to see the status. LinkedIn can tell you where the message is en route to your desired party. If your shared connection has passed it along and the recipient hasn't received the message, you might e-mail the shared connection and ask him to help you to get the e-mail sent to the desired party.

When you look at your list of connections, consider which person is best to pass your message along. Are you going through the best connection on your end? As stated in previous chapters, a CEO is more likely to get someone's attention than others you might choose.

Also remember not to "burn out" your network with too many requests; your connections might start to feel used and not help you so readily.

Managing Declined Messages

As you contact other LinkedIn members and other members contact you, your invitations may be declined by others whom you're trying to contact, and you may have to decline invitations from others who want to contact you. So you need to learn to manage declines both as a receiver and as a sender.

If You've Been Declined

When you receive a declined message in response to a request, the first question you must ask yourself is, "Am I bringing this person something of value and will his professional life be enhanced with my invitation or my desire to speak to them about something?" In other words, is there a good enough reason for the recipient to answer this request or invitation?

The declined message you receive should give you some idea as to whether you should connect again and, if so, some ideas on how to reach out again. You must ask yourself whether you have reached out to this person to make a real connection or are you just using him to make your network as big as possible. If you're just trying to expand your network, you shouldn't contact the person again unless you have a compelling reason or message, as explained earlier in this chapter. Remember that your goal is to make your network as valuable as possible not only to yourself but also to other people in your network. The more valuable your network is, the more desire you'll build in others to be one of your connections.

If a connection has been gracious enough to give you his e-mail address, then take the time to write a little bit about yourself and why it makes sense that you get to know each other professionally. Doing so may not pay off in the near future, but adding some information about yourself could mean that a member will forward your information to a valuable contact or accept your request to connect.

If You Need to Decline

If you find that you need to decline an invitation you receive, there are polite ways to go about doing so. Scott Allen, coauthor of *The Virtual Handshake: Opening Doors and Closing Deals Online* (AMACOM, 2005), has a very good approach to declining an invitation or a request. He writes the following message, and you may want to use a similar message:

> Thanks for inviting me to connect on LinkedIn. I would love to start a dialog, get to know each other, and find out how we might be of service to each other. You have my email, so feel free to drop me a line and we can get started. However, I do use LinkedIn as they recommend and as my experience has shown to give me the best return on my time investment, and I only connect (create a permanent referral link) with people I know well professionally, and in most cases have actually worked on some kind of project together.

What's Next?

Now that you know how to use LinkedIn and manage it to your advantage, it's time to learn how to use it with complementary networking products. LinkedIn already works with the del.icio.us social bookmarking site and the Digg content-sharing site, but those are only two of the many other sites available on the Web. In Chapter 12 we look at five other networking options that you may want to use in combination with LinkedIn to maximize your online networking power.

Other Business Networking Web Sites

In addition to LinkedIn, many other networking solutions are available on the Web. Some require that you download software to your computer, and others are Web-based solutions. In this chapter, we provide an overview of five solutions that can help you expand your network and/or find the information you need.

illumio

With the ever expanding number of social networking Web sites, blogs, and other Web content available for a wide variety of interests (see the Wikipedia article http://en.wikipedia.org/wiki/List_of_social_networking_websites for a list of notable social networking sites), it's difficult to keep track of it all. Tacit Software brings a unique approach not only to managing all that information but also to garnering expertise with their illumio product, which is available at http://www.illumio.com, as shown in Figure 12-1.

The illumio software program is free to download, though it is available only on the Windows platform (a Mac OS version is in development as of this writing). Once you use the installation wizard to install the program, illumio frees you from manually tracking personal and/or business information that matters to you. Instead, illumio monitors the feeds you choose and the groups you join, and it delivers only the information that is important to you. This information is presented in a "dashboard" format, listing your information and the groups and feeds you belong to. After you install illumio, it begins to "train" itself to know which information matches your interests. When illumio receives matching information, it alerts you to it on your desktop.

 *Figure 12-1.* **The illumio Web site**

You can stay connected in two ways. You can monitor your own Really Simple Syndication (RSS) feeds with content such as blogs, discussion forums, and news that is streamed from Web sites. You also can join illumio groups that other illumio users have created. If you decide to participate in an illumio group, you can ask a question from the illumio program, as shown in Figure 12-3, and the software sends the question to people whose interests match the subject of your questions. You can also send your question to all users in all groups, or you can limit the visibility of your question so that only group members can see it. If illumio identifies you as a match for a question asked by someone else, the system notifies you privately. You can control who views your answers to questions from other illumio users in the same way.

As a solution, illumio is particularly helpful within large enterprises where experts are regularly sought out for consulting opportunities. If your business is such that doing business with a large enterprise is of interest to you, then consider illumio as a solution.

Figure 12-2. **The illumio window**

Doostang

Doostang (http://www.doostang.com) focuses on bringing together recruiters and candidates. Though this solution has a bit of a micro focus on groups of people in their twenties and thirties, people with business degrees, and people with an interest in finance, its reach is expanding to Internet, media, and software companies. As the Doostang Web site shows (Figure 12-4), you must be invited (as with many other social networking sites).

Figure 12-3. **The illumio Ask a Question window**

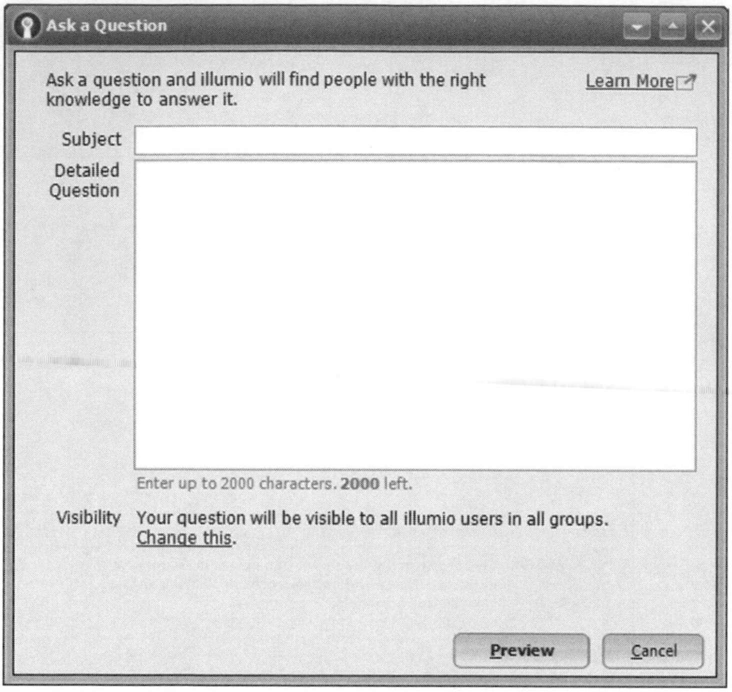

Figure 12-4. **The Doostang Web site**

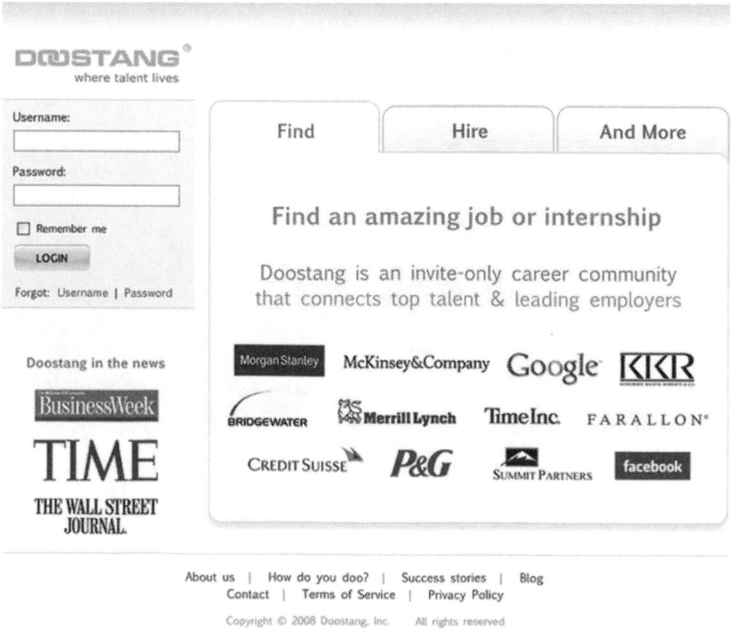

You might visit the Web site for a variety of reasons, including:

- Looking for a job
- Posting a job
- Joining a group of common interest
- Looking up your college classmates
- Joining a forum to engage in a variety of topics
- Looking for candidates if you are an employer
- Posting a discussion topic
- Asking a career question

As with LinkedIn, you can search for jobs, companies, and people by using keywords. Doostang tries to limit the number of resumes going into companies by asking you to be a member of groups with similar backgrounds. For example, if you are looking for a business development job, you may have to be a member of a group consisting of business development talent. This restriction offers an advantage over LinkedIn in that recruiters and employers can limit the number of resumes they look at. Of course, many candidates are uncanny in getting around this requirement, so recruiters and employers should be aware that people can justify being in just about any group, especially if their careers include a variety of positions.

Recruiters and employers are allowed to look at the backgrounds of candidates' friends as well. Therefore, while they are looking at one person's profile, they can glance at her friends' profiles to check out their backgrounds and perhaps find a better fit for the position.

Doostang also does not allow recruiters to contact job postings for any reason. If they do, they risk being bumped from the site. The primary drawback to this is obvious: If you are a recruiter with a great position, will you advertise it on Doostang?

Even as the need for talent gets greater and greater, Doostang may not be the best place for recruiters to advertise their jobs. But if you are looking for strong business talent in the areas Doostang focuses on to add to your organization, you may find candidates here.

Plaxo

Plaxo (http://www.plaxo.com) is an online address book and networking service that was founded in 2001 in part by Sean Parker of Napster (yes, the infamous music file sharing service). Plaxo not only keeps your address book up-to-date, but, if you make changes to your address information, then your contact information is automatically updated in the address books of others who have your information.

You can use the online version and/or download the Plaxo toolbars. Either way, you can synchronize your address book in Outlook (shown in Figure 12-5), Outlook Express, Mac OS X, Thunderbird, Windows Mobile, and your mobile address book with the Plaxo online address book.

Figure 12-5. **The Plaxo toolbar for Outlook**

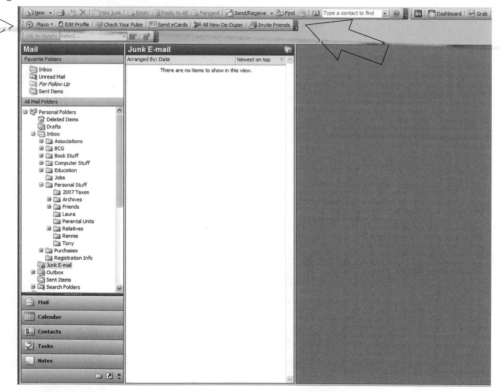

As with LinkedIn, you can connect with other Plaxo users and view the status of those connections, as shown in Figure 12-6, as well as connect to other people with whom your connections have recently connected.

Also as with LinkedIn, you set up your own profile to include information about yourself (including your photo), your professional summary, and personal and professional information, as shown in Figure 12-7.

Although Plaxo looks pretty similar to LinkedIn, it differs in a few ways. For example, Plaxo's address book shows not only contact information but also a Yahoo

⌒ *Figure 12-6.* **The Plaxo Web site**

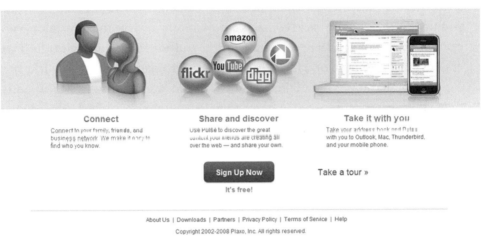

⌒ *Figure 12-7.* **Eric Butow's profile on Plaxo**

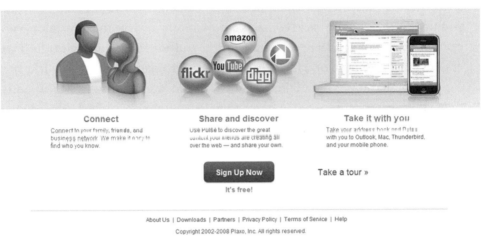

map with the work address. Just as shown in Figure 12-7, Plaxo has recently introduced Pulse, a feature in the up-and-coming version 3.0 of Plaxo that works with a number of other content-sharing Web sites, including Digg, MySpace, and Flickr. You can tell Plaxo 3.0 about the sites where you post online content and how you want to share it using Pulse. If you share these sites with others in your Plaxo network, when you update them, your Plaxo contacts automatically receive the new information. For example, if you upload a new photo to Flickr and you share your Flickr feed with others in your Plaxo network, those in your network receive your new Flickr photos.

The basic version of Plaxo is free. If you want to use LinkedIn with Plaxo, then you might be interested in purchasing Plaxo Premium, which synchronizes with your LinkedIn network so that you can have more detailed contact information about your LinkedIn connections in your Plaxo address book. The cost of Plaxo Premium is $49.95 per year.

Spock

If you want to know where people in your address book are on the Web, you can use the Spock people search Web site at http://www.spock.com, as shown in Figure 12-8. When you join the Spock Web site, you can network with other members to find out where other people are on the Web. For example, when I look for my friend Tony Barcellos on the site by typing Anthony Barcellos in the Search box, I receive information about him in the results page, as shown in Figure 12-9.

As you build relationships with other Spock members, you also can search other members' networks (and they can search yours) to find the people that you (and they) are looking for. The Spock Web site claims that it has indexed more than 100 million people from more than 1.5 billion data records, including information from LinkedIn. For Tony's results, the information listing page in Figure 12-9 includes not only his current position as a math instructor but also where he went to school.

Spock also automatically adds tags to people it finds, and you can add tags of your own (such as where the person worked before), identify relationships between people you find, and upload pictures to go with the record of the person you've found. For example, in Figure 12-9, the tags appear as green links underneath Tony's name. When I click on the link, Spock lists other people who also have that tag.

Though Spock currently doesn't connect with LinkedIn, it's good as an additional site to find people on the Web and to build your own in-depth contact database. People are excited about Spock because of its people-searching capabilities, which are

⌒ *Figure 12-8.* **The Spock Web site**

⌒ *Figure 12-9.* **Information about Tony Barcellos in Spock.com**

beyond the capabilities of current search engines, thanks to a concept called entity resolution, or the ability to disambiguate people and collapse multiple sources of information into one entry about a person. Spock still is in beta form as of this writing, but it could pose a serious challenge to Plaxo down the road.

Jigsaw

If you want to build your database of contacts more quickly than you can in LinkedIn, Plaxo, or Spock, Jigsaw (http://www.jigsaw.com) builds its network on one of the staples of business life: the business card. Jigsaw is a free service that lets you buy and trade business cards, as shown in Figure 12-10. Jigsaw contains more than 7 million contacts that are complete with the full name, title, postal address, e-mail address, and telephone number of people you want to reach. Members add business cards and earn points for entering complete business cards and lose points for adding bad or incomplete contacts. These points can then be used to buy contact information from the Jigsaw database. If you update your contacts with complete informa-

Figure 12-10. **The Jigsaw Web site**

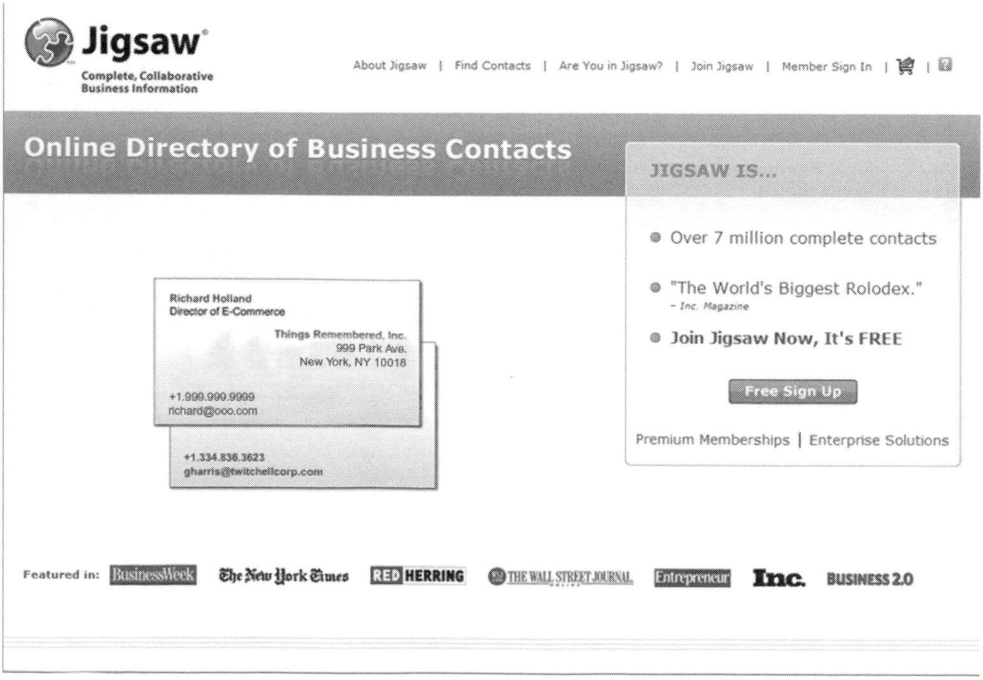

tion, you also get points. When you join Jigsaw, you get 10 free points, and you get additional points for referring someone else to join.

You can also upload your contacts on the site, from a file, or from your Outlook database. If you would rather not add contacts, you can buy them when you pay for a premium account, with plans starting at $25 per month. Jigsaw also contains a number of paid options for sharing contacts within your organization, for mailing lists, and for removing obsolete and duplicate records from your customer relationship management (CRM) system.

The Jigsaw solution has given rise to some controversy because business cards, complete with your phone number and e-mail address, are added to the Jigsaw network, which has brought up issues of privacy. The counterargument is that the information on the network is public—people freely give away their business cards with this information, and business cards have always been passed around just as freely. If you want to find out whether you're in Jigsaw, click the Are You In Jigsaw? link at the bottom of the Jigsaw page. You can then type your e-mail address in the Are You In Jigsaw? page, as shown in Figure 12-11, to find out whether your business card is in the Jigsaw system.

Figure 12-11. **The Are You In Jigsaw? Page**

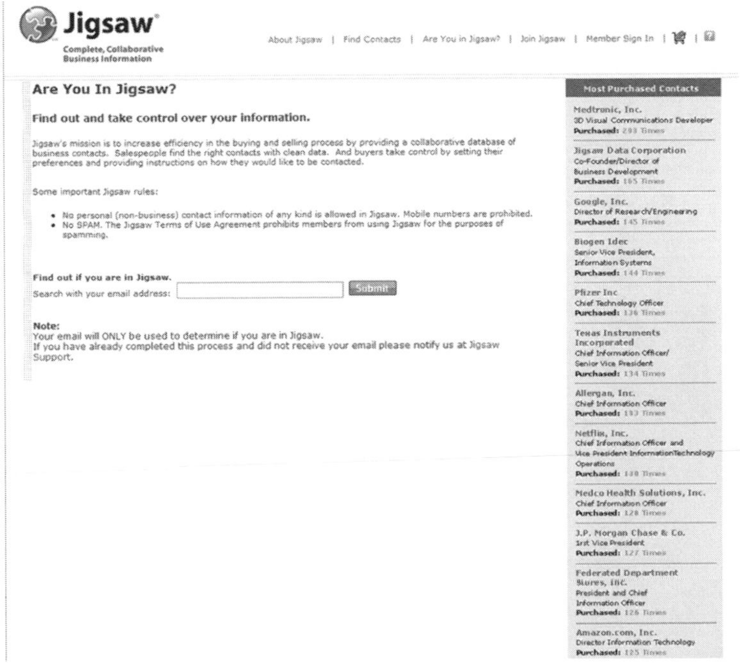

You can use Jigsaw as a complementary tool with LinkedIn to find more people. As with any other such service, be cautious when inviting people you find on Jigsaw into your LinkedIn network. Tell the person where you got their information and why you want to invite him into your network. If you provide as much information as possible about yourself and why you want to connect with the person, you stand a much better chance of having him join your network.

These tools are all about making as many connections as possible, and you can use them to augment the networks you form on LinkedIn. The more connections you make, the more opportunities you have to help others and to get help yourself. Now that you know how to use LinkedIn to build your online network, have fun using LinkedIn and the related tools listed in this chapter to build a richer networking experience for yourself and others.

Index